Intimacy and Separateness in Psychoanalysis

Clinical psychoanalysis serves as our best laboratory for exploring the riddle of what it is to be a person, and how a person is at once singularly unique while always a piece of the interpersonal fabric of humanity. In *Intimacy and Separateness in Psychoanalysis*, Warren Poland casts a freshly erudite eye on this paradox, resisting individual or intersubjective bias and avoiding the parochial allegiances common in our age of pluralism.

Poland combines vivid reports from clinical analyses, literary readings, and his own life – all unfolding original observations on a person as both *a part of* and *apart from* human commonality. His consideration of how one person's witnessing facilitates another's self-definition, a concept extended here in his study of outsiderness as part of human nature, has been marked a keynote contribution. Clinical illustrations of moments that matter but are usually omitted from public presentation are set alongside examples of reading powerful fiction to show how analyst and author both incite fresh openness in a person's mind. Poland goes farther, exposing the personal power of union and separateness in its keenest form, facing the ultimate separation of one's own actual death.

Only with separateness can true intimacy grow, and only within the fabric of others can true individuality exist. This evocative book, ranging from the lightness of whimsy to the dread of dying, allows every reader to taste and to learn from Poland's thinking. Psychoanalyst or patient, writer or reader, each one living one's own life – all can find new understandings in this work.

Warren S. Poland, M.D., has practiced clinical psychoanalysis for over half a century. His observations and reflections, including in his early book *Melting the Darkness: The Dyad and Principles of Clinical Technique*, were honored by his receipt of the Sigourney Award in 2009. In personal essays, in considerations of literary works, and centrally in his clinical psychoanalytic studies, he explores the paradoxical simultaneity of intersubjectivity and individuality. He is also the former editor of the *JAPA Review of Books*.

"This is no ordinary psychoanalytic book. It has no peer in the way it struggles to come to terms with the paradox of the essential otherness of people to one another despite all we hold in common. This book is also like no other psychoanalytic book in the way it draws on language as the custodian of our accrued experience as a civilization. What a pleasure it is when once in a great while we come across a book such as this one where we find ourselves pausing after reading a sentence, reading it several times before going on, or simply taking time to sit with its reverberations and echoes." – **Thomas H. Ogden**, author most recently of *Reclaiming Unlived Life: Experiences in Psychoanalysis*

"I was moved to tears a number of times by this book, as Warren Poland cut through the psychoanalytic jargon and took the reader to the heart of what it is to be human – messy, vulnerable, mortal and incapable of living up to what we would like to be. Yet a form of hope emerges from his writing that I find downright inspiring. I will return to this book again and again." – **Glen O. Gabbard, M.D.**, author of *Love and Hate in the Analytic Setting*

"Wisdom is a quality rarely encountered in life or literature, still more rarely in writings on psychoanalysis. Warren Poland has given us that rarest of gifts; a book rich in the wisdom that only a clinician of long experience, striking originality, and unique sensitivity to the paradoxes of our human condition could produce. This is a truly wonderful book, the culmination of Warren Poland's invaluable contributions to psychoanalysis." – **Ted Jacobs**, Clinical Professor, Emeritus, Albert Einstein College of Medicine, Training and Supervising Analyst, The New York and IPE Psychoanalytic Institutes

"Warren Poland writes of analysis as contact between separate people, a contact that leads to change in both. In his writing he achieves a similar contact. He describes the psychoanalytic experience with such clarity and emotional depth that his words touch the reader as words in an analysis touch the other. This book is for all analysts, to be returned to again and again, both for the knowledge it contains and for the pleasure provided by his beautiful and accurate description of what actually takes place during psychoanalysis." – **Judith Fingert Chused, M.D.**, Clinical Professor of Psychiatry and Behavioral Sciences and Clinical Professor of Pediatrics, George Washington University School of Medicine, Emeritus Training and Supervising Analyst, Washington Center for Psychoanalysis

Intimacy and Separateness in Psychoanalysis

Warren S. Poland

Edited and introduced by
William F. Cornell
With a preface by Nancy Chodorow

Routledge
Taylor & Francis Group
LONDON AND NEW YORK

First published 2018
by Routledge
2 Park Square, Milton Park, Abingdon, Oxon OX14 4RN

and by Routledge
711 Third Avenue, New York, NY 10017

Routledge is an imprint of the Taylor & Francis Group, an informa business

British Library Cataloguing in Publication Data
A catalogue record for this book is available from the British Library

Library of Congress Cataloging in Publication Data
A catalog record for this book has been requested

ISBN: 978-1-138-09775-9 (hbk)
ISBN: 978-1-138-09776-6 (pbk)
ISBN: 978-1-315-10472-0 (ebk)

Typeset in Times New Roman
by Swales & Willis Ltd, Exeter, Devon, UK

Psychoanalysis is ...

... a celebration of the emergence of the self, a unique, unprecedented event in the history of the universe, an awareness of the continuity of experience in a unique entity, one that never existed before and will never exist again. This miracle is confirmed by the others, the witnesses to one's uniqueness, just as the self gives meaning to the uniqueness and individuality of others ... This is the dramatic element in psychoanalysis, a continuous, mutual reaffirmation of two independent but related selves, something that makes the long hours and the tremendous cost of psychoanalysis a very special and worthwhile experience. Psychoanalysis defines and celebrates both the changing uniqueness and the continuity of the self over time and experience. The self thus stands as a commentary on the essential nature of time, and vice versa. We are witnesses of and witnessed by the others and by the universe. They will always be there, no matter how brief a sojourn we have in time and life. It reminded me of the lines of Lamartine's "Le Lac":

> *L'homme n'a point de port, le temps n'a point de rive ;*
> *Il coule, et nous passons !*

Jacob Arlow
Personal correspondence

Contents

Preface

Warren Poland: humanist, ethicist, friend

Nancy Chodorow

As analysts, we meet our patients in the consulting room, but we often meet our colleagues and forebears, beginning with Freud, through their writings. I first met Warren Poland, I do not remember when, through his writings – highly theoretical, deeply clinical, straightforwardly personal, pervasively ethical, and flat out gorgeous – writings that I return to again and again. He is one of psychoanalysis's great writers. As we read him, we are bathed in the language of the patient, in his empathy for his patients, and in what he says to them and feels about and for them, so eloquently and to the point. We are bathed in his always-pertinent self-reflection and self-observation but never inundated by the analyst's subjectivity. And we find references to Shakespeare, Proust, Vuillard, the Nabis, Yiddish tales, Japanese Noh mask carving. Analyst and author, author and analyst, seem to go seamlessly together, both underpinned by an ethical humanity.

Warren Poland is among our most elegant, sophisticated, and as right as you can be contemporary writers about the simple and straightforward, yet complex and amazing, work that is psychoanalysis. He gives us clear concepts and rich case descriptions that seem to provide in themselves guidance to how we want to work. His clinical sensitivity, the cases he describes, Warren's own feelings as he works – these all come alive as he creates narratives about the deepest feelings, meanings, and histories of his patients, about their work together, about change and the internal and external impediments to change. "Vignette" does not do justice to Warren's case writing, and "theory" does not do justice to his seamless, grounded accounts of the clinical consulting room and the goals of analytic work. We wonder, as we also wonder about our other great writers, beginning with Freud – and for each of us, a select additional few – are they separable, being an analyst and being a writer? For Warren, they seem to be inextricably intertwined.

In *Melting the Darkness*, Warren writes,

> It is misleading to speak glibly of one-person psychology versus two-person psychology. No single person exists outside a human, object-connected field; the analytic space colors how such a single person comes to understanding by the other and to insight. At the same time, the mind of any individual can be engaged by another yet is always crucially apart, a private universe of inner experience.

Later in that same work, he adds, "The goal of psychoanalysis is the exploration of the mind of the patient. Attention to the dyadic aspects of the development of insight does not imply alteration of that goal or of customary technique."

In these statements, we find the core of Warren's analytic understanding: an insistence on the patient's separate humanity and individual uniqueness, and, by implication, an ethical and clinical conception of the analyst's role that grows from the essential and separate humanity of the analyst. Since that time, Warren has been elaborating upon these core understandings and commitments in a series of articles, presentations, and reflections that together define and elaborate a foundational psychoanalytic attitude and pragmatic. This taken-for-granted, deeply ethical internal stance toward the other, and the actions that such an ethic entails, are the gifts that are elaborated for the reader in *Intimacy and Separateness in Psychoanalysis* through formulations about the analytic project that are always focused, as Warren notices in his opening chapter, on regard for otherness.

Warren has written that he sees philosophy as the lectures and psychoanalysis as the lab. If so, I think we could see Warren himself as somewhere in between. He has become our field's leading ordinary language psychoanalyst and ordinary language ethicist, advocating a focus on the patient and on what we do, or try to do, for him or her. Just as ordinary language philosophers are not telling us to use a different language, and pragmatists and social phenomenologists are not telling us what we *should* be doing as practice, so also Warren unpacks for us the full meaning, the full implication for practice, for the internal analytic setting and for the analyst's subjectivity as analyst, of what we claim we stand for and do. From these writings, we get some of our most felicitous concepts and clinical admonitions, all in plain, everyday English: "the patient as a unique other"; we serve as a "*recognizing other*" for the patient; the patient as a "private universe of inner experience"; "witnessing"; "the marvel of otherness"; the "interpretive attitude." Reminding us of Freud's "powerful curiosity about meaning," Warren points again and again to the centrality of curiosity for both patient and analyst.

"Regard for otherness," it would seem, is Warren's fundamental rule for the analyst, and he has chosen to open this volume with "Regarding the other," a short contribution that sums up his psychoanalytic credo. Regard for the other and otherness, he implies, is of much more importance than whatever fundamental rule, changing over the years and according to location and tradition, that we require, or do not require, of our patients. Regard for otherness affirms the individual selfhood of the patient and their otherness to the analyst, which is at the same time their (potential) selfness to themselves: the capacity to think, to self-observe, to have their own mind. Recognizing the patient's specific selfhood, we hope to give patients tools to elaborate their own self-recognition and self-understanding.

Regarding the other entails what Warren names three foundational principles: individuality, otherness, and outsiderness. In the context of our field's pervasive shift toward a focus on the analytic dyad, the relationship, transference-countertransference in the room, and the analyst's mind, Warren emphasizes that "the analysand is the central person in any analysis." Here he becomes ethicist, and his is a cautionary tale. The analyst, far from being co-creator, co-author, or psychological subject equivalent to the patient, is the patient's other. The analytic field consists in a "total field of intersubjective engagement between the clinical partners," but at the same time, "the patient comes to an analysis for the sake of personal growth, and the analyst works therein to further that patient's personal analysis." As Warren puts it, "it is the patient and the patient's life that are the top priority." In this context, Warren becomes also a pragmatist. He reminds us repeatedly that the analyst is "engaged to be a professional assistant." He asks, "what can the patient *use* after termination?"

Regard for otherness calls for what Warren has named, in a lasting and brilliant formulation, again in everyday language, a "two-person separate" view of the analytic encounter. "Two-person separate" describes two distinct people, two subjects, in interaction, an intersubjectivity that is not a fusion or unity, not the "two-person unified" – also Warren's term – of relational psychoanalysis, field theory, co-creation, or the bi-personal field, and not the one-person mode of classical analysis. "Two-person separate" describes the epistemology and methodology that underpin not only regard for otherness, curiosity, interpretation, and all other of the analyst's provisions for the patient. It recognizes also the separate and unique individual selfhood of the patient, whose mind and experience go beyond the consulting room.

"Two-person separate" was first named in "The analyst's witnessing and otherness," Warren's 1997 plenary address to the American Psychoanalytic Association. Witnessing affirms the *individual selfhood* of the patient, their otherness to the analyst, which is at the same time their (potential) selfness to themselves, the capacity to think, to self-observe, and to have their own mind. The analyst, in Warren's view, accompanies as a guide. This is a taken-for-granted, deeply ethical internal stance toward the other, and an analyst who is first and foremost an ethical human being, for whom all theory, all technical precepts, all rules – work from the surface, interpret, work in the transference, analyze the resistance, explain free association, and similar analytic precepts from throughout the world – are *"in the service of the other."* In witnessing our patients, Warren tells us, we are "in attendance to hear," we "serve as other," we "stand by," we "travel with."

Through witnessing, the analyst is able to recognize personal trauma – Warren's young woman patient, who reports that she must undergo a hysterectomy. Warren suggests that we *witness* suffering: we cannot always interpret or try to "empathize." I have found, in clinical work and in teaching, that the idea of witnessing also gives young clinicians (and ourselves) guidance in working with patients who have experienced trauma from without – political trauma, torture, forced migration, economic disaster, racism. Here also, interpretation is beside the point, while witnessing is emphatically (and empathically) very much what is needed.

Throughout this book, Warren also witnesses himself, with all his commitments and all his foibles, as analyst, as citizen, parent, child, and husband, as colleague and friend. He bears witness to the trajectory of the analytic profession, to what we should be and represent, and to what we do. He testifies to the analyst's primary goal or mode of being, which could serve as this book's alternative title and expresses its pervasive ethic: *Regarding the Other*. For me, all of Warren's writing is inspiration and companion as I work, but "The analyst's witnessing and otherness" and "two-person separate" especially transformed my conceptualization of the possibilities of psychoanalytic theory and practice.

The reader notices throughout this book that there is no jargon in Warren's formulations, no terms that any educated person would not understand, even as this writer and analyst gets right to the heart of the matter. Warren's writing contrasts sharply with my own drive to theorize and that of so many of our colleagues – our pull toward the abstract and theoretical. You can contrast Warren's everyday language formulation, "two-person separate," completely straightforward, in ordinary English, with my own formulation, "intersubjective ego psychology," the theory and epistemology that I named to describe an American Independent Tradition, beginning from Loewald and Erikson and including, as a prime exemplar, Warren (who, to my eternal gratitude, has generously acknowledged the identity – and both independence and tradition here are key). "Two-person separate" bears a family resemblance, which I think Warren would own, to Loewald, just as Warren's "private universe of experience" reminds me of Loewald's human mind as "a universe in its own right."

On the side of development Warren has contributed profoundly and movingly to a view of development as a lifelong process. Throughout this volume, and especially as the reader moves toward its conclusion, "Endings in poetry, psychoanalysis, and life," she finds reflective, illuminating, sympathetic, in-the-room accounts of Warren himself as someone traversing the life cycle along with his patients. Warren reflects on his previous analyses not so much to tell us about himself and his inner life, but to develop his thoughts about experiences that affect us all: aging, the life span, and the cycle of generations. He does not shy away from talking directly about the fundamental transience of human existence, of life and death. Such a focus is in our field rare. We can forget, but Warren does not, that Oedipus is as much about generation as about gender. We are in the vicinity of ego integrity.

In this final section, Warren begins, in the service of his colleagues as well as his patients, to take account of his own life and life cycle. We learn of his relation to his father and his son, himself going from youth to middle age and to what he describes as the fading of old age (perhaps we could include ripening here and the deepening of maturity, in addition to inevitable loss, all of which we take so abundantly from Warren's writing presence in this volume). Earlier, he has begun "The analyst's witnessing and otherness" with an unforgettable case vignette about the disruption of generation and generativity. His young female patient who must have a hysterectomy will not be able to contribute biologically to the ongoingness of the generations. Warren, male, of a different generation, already a father, gets it. He understands that in the face of this radical tragedy in the life of a young woman, he can only witness. He cannot comfort, explore, or analyze.

In "The analyst's fears," Warren becomes his own other. He notices that, in his youth he could focus clinically (and, one infers, personally) on one pole of the Oedipus conflict: sexuality and gender. Rich echoes of these interests are found in this volume in Warren's playful writings about – and his brilliant naming of – "polymorphously normal," "ungendered" sex and protean gender in Shakespeare's comedies (I could, with pleasure and delight, focus another preface entirely on Warren's reflections on Shakespeare – *A Midsummer Night's Dream* and *Twelfth Night*, with its tragic off-center in Malvolio). Now, he describes a dying patient who wishes Warren to meet once with his son after he is gone, to give the son another way of connecting to his father, and another patient whom Warren sits with over the period from diagnosis of a fatal illness through to fading and death.

Especially in "Ephemera" and "Slouching towards mortality," Warren writes movingly and with palpable emotional immediacy on a topic rare in our literature: how the analyst's place, Warren's own place, in the life cycle and his own aging have affected his sense of self. We find a facing of mortality and death, a drawing once more upon Shakespeare as well as upon his own clinical experience, but especially upon his own ego integrity, a facing of the life that he has lived and will live as his one and only life. Warren has discovered, he tells us, that fears and dangers have shifted across his life span (even in a preface, it is impossible to write about Warren Poland without direct quotation):

> That brings me to one other experience that I want to acknowledge candidly as having a personal truth, one that I believe at least some others must share ... It has to do with my personal sense of increasing vulnerability to the contagion of fear. I believe that my clinical skill has for the most part increased with years of practice. Yet my growing experience and possibly my growing skill have either led to or permitted me more openness to dread and sadness. Pleasures have also grown, even greater appreciation of the delight of very small pleasures, but the awareness of more freely feeling fear has brought with it a sense of poignancy that I did not know when I was younger ... Something about aging in a life immersed in other people's analyses has been incredibly enriching but has changed me so that I feel more open to anguish.
> (p. 79)

And here is how Warren leaves his readers in "Regarding the other," his good-bye as author of the "Clinician's corner":

> The analyst's desire to work in the psychoanalytic service of the other is manifested in an underlying regard for the uniqueness of the patient's individuality, the authenticity of the patient's otherness, and the vulnerability of the patient's sense of essential outsiderness. No two people are the same. Knowing an other is always partial and somewhat askew. Each person is inherently vulnerable in the presence of an other person whose life and experience the first one cannot ever fully know.
> (Poland, W. S. (2011). Regarding the Other.
> *American Imago* 68(2):358)

In 2015, I was fortunate to chair a "Meet the Author" session honoring Warren at the Meetings of the International Psychoanalytical Association. There I noticed that I taught Warren's "The analyst's witnessing and otherness" as much as any writing beyond that of Loewald (the equivalent for any other analyst of any analytic writer beyond Freud), and that "two-person separate" had years ago provided me with the most succinct and clear conceptualization of what I was reaching to describe in my own clinical identity and my own writings. I advocated on that occasion for this book. I said that it would be a book that I would refer to again and again and that would find a welcome on my bookshelf of most-consulted books, a single shelf built into a mid-century Danish modern desk that contains Freud's twenty-four volumes, Loewald's *Papers on Psychoanalysis*, Erikson's *Childhood and Society*, and a few other works, including *Melting the Darkness*.

My wish has come to fruition. Readers of *Intimacy and Separateness in Psychoanalysis* will expand and deepen their analytic identity and practice and any other professional endeavors in which they are engaged. They will be wiser and better people. We are so fortunate to have this collection for our further education and development as analysts and as human beings, and, quite simply, for the pleasures of reading.

Acknowledgments

In Sebastian's words, "I can no other answer make but thanks, and thanks, and ever; oft good turns are shuffled off with such uncurrent pay" (Shakespeare, *Twelfth Night*). The strength of my appreciation is poorly betokened in the insufficiency of my words.

First come my teachers, the name for a family that extends from my early masters through all of my patients, the most valuable teachers of my adulthood. When young, I thought such crediting of patients by authors was a social posture, perhaps a pose of modesty. How naïve, how wrong, I was.

Those who welcomed me alongside them on their personal journeys of introspection have taught me about how minds work and about how the world works, with a richness I could have had no other way. Each has been different, but all have borne my slowness in understanding, even if not always with patience. They merit being named one by one, but respect commands anonymity. They are not anonymous to me.

It is a truth universally acknowledged that a writer in possession of a manuscript must be in want of an editor. This book would not have come to fruition had it not been for the energy, enthusiasm, effort, and incisive wisdom brought by its editor, William F. Cornell. To my benefit and admiration, he has contributed more than mere redaction, enriching me as well as this book. Bill Cornell has a rare sense of what it means to be human, one that extends from the depths of psychoanalytic thought, on to the centrality of bodily experiences, extending further on to the breadth of intersubjective and relational processes, the workings of social groups. Thinking I had found an editor, I was delighted to discover I had found such a teacher.

So is it also with Nancy Chodorow. She is a wonder, a fact recognized around the world. Her highly valued, deeply analytic work in cultural anthropology and sociology already of historical importance, her clinical training and experience, have only further expanded her value to and impact in the field of psychoanalysis. Her creativity continues unabated. A dear friend who always makes my mind stretch to keep up with hers, she has uniquely helped me to augment my fragile personal objectivity, a gift for which I am particularly grateful.

Thomas Ogden is known to the world as an original thinker who has added importantly to psychoanalytic understanding, advancing it to a level lacking without him. While I have profound respect for that work, it is the uncommonly gifted, ferocious intensity of his dedication to the quality of writing and its realization in his remarkable creativity that have come to me as an unexpected pleasure. His friendship has dispelled the insidiously creeping ennui of age, rekindling for me the vigor of literary passion from school days. His epistolary friendship places him side by side with Samuel Johnson in the cherished inner circle in my mind.

My vision of the world has broadened, become deeper and more subtly complex thanks to Theodore Jacobs, as well as to Judith Chused, Ilany Kogan, Eugene Mahon, René Major, and Donna Orange. Each has taught me ways to look at the world afresh, and each has been wondrously and endlessly generous of friendship. To live with such friends is to live among poets. From all of them I have learned about patients, I have learned about friendship, I have learned about myself, and, thrillingly, I have learned something of how to use language.

Peter Rudnytsky has helped me develop my writing with consistent support and with a rare scholarship I greatly admire. Similarly, the volley of ideas with Dale Boesky and Lee Grossman has forced me to continue to learn, each doing so with refreshingly uncommon wit.

In addition to them, Glen Gabbard, Robert Gardner, Jay Greenberg, Charles Hanly, Mick Landaiche, and Elias Poland have also warmly and helpfully sharpened the thinking that is developed in this book. As already granted, such mere mention is most uncurrent pay.

My gratitude to Janice Poland, my wife, transcends the limits of that word, since to my pleasure she and her customs have become so much part of my own, indeed of myself. Beyond the infinite ways she has enriched my life, her editorial hand in my writing has been essential. She is devastating when confronting unclear thinking, cruel when facing clumsy sentences.

There is one other point that requires specific statement. I am, of course, responsible for all the views expressed in this book, but I would not and do not claim originality for all of the ideas. It is not possible to cite all of the vast community of colleagues who have created the cumulative scholarship that has become part of all of my thinking. The way I integrate and express my thinking is my own, yet there can be no question that I do so only by virtue of all that has already been said, taught, and written in the psychoanalytic world at large.

Whatever the imperfections and errors included in his thinking, some of which I discuss in this book, Freud inspires me with unending awe. His combined genius and humanity have created the very language in which the rest of us write. I am aware that some would deem this idealization, just as they judge the appreciative awe and wonder with which Shakespeare fills me endlessly. I believe I am simply being fair in my evaluations.

And *you*, dear reader, are indeed keenly present in my list of those to whom I feel indebted. You will, as you must and should, turn my text into a responsive dialogue. Without you, these words would be dead; with you, they can take their place in the continuous conversation that is the sinew and blood of human progress. None is intended as the last word. I thank you.

Parts of this volume have already been published, some in earlier and less developed form. For permission to publish versions of that work, I thank the following:

American Imago:

The analyst's fears, 2006, 63:201–217.

Polymorphously normal sexuality, 2006, 63:479–483.

The limits of empathy, 2007, 64:87–93.

Oedipal complexes, oedipal schema, 2007, 64:561–565.

Beyond bedrock, 2011, 68:31–36.

Rather my own shortcomings, 2011, 68:121–125.

The International Journal of Psychoanalysis:

Problems of collegial learning in psychoanalysis: narcissism and curiosity, 2009, 90:249–262.

The Journal of the American Psychoanalytic Association:

The analyst's witnessing and otherness, 2000, 48:17–34.

The interpretive attitude, 2002, 50:807–826.

Reading fiction and the psychoanalytic experience: Proust on reading and on reading Proust, 2003, 51:1263–1281.

Ephemera – unfinished thoughts on psychoanalysis, poetry, endings, and death: commentary on Caston, 2007, 55:31–41.

Slouching towards mortality: thoughts on time and death, 2016, 64:795–802.

The Psychoanalytic Quarterly:

On immediacy: "vivid contrast between past and present," 2002, 71:113–115.

Whimsy, 2010, 79:235–240.

Outsiderness in human nature, 2012, 81:931–953.

The analyst's approach and the patient's psychic growth, 2013, 82:829–847.

Reference

Shakespeare, W. (1971). *Twelfth Night or What You Will*. New York: Penguin Books.

Editor's introduction

A freedom of mind: Warren Poland in word and deed

William F. Cornell

> *Making art, making poetry, yes even analyzing – these create meaning and value perhaps best not as a denial of horror but defiantly in the face of horror.*
> (Poland, 2007, p. 40)

It is a rare contributor to psychoanalytic discourse who insists on the independence of his own mind while granting full freedom and agency to the mind of the reader. In *Intimacy and Separateness in Psychoanalysis*, Warren Poland takes up many of the themes and controversies that often enliven – and at times deaden or divide – contemporary psychoanalytic conversations. His thinking on the mechanisms of therapeutic relatedness in particular is notably more nuanced and integrative, avoiding such simplistic demarcations as "one-person" vs. "two-person" models of psychoanalytic theory and technique. As Poland articulates his own searching positions, he never invites the reader to disclaim or acclaim one point of view over another or to simply take up his. Rather, he insists that the reader engage her or his own thinking anew.

Engagement with paradox constantly informs Poland's work. He argues for the necessity of an approach to theoretical discussions from both unobstructed and disciplined frames of mind in the service of professional maturation. By "unobstructed," Poland may well be invoking the true meaning of Freud's notion of neutrality – to be open, curious, and deeply receptive – applied at the level of analytic theorizing as well as to analytic listening. "Discipline," as Poland defines it, necessitates and relishes "rigor in conceptualization, regard for prior learning, and tolerance in the face of unyielding paradox" (p. 88). Inherent, too, in Poland's valuing of discipline is his repeated demonstrations of the centrality of self-analysis that is fundamental to his clinical work. He wryly observes that while each clinical analysis does come to a defined point of termination, the need for self-analytic reflection never ends.

It has been only recently that I met Warren in person. My knowledge of his work had previously been through a series of encounters with his writing over many years and then through an occasional exchange of letters. My own graduate school training was in phenomenology and existentialism, followed by transactional analysis, not psychoanalysis. I have always been grateful for that, because as I undertook my own professional exploration of diverse psychoanalytic authors, I have felt freed of the burdens of the orthodoxies that have so often rendered the psychoanalytic literature as gospel rather than as guidance and inspiration, the orthodoxies so many of my analytically trained colleagues have had to so achingly climb out from under. My non-analytic grounding has undoubtedly been an important part of what drew me to Warren's writing over the years. His has been and remains an independent mind in which I found a kinship that excited and challenged me. It was this kinship and valuing of Warren's singular voice that led me to offer to edit his more recent papers for *Intimacy and Separateness in Psychoanalysis*.

I use the phrase "encounters with his writing" quite intentionally. The notion of encounter is central to existential thinking. Reading Poland's work over the years has had for me the quality, the impact, of encounter – a coming up against my self, my assumptions, and my therapeutic comforts. His writing does not yield ground easily to the preferences of the reader, nor does it attack them. Rather, it simultaneously invites the reader to pause, to wonder, to grapple with familiar knowns, and to consider the unfamiliar and the unwanted. Warren does not shy away from his own encounters: with colleagues, with the literature, with his patients, with himself, with life and death.

The writer and the reader

> One lets oneself go in order to take something in, but what is taken in is not swallowed whole; it is selectively chewed over and only then digested. That is so as you consider what I write; it is so when the lights come on between acts at the theater; it is so when an analyst emotionally steps back to think about what has been heard and felt; it is so when a patient contemplates an interpretation; and it is so when a reader pulls back after being lost in a book. The *becoming as-if-one-with* and the *separating from* are at the heart of both reading and analyzing.
>
> (p. 122)

Poland's is the voice of a man who loves language. His immersive embrace of literature and theater echoes through almost every essay contained in this book. For Poland, psychoanalysis shares much more in common with the literary arts than with the scientific traditions, arguing that both psychoanalysis and literature seek the articulation, through language, of the frailties of human existence coupled with its transcendent potential. He reminds us of Freud's frequent efforts to bring psychoanalytic understandings to the literature of his time (and of the eras that preceded him) and to bring the wisdom and creativity of literary minds to psychoanalysis. Poland argues, quite fiercely, that the immersion of psychoanalysis in the culture of its time – art, literature, politics, history – is not merely "applied" as opposed to "clinical" psychoanalysis, but rather an endless source of vitalization to psychoanalytic thinking. A retreat to purely clinical theorizing may protect the clinician from the impact of cultural and social intrusions, yet it impoverishes the reach of psychoanalytic inquiry. As Poland wrote in his book *Melting the Darkness*, "sensitive involvement with reading, drama, music, and visual arts can open inner emotional areas that have been closed" (1996, p. 258).

Through his essays on literature, theater, and poetry included in this volume, we witness Poland's holding of the inevitable tensions between the arenas of commonality evoked by the timeless power of great art and those of the deeply, and often darkly, held regions of one's psyche that art can bring to the surface – often unbidden and at times unwanted. He quotes Proust's observation that although the reader is involved in a conversation with the author, each of us reads in the midst of our own solitude. So, too, Poland argues that what is ultimately assimilated in an analysis occurs within the privacy of the self.

The analytic approach

> Thus, not only does the patient benefit from the content of what the analyst says focused on the specific issue of the moment, the patient has the benefit of observing, and observing repeatedly, the analyst's way of handling conflicts, the analyst's preferred ways of delaying impulsive discharge and instead turning inner conflict into data for consideration. The analyst's approach informs the patient *how* the analyst analyses.
>
> (p. 67)

In his clinical articles, Warren places great emphasis on the analytic *approach*, in contrast to analytic *technique*. He argues that over the course of an analysis, while a patient may well profit from the moments of insight and other forms of analytic content, it is the attitude and approach of the analyst – gradually observed, experienced, and internalized – that is the primary factor in the patient's psychic growth and the lasting gift of psychoanalytic therapies. So, too, in reading the essays in this book, the reader has the benefit of watching and experiencing Warren's ways of thinking and working inside and outside the consulting room. For me as a reader – as well as a therapist and author – this has opened up a much appreciated space for reflection.

Warren repeatedly challenges the parochialism that can infect psychoanalytic communities and foster defenses that limit open dialogue among professionals. Observing that "the anxious uncertainty intrinsic to creativity stimulates the pressure for team loyalty" (p. 94), Warren describes the conscious and unconscious forces that too often make it difficult, if not impossible, for colleagues of different theoretical preferences to truly listen to one another. Here again he speaks to the essential paradox inherent in maturational processes:

> Narcissism speaks of the emotional investments aimed inward, while curiosity refers to those aimed outward ... like conjoined twins, the two always go in tandem even when in conflict. ... Self-concerns and experience of the other are unitary in the process of creating meaning.
>
> (p. 97)

Not only in clinical engagement, but in professional and theoretical engagements as well, our work carries the responsibility for self-analysis when the capacity to listen receptively falters. Curiosity and uncertainty live at the heart of open clinical inquiry. At its best, Warren contends, "theory reminds us to wonder," but theory can also serve "the defensive comfort of closure ... insistent knowing so as not to feel uncertain" (p. 84).

Warren argues forcefully for an "exploratory rather than revelatory approach" (p. 51) in listening to and speaking with patients:

> The analyst provides a holding environment, an empathic ambiance, and a capacity to contain the anxieties and conflicts taken in from a patient's projections. The analyst respects, listens, hears, regards, and witnesses.
>
> (p. 69)

But these services to the other are not those of submission, acquiescence, or union with the other. Poland holds his mind quite distinct from that of his patient while holding the mind of his patient quite distinct from his own. It is in this terrain that we see Poland at work in a subtle, ever-evolving nexus that involves the other, the quality of otherness, and the experience of outsiderness. In his clinical papers, he offers discussions of the interpretive attitude, empathy, containment, intersubjectivity, witnessing, and regard – each and all as necessary elements of an analysis and each, as presented in his unique voice, fostering psychic separateness and maturation.

The therapeutic attitude

Poland seeks to expand the meaning and function of interpretation, shifting the focus from content to process, from what to how. While he does not deny the relevance of the declarative interpretation as an effort to bring new meanings and connection to a patient's awareness, his emphasis is on the interpretive *attitude* as embodying the lived experience of curiosity, investigation, and discovery that is the core of a free mind:

> That curiosity about as yet unknown deeper explanations is what places the unrestricted interpretive attitude at the heart of the psychoanalytic approach.
>
> (p. 58)

Essential to the lasting productivity of an analysis is the patient's gradual internalization of a self-interpretive capacity, one that serves the coherence, efficacy and delight of finding and keeping a mind of one's own. The analyst works in service of this maturational process:

> Any transference exploration and resolution is possible because the mature strengths of the analyzing partners can be brought to bear on the experiences that had originally developed when the analysand was less mature.
>
> (p. 52)

Poland does not presume that all transference relations are backward-looking, nor that all interpretations need to articulate their archaic roots. Eros is alive in transference relations, pressing for more life, seeking, even demanding a future different from the past. The exploratory attitude of interpretation is based in the belief that there is something new to be found.

Witnessing

> By "witnessing" I refer to an analyst's activity: the analyst's functioning as a patient's other who maintains an actively observing presence, who recognizes and grasps the emotional activity in the mind of the patient at work, and who is himself recognized by the patient as a distinctly separate person in his own right, not merely as a transferential object. ... Recognition of autonomy and respect for otherness are central to witnessing.
>
> (p. 18; emphasis in original)

In his elaboration of the analytic function of witnessing, Poland provides a stark contrast to the notions of therapeutic empathy:

> At moments of pain as one deals forthrightly with personal responsibility for one's role in what had been painful to oneself or others, at those moments it matters that another know, that another understand, that another have some appreciation of the implications. Recognition, not exoneration, is what is then called for.
>
> (p. 18)

Witnessing does not alleviate suffering but acknowledges it.

As catalyst to the patient's capacity to know and to define a self as unique among others, witnessing enables a deepening personal testimony and meaning. Poland suggests that the credit due an analyst at the end of a challenging analysis is rarely for interpretive virtuosity but much more likely for the analyst's capacity to keep the faith in the face of recurrent and often disheartening periods of frustrating, draining, and corrosive constriction.

When taking up the place of empathy in contemporary psychoanalytic practice, Poland throws down a gauntlet: "[Empathy] has been seen lying at the heart of growth and development; its lack has been posited as the centerpiece of pathogenesis; and it has been put forward as the essence of what is mutative in the analytic process" (p. 103). He goes on, "This misuse of empathy sidesteps the observer's need for the uncomfortable work of self-analysis ... [and] is an under-mining of the patient's separateness and uniqueness" (p. 103). He offers a powerfully different casting of the function and place of empathy in the analytic project:

> Empathy, which refers to how one person perceives another when two sep-arate people come together, can be valid only when founded on profound respect for otherness, the full respect of the observing person for the singular-ity and particularity of the other.
>
> (p. 106)

Poland's insistence on respect goes both ways as he argues that the patient, too, must come to see the analyst as a separate and unique person: "No. I am not you, nor am I one of your ghosts. ... No, I am not your fantasy actualized" (p. 23). It has been in this terrain that Poland's perspective has deeply fos-tered my own self-analysis in my work with those patients who have pressed relentlessly for "empathy," which too often conflated agreement with the patient's perception of events as a form of compassionate understanding. As a younger therapist I often fell mute in the face of these transferential pres-sures. Even as I knew such merger and pseudo-comfort would not serve my patients, the resonance with my own family history and my functioning within the family stopped me in my tracks. Warren's papers, with those of James McLaughlin and Christopher Bollas, gave me a way to begin to think more effectively. Gradually I could find ways to bring my self to these patients, neither as a merging object nor as an invasive, controlling object, but as one of two separate people deeply engaged in looking at the world (and selves), side by side.

In the opening paper of this volume, Poland elaborates the concept of "regard," suggesting that it might be a word that captures this intention of therapeutic engagement better than his original use of "witness." The English for this alterna-tive word is derived from the French *regarder*, which conveys the meanings of watching, looking, guarding, and protecting. It is an active perspective – attentive, sustaining, a keeping of the faith.

Encountering strangers

> The underlying analytic process is premised on a shift from what is conven-tional to the emphatically unconventional process of openness beyond the usual taboos, an intimacy structured for expression, exposure, and explora-tion. *In this new world of the analytic situation, each partner approaches the other as a stranger.*
>
> (p. 40; emphasis in original)

It has been more than 20 years since the publication of Poland's first book, *Melting the Darkness: The Dyad and Principles of Clinical Practice*. In that earlier volume, Poland explored facets of the clinical partnership engendered through the analytic process. Offering numerous case examples, he demonstrated a clinical attitude grounded in the interplay of two distinct, individual psychologies, a perspective that he came to call "two-person separate."

This new volume of essays more fully articulates Poland's fundamental respect for the uniqueness and separateness of the patient's and the analyst's psyches emerging from the profound intimacies afforded through the psychoanalytic encounter. *Self* and *other* have been fundamental organizing concepts in psychoanalysis for decades, bringing the inevitability and vitality of clinical attention to the therapeutic dyad in all of its myriad manifestations. Poland does not diminish the importance of the dyad, but he offers a profound regard for "the private universe of inner experience", thus placing the interpersonal in dynamic tension with the private. His focus in many of his recent essays shifts significantly to the exploration and elaboration of this terrain. Writing during a time of theories valorizing co-creation, mutuality, empathy, and intersubjectivity within the analytic dyad, Poland instead invites the stranger, the alien, the unknown, and the unwanted self into the consulting room for the reader's careful consideration. He underscores the courage and risk both parties bring to the fore in entering this field of analytic endeavor. Poland makes it clear – especially in the essays "The analyst's fears" and "On long analyses" – that the analyst is rarely the master of his or her own house. It is fundamental in all of his writing that it is only through rigorous, ongoing self-analysis that the analyst can ensure the clarity and receptivity of his mind to that of the patient. Self-analysis is the greatest insurance of the analyst's capacity to hold the other in true *regard*.

Poland argues that there are aspects of psychic life and the therapeutic process that are not contained or best expressed in dyadic terms. He challenges the ways in which the valorization of the dyad can offer hiding places and deflections from facing the quite separate realities of the analyst's and the patient's actual and psychic worlds. While curiosity and uncertainty are essential to an analytic process of any depth and significance, Poland speaks to the analyst's vulnerability in the face of the inevitable limits to the understanding of the patient's psychic world. "*Each partner approaches the other as a stranger.*" Here again is a paradoxical pairing: that of a unique form of intimacy with an unavoidable strangeness, the profound depths of otherness and differentness that will constantly haunt the emergent and fragile "we-ness" of the analytic process.

It takes two to witness the unconscious, in Poland's view. But he asks, what is the nature of that two-ness? He repeatedly returns to the question of how to integrate human commonalities and fundamental singularities within the ongoing analytic endeavor. In the contemporary analytic literature, intersubjectivity often takes center stage as an answer to this vexing question. Does an individual ever truly exist outside of a relational context? Relational and intersubjective theorists seem to answer "no" to that question. Poland brings a unique perspective. He posits two forms of intersubjectivity. The more common contemporary usage connotes a therapeutic pair in which experience and understanding are co-created through the formation of an essential unity: two into one. While acknowledging this aspect of therapeutic engagement, Poland questions whether it is a primary mutative factor in psychic growth and maturation. He posits instead a second perspective on intersubjectivity, that of "the communicative emotional flow between two different parties" (p. 25). Separateness again comes to the fore. He brings our attention to the quality of intersubjectivity created by the reciprocal experiences generated by subject–object separation and differentiation.

Otherness and outsiderness open different terrains. Otherness refers to the emotional realization that one's self is different from the lived actuality of others. In otherness there are aspects of one's self experience that will remain inevitably "other" to others, embodying unique and private aspects of the individual psyche that can never be fully grasped and known by someone other than oneself. Outsiderness has its own particular lived quality, one of being fundamentally apart from the world of others. Outsiderness is not just about being different, it is about being *apart*, not fitting, not belonging. Outsiderness has long been the subject of the existential literature but has been little explored in an analytic context. Poland brings this experience into an analytic frame as he outlines the near universal vulnerability to feeling outside – *alien, unbelonging* – over the course of one's life span. Once again, he addresses the paradox of outsiderness. He posits that analyst and analysand begin their work together each being an outsider to the other's experience; they meet as strangers. Each lives with the possibility and vulnerability to painful misunderstandings. And then the work unfolds as "the world of transference and dream can come alive" (p. 41). Analyst and patient "share the effort to move from strangeness to familiarity, from parallel outsiderness to a mutual and growing, shared *insiderness*" (p. 40). But the work does not stop there. Poland argues that to be satisfied with the achievement of mutuality and insiderness would be to cut short the final emergence, recognition, and regard for the compelling individuality of each – therein lies the unique quality of intimacy afforded through psychoanalytic exploration.

Poland draws on Freud's brief but exquisite essay "On transience," which to my mind speaks to the heart of the existential perspective that the impermanence of life makes all we do more precious and vital. This is the terrain in which the individual psyche reaches the full, fragile depths of the self. Poland concludes that some things can be accomplished and realized alone that cannot be accomplished with someone else. Patient and analyst part no longer strangers yet still left ultimately with their own resources to encounter the disappointments, the travails, as well as the unending richness of being alive, while awaiting death.

Encountering darkness

> Does our therapeutic zeal lead us to put an unduly happy face on endings in order to salve our own anxieties of uncertainty and helplessness? Might we do better with a bit less encouraging inspiration and a bit more respect for the verities of loss and death? Those are questions not only for psychoanalytic technique but for living life itself.
>
> (p. 160)

The essays in this book were written in the latter years of Warren's life and career. Now "darkness" does not so much "melt" as surround, encroach, and enrich. Here the existential underpinnings of Poland's thinking sweep to the surface: "impermanence is an essential organizing principle that defines our species. ... Transience is in the very structure of our minds" (p. 164).

One of my favorite essays here is his brief "What play did Shakespeare write when he wrote *Twelfth Night*?" Warren brings a warm and humorous touch to his personal accounts of his reckonings with the dodge and chase of one's maturational efforts. In his taking up of *Twelfth Night,* he describes the multiplicity of meanings he has discovered over the course of his life through many readings and viewings of this play. He takes notice that the text of the play could not itself have actually changed, but then wryly comments, "It took a long while before I recognized that it has also consistently served as a precious interpretive companion, one profoundly valuable to mark the self analysis by which I struggle to mature, trying to make maturity keep up with age" (p. 154). We again witness the generative interplay of Poland the reader, Poland the audience, Poland the writer, and Poland the analyst. As it is a play that I, too, have seen in several versions over the years, I could easily relate to Warren's evolving experience of it. Even more so, I could relate this essay to my own readings and rereadings over the years of various favorite papers by Freud, Winnicott, Berne, Reich, Bollas, McLaughlin, Dimen, and of course Poland, which unfold in greater depth and meaning as I struggle and mature (hopefully) in expertise as well as age.

I find the essay "The analyst's fears" to be the heart of this book. First written when Poland was in his late 60s, he noted with "chagrin," only after working and writing for more than 30 years, that "my looking directly at fear comes so very late, nearer the end rather than the start of my thinking" (p. 74). It is a frank and unflinching examination of human and analytic frailty. Here again, we meet paradox as Poland observes that as his analytic skills have deepened over the years of practice, this very fact has "either led to or permitted me more openness to more deeply felt dread and sadness" (p. 79). In his reflections on *Twelfth Night*, it was not until his fifties that he was able to see "how dark a stain ran through the play ... a nakedly mean, ruthless malice" (153–154).

> Just as I was forced to accept in my own world the persistent presence of disappointment, a view of the universe far different from the wonders

of delight I had imagined in my adolescent idealism, so too the play now exposed evil, not only its brutality but also its eternal presence.

(p. 154)

Poland as reader, analyst, and self come into a blunt encounter.

This brief essay and "The analyst's fears" echo through my life and my own personal analyses, each essay evoking memories of those moments when I finally encountered and truly faced the consequences of my persistent refusal to meet head on the tragedies and losses that I had so fervently disavowed in my life and in the lives of those I have loved. So, too, I think of those moments in treatment and in my intimate relations when I came to confront the nasty aspects of my character and of those poignant, essential moments in therapy when a patient begins to take ownership of the potential for malice that lurks in each of us.

The sense of psychic frailty is a quiet presence throughout Poland's work. In "Fears" he brings a fierce attention to the reality that "fear is not a theoretical concept; it is something that lies cold at the bottom of the stomach" (p. 77). He leads us through a series of clinical vignettes in which he had to confront and resolve his own fear in order to do his work. His final vignettes are of a patient whose father was dying during his analysis and of a woman who was herself dying during her analysis, presented so as to illustrate bluntly that "an analyst is not invulnerable to the perils of reality" (p. 78). Poland insists that we look at the actual dangers that exist in life interfering with and facilitating therapeutic efforts – again paradox. He goes on to delineate the sense of clinical and life dangers that foster fear in the analyst. He returns to a recurrent theme of the misuse of theory to ward off the uncertainty and fears of entering uncharted territories with patients. He concludes:

I analyze, in part ... to take revenge on reality, to try to prove to myself over and over and over and over that insight truly can gain some dominance over terror. Yet I learn repeatedly that fear can be tamed but never fully vanquished.

(p. 84)

In life and in death

Warren and I share an abiding passion for the arts, yet there is just enough difference in our ages that Warren and I are from different generations in the art and music that filled our formative years. As a young man, I was immersed in a particular generation of poets and artists. I spent countless hours reading the Beat poets – Allen Ginsberg, Gary Snyder, Kenneth Patchen, William Everson, and Philip Whalen – whose photographs hang in my consulting room. I had the good fortune to meet many of them and so to hear their voices as well as read their words on the page. Their poetry, when I first encountered it, was passionate, ferocious, rebellious, and relentlessly sexual. Inevitably, as they aged, Eros met Thanatos. Their work faced and brought voice to loss and death, as has my own (Cornell 2014).

William Everson, a poet of ferocious intensity and eroticism, was diagnosed with Parkinson's disease. As he turned 65, he wrote of his then standing "in the center of a twilight field, distantly circled by dark woods" (1980, p. 1). He did not find himself fearing death. Rather, he feared "the passing of rapacious joy, that appetitive sensuality and intellectual thirst" (1980, p. 1).

Warren closes *Intimacy and Separateness in Psychoanalysis* with "Slouching towards mortality: Thoughts on time and death." I first *heard* rather than read this paper. It brought me to silence. It brought me to tears. When Warren finished speaking, it was as though I was witnessing the end of a brilliant theater performance, one where I am not clapping or standing for the ovation but am sitting in utter silence, alone even though I am surrounded by a loud and enthusiastic crowd. To *hear* Warren's quietly passionate voice speaking to the wizened creativity that age and risk-taking can spark into life brought a new understanding to his words that I had been reading for many years. Warren speaks to the deeply personal meeting of intimacy and loss, vitality and reality, Eros and Thanatos – "facing Thanatos stirs the defiant vitality of Eros" (p. 166). In so doing, he offers his final paradoxical pairing.

He closes the essay with the story of a patient dying in his early 50s during his analysis, his son still an adolescent. The patient asked Warren to meet with his son, whenever his son was ready, and speak for him of his father as a man, of his profound love and regard for his son. Warren did, carrying for his dead patient a voice he had not himself been able to bring to his young son. He was able to convey this father's wish for his son to flourish in his own life.

I have been in this work for nearly 50 years now. As a student and then young therapist, my days were often filled with the dark but idealistically defiant music of Bob Dylan, Patti Smith, and Lou Reed. These are artists whose work has stayed alive and maturing from one decade to the next. Each has faced profound losses and the deaths of loved ones that they have transformed through their music. Lou Reed was a poet and performer of relentless, unyielding self-scrutiny. As I prepared to write this introduction and reread the papers in this book, especially the closing chapter, I kept thinking of Reed's image of a "talking book," written for a theatrical collaboration with Robert Wilson. Reed described his wish for a *talking* book, not just words on a page, but a book that talked and could *speak* the "keys to past and present memories" and *speak* the name of someone now gone, so that they would "still remain more than a picture on a shelf" (2000, p. 430).

Warren gives us just such a talking book. He writes,

> Generosity of spirit, creative generativity, is the way Eros defies Thanatos, the way one generation can deeply regret its own death yet be comforted by the continuation of loved others. ... And what is the essence of that word "generation" but a group defined by engendering those who follow?

(p. 168–169)

Intimacy and Separateness in Psychoanalysis is a generous book, a talking book of hard-won and heartfelt generativity. It is a book that I hope will speak to our future generations of psychoanalysts and psychotherapists for many years to come.

References

Cornell, W.F. (2014). Grief, mourning, and meaning: In a personal voice. *Transactional Analysis Journal*, 44:302–310.

Everson, W. (1980). *Sixty Five*. Boston, MA: Anne & David Bromer.

Poland, W.S. (1996). *Melting the Darkness: The Dyad and Principles of Clinical Practice*. Northvale, NJ: Jason Aronson.

Poland, W.S. (2007). Ephemera: Unfinished thoughts on Psychoanalysis, Poetry, Endings, and Death – Commentary on Caston. *Journal of the American Psychoanalytic Association*, 55(1):40.

Reed, L. (2000). *Pass through Fire*. New York: Hyperion.

Part I

Opening conclusions

Chapter 1

Regarding the other

Regarding the other

"Regard" – what a wonderfully elastic word that is. It stretches across the breadth of engagement from a fully detached surveying of a broad field to a more focused but still removed looking at a narrower specific focus with an interested curiosity in which other emotional investment is absent, then extending all the way to an observing that is participatory and includes such personal emotional engagement as caring.

The *Oxford English Dictionary* makes clear that the word "regard" has covered the full diversity of levels of dispassion and passion throughout its history. The word comes to us from the French *regarder*, to look at or watch, with that word deriving from the Old French *reguarder*, implying guarding or protecting. Indeed, *reguarder* is tellingly linked to its sibling, the Old Northern French variant *rewarder*, to give a reward. Regard, warden, and guard all belong to the same small genetic family.

The expanse of implications of the verb "to regard" shows through in a specific incarnation, the vast range of ways analysis has, through its history, thought of the analyst's relationship to the patient – from fully detached examining to a beginning consideration of an analyst's engagement as seen only as an interfering artifice, then on to appreciation of the place of participant–observer oscillations, from there on farther to valuing of the dyadic mutuality as the very medium of the analytic process, and even reaching at times to a radical relationalism in which separate individualities are absented.

Is one of these views to be taken as valid and are the others to be deemed mistaken? At times, polemical debates between analysts sound as if that were so. Can all of these views have simultaneous validity, even as they can appear to be contradictory? How is one to conceive the nature of the analyst–patient engagement? How do so-called one-person and two-person psychologies mesh or conflict in shaping understanding?

Our minds strive to comprehend experience by breaking it into bite-sized pieces so that we can grasp, identify, and categorize them. Our literature reflects, often with an excess of fervor, the endless variety of such points of view, yet our minds seem ill equipped or insufficient to integrate fully the implicit paradoxes of such varied considerations.

This is the hard problem of psychoanalysis. Neuroscientists have used the term "hard problem" to describe the enigma of consciousness. How is it that among the overwhelmingly complex multiplicity of brain activities, there is one process that leaps from insensate function to the creation of consciousness? That challenge for neuroscientists demands their bridging the separate phenomenological universes studied in the distinct disciplines of biology and psychology.

Psychoanalysis has its own internal hard problem, and it is one that is entirely internal to the discipline of psychology. It is the challenge to integrate the phenomena of human separateness and commonality. How can one best conceive of a person as a particular distinct individual while simultaneously holding in mind the implications of the view that there is no such thing as a person outside the common human fabric? How well can anyone keep in mind separateness and unified human experience all at once?

The words we use serve us to conceptualize and express ideas. By our reflecting on them, they also can inform us of how our minds struggle to combine denotations that have specificity of viewpoint with connotations that keep open varied aspects of understanding. As we have seen, the word "regard" has the flexibility we require for consideration of the clinical analytic process.

The problem, of course, is more than clinical. At its heart, even beyond its therapeutic application, psychoanalysis is a form of inquiry, a disciplined technique developed as a specific tool for allowing exploration of the hidden parts of a mind at work. It is a tool for knowledge, a tool that makes possible a unique way of knowing.

In knowing something, the dilemmas are present. What do we mean when we say we know? I do not attempt to open the vast continent of epistemology, now wishing only to note that the word "know" is as varied in its connotations as is "regard." On this abstract level as on the experiential clinical level, the word extends from descriptive perceiving to inferential understanding, those themselves both ranging from disinterested objectivity to emotionally detached engagement, then reaching all the way to the connection of what might be termed emotional tasting, extending yet farther to merger, becoming a part of and unifying with the object, as in knowing sexually ("to know in a biblical sense").

When trying to name the experiences I describe in the chapter on the analyst's witnessing, I felt that the word "witnessing" was never more than almost right. First, one tends to link the work to legal matters, where testifying is implicit, and testifying is importantly excluded from witnessing as an analytic function. Also, the word carries powerful emotional and even religious undertones as a result of the Holocaust. Can any word ever be quite right?

If one looks closely at any analytic unfolding, the enigma of separateness and commonality is always present. Perhaps that is so for all human endeavors, yet it is only in retrospect that I have recognized that this dilemma has always shaped my thinking and my work. It is the reason I feel "regarding" to be the word that comes nearest to covering the multiple ways an analyst approaches, experiences, and engages with the other person in the analysis.

Concluding reflections en route

Perhaps I should have recognized this earlier. Looking backward, I see this concern for clarifying the relationship between self definition and otherness as having shaped my thinking beyond my awareness. I see it now evident even when as a young analyst responding to a request for a statement on self analysis I wrote,

> For me, grasping reality always requires a stretch to try to realize what self and otherness mean, to struggle to contain with great difficulty the awareness that, while you and I share the same world, we have different and equally valid realities.
>
> (Poland 1996, p. 246)

It shocks me now to realize that I have spent well over 50 years behind the couch. Even now, it still is as it was at the start: I am trying to learn *how* to analyze. I feel keenly identified with an elderly Japanese Noh mask carver I met who said of the same point in his career,

> People ask me if my carving has improved over the years. I really can't answer that. Each mask is different. I approach each one as if I am carving for the first time. Work done slowly, carefully, patiently and with *the open mind of a beginner* will be good.
>
> (Personal communication)

"The open mind of a beginner" – analytic candidacy is the start of training, not its end.

Finding a face buried in a block of wood and helping someone with self inquiry are both bound to fall short of perfection. That each time is "for the first time" is vital so that a patient's *self* inquiry not be carved to the design of the analyst's favorite theory or view of the world.

Aware of the power of self delusion, we know the wisdom in the tennis coach's saying, "Practice makes permanent." Long practice can lead to growing skills, but merely repeated experience can also lead to calling something growth that in fact is only personal comfort.

There is a point where mask carving and analyzing split ways. An irony innate to analysis is that while a patient asks an analyst's help, analysis by its very definition is the study of whatever it is that people do *not* want to know about themselves. The wood gives itself up to the carver. A patient, however, is in conflict, torn, pulled from as well as toward insight.

What I have written is not intended either to proclaim or to promote a point. Writing is my way of trying to understand; what I offer is meant not as last words but only as how I grasp a topic at this point. This mirrors how I work, or try to work, in practice, always in an inquiry to try to find whatever meaning lies behind what has unfolded. Analyzing is like extending a clearing in the forest.

When advancing, one always works at the edge of darkness, and too much clarity at work raises concern that what is uncertain has been left for the safety of what is congenial.

When I passed the 50-year marker, I asked myself what was the most important thing I had learned in that half century. Perhaps I should not have been, but I was surprised to recognize that the hardest thing for me to learn was the most obvious. It is that *the patient is somebody else!* Not me, not part of me, but really somebody else, somebody with a full life that does not include me. Not simply a patient in *my* office, a character in *my* mind, a person in *my* life, but somebody truly "else," a person entire in his or her own life. I am the other's other.

Indeed, I am actually only one person among very many others in the patient's life. Yes, I am one with a privileged position inside that person's mind, but I am there only at that person's invitation, asked in for a specific purpose and consequently for a limited time.

When I think of all I have written as my part in what Dr. Johnson called the epidemical conspiracy for the destruction of trees, one of the few sentences that satisfies me is one that seems almost a throw-away line, the final sentence in an early paper on neutrality: "All the technical principles ... are reasonable, logical, and inevitable consequences of remembering *who* the analyst is and *why* the analyst is there" (Poland 1996, p. 100).

Whatever the desire to extend psychoanalytic knowledge, the analyst's clinical participation in another's introspective journey is always primarily in the service of that patient. The ethics of clinical responsibility toward the patient take priority over purely academic exploration. The analyst works in the service of the other.

Experience has led me to conclude that there is a contribution the analyst makes even more basic than that of advancing the patient's self inquiry. It is the analyst's respectful recognition of the patient as having a self in its own right, distinct and with its own values, regardless of those of the analyst. Not only is such an attitude essential for exploration to unfold, but also it has a fundamental beneficial import in and of itself.

It is crucial for a patient, for any person, to be seen, acknowledged, and appreciated for that person's unique self. Being seen and being gotten, without being acted on for the sake of the other's purposes, even therapeutic – that is vital and essential.

As we know, psychoanalysis is not a spectator sport. The analyst has many differing ways of coming to understand. One is conscious attention to unfolding associations. Another has to do with experiencing the patient's emotional world, doing so in a way that oscillates between engaged empathy and detached reflection. The analyst's self analysis is essential for this to succeed, for experiencing but not getting lost in the patient's dream world brought to life.

Any clinician soon learns that the analyst's self analytic in-and-out is not as easy as it may sound, yet it is basic to the process. The analyst's *silent* self analysis is something a patient picks up. It is through that picking up that the patient develops the patient's own ability similarly to shift between conflictual and observing spheres of the mind, the patient's own ability to oscillate between subjectivity and objectivity.

Technique is not simply explicit activity consciously planned. Much more significantly, technique is attitude actualized. What is in the back of the analyst's mind, including *how* the analyst's mind works, shapes the analyst's functioning ... and the patient picks that up, whether wittingly or not.

In terms of self-other differentiation, whatever the analyst says, from the most trivial clarification to the most profound interpretation, whatever the content of the words, also communicates an implicit individuating message:

> *No*, I am *not* you, nor am I one of your ghosts, but as separate people we can speak to and with each other of what is going on. No, I am *not* part of your dream, but as a person separate from you, I can help you find the words to say it.

Contact between separate people replaces merger.

This consideration was recognized early by Stone when he wrote, "The psychoanalytic situation is one in which two persons in the state of 'intimate separation' ... express the whole gamut of tensions which may rise between them" (Stone 1961, p. 91). "Intimate separation" is essential and intrinsic to the fundamental psychoanalytic situation, whatever the derivative manifestations – for instance, the tendency to merge or, inevitably, the development of a psychological couple – whether viewed in terms of the dyad, the analytic third (Ogden 1994), or the bi-personal field (Baranger & Baranger 2008).

Analysis cannot be conceived without appreciation of the intersubjective context within which it unfolds. Nonetheless, when the work goes well, the patient's individuality, profoundly respected from the start, grows in autonomous strength through the collaborative work.

This is what I attempt to explore in what follows. I do so in the presence of unresolved concerns ever present. For illustration I mention two, the misuse of theory and the psychoanalytic tendency to pathologize life. I will make a brief comment on each.

First, the misuse of theory. I could not overestimate the value of what I have learned from my teachers and colleagues, that cumulative knowledge combined and codified into what we call theory. Not to appreciate theory is to believe that ignorance actually is bliss. Closing one's mind to learning is mental suicide.

Nonetheless, rapid resort to theory is counter productive, closing questions rather than opening them. It is too easy to fall back on theory to minimize the discomfort of feeling lost when facing the edge of darkness, the land where inquiry lives. There is no GPS for exploring *terra incognita*. To paraphrase Clive James (2007, p. 606), a sense of experience reveals variety, and an ideology conceals it.

A second unsolved difficulty has to do with flaws intrinsic to psychoanalytic thinking itself. The primary data of analytic knowledge necessarily come from clinical practice, from analytically disciplined work with patients. An undesired consequence of work done in such a clinical laboratory is the tendency of psychoanalysis to pathologize life. We must find a way that when we search the index of our knowledge, the listing for "How the mind works" does not say "See Pathology."

Dilemmas notwithstanding, it is hard not to feel awe at what an astonishing world was exposed when Freud pulled back the curtain hiding unconscious forces and at how fortunate we are to be lost in exploring such terrain. How privileged we are to be welcomed into the lives of specific, singular, and unique individual others to share such a project.

References

Baranger, M. & Baranger, W. (2008). The analytic situation as a dynamic field. *International Journal of Psychoanalysis*, 89:795–826.

James, C. (2007). *Culture Amnesia: Necessary Memories from History and the Arts*. New York: Norton.

Ogden, T.H. (1994). The analytic third: Working with intersubjective clinical facts. *International Journal of Psychoanalysis*, 75:3–19.

Poland, W. (1996). *Melting the Darkness: The Dyad and Principles of Clinical Practice*. Northvale, NJ: Jason Aronson.

Stone, L. (1961). *The Psychoanalytic Situation: An Examination of Its Developmental and Essential Nature*. New York: International Universities Press.

Chapter 2

Rather my own shortcomings

Lord, help me find the truth, and, Lord,
protect me from those who have already found it.
                                        — An ancient prayer

Most of them met at art school, the Académie Julian, gifted youngsters eager not
only to learn from their masters but also to move beyond them. Influenced by
ideas Sérusier had brought from Gauguin in Brittany, the young Vuillard, Denis,
Bonnard, and others banded together. Wanting to leave the prevailing style of
impressionism behind, they called themselves Nabis, prophets, and together with
a few added colleagues set out to find a new approach to painting and color.

Denis became their theorist. In 1890, when only 19 years old, he published
his *Définition du néo-traditionnisme*. Its first paragraph famously set down the
basic premise from which the other principles of the Nabis derived: "Remember
that before it is a warhorse, a naked woman, or a trumpery anecdote, a painting is
essentially flat surface covered with colors assembled in a certain order" (Russell
1971, p. 20). As is common with any diktat of theory, implications for possible
rules of technique soon followed.

As time passed, the individuals among the Nabis painted and experimented,
some staying close to the principles set down by Denis and some moving away.
Troubled by a style felt to be insufficiently true to the theory, in 1898 Denis sent
Vuillard a letter of concern about Vuillard's having wandered too far afield. In a
long reply, a letter that seemed at once an effort at self-defense yet also a genuine
striving toward self-definition, Vuillard wrote, "To sum up, I have a horror (or
rather, an absolute terror) of general ideas that I have not arrived at by myself. It
is not that I deny their validity. I'd rather own up to my shortcomings than pretend
to an understanding that I don't really possess" (Russell 1971, p. 65).

So much is present in those three short sentences. Vuillard does not rebelliously
repudiate the principles offered but respectfully values their validity. Nonetheless,
he insists on his need to digest and assimilate those principles for him to make
them his own rather than accept them as a formulaic recipe for technical procedure.

This is no mere bit of vanity; it matters. Struggling toward authenticity, Vuillard prefers to acknowledge personal shortcomings rather than become a *poseur*, one who gains acceptance by assuming whatever is thought to be the preferred way of doing things. Even within the tenets he valued in a specific school of art, he would not make art that was not essentially his own. Instead, he labored to translate those cherished concepts into what was true to his personal experience. He knew that imitation could grow into mastery only through the difficult struggle of integrating principles, not by perverting them into external rules.

From visual art to psychoanalysis

What might this say for psychoanalysis?

Clinical analysis involves one person putting his mind into the service of the mind of another. In the service of the patient's introspection, in what Robert Gardner (1983) has spoken of as reciprocating self-inquiries, the analyst structures a special situation, one with controlled limits and regularity of routine, in order to facilitate the patient's calling forth the hidden forces within the patient's mind. The analyst's discipline, the analyst's efforts toward neutrality and abstinence, are not goals in themselves but are modulated techniques designed to move the relationship from the conventional and toward opening what is buried and hidden. It seems appropriate that an analytic session is called a *séance* in French.

Yet, if the analyst imposes a personal view of the way the patient's world is likely to be constructed, the validity of the search is corrupted into an effort at persuasion. True psychoanalytic efforts are struggles of inquiry, not indoctrination.

It may be psychoanalytic theory itself that most often intrudes. Basic concepts, including the one that says that behind every expression lie other meanings as yet unexposed – those fundamental principles allow investigation to take place.

Higher-level theories, such as those of infantile sexuality or defense mechanisms, and so on – all of those matter mostly to remind the analyst to wonder (not conclude) about important out-of-awareness forces that might be passing unconsidered. The more abstract the theory, the greater likelihood that it may not be apt in any individual instance.

Rather than open new possibilities, theory can also be misused, brought in not to open new potential understandings but to comfort an analyst's mind in the face of uncertainty. Misuse of the analyst's theoretical thinking may be most innocent with young analysts in training, albeit no less disorienting and potentially harmful to genuine exploration. Such is the nature of learning: identifying with a valued teacher, taking in what is new, perhaps even imitating the teacher, and over time digesting and assimilating the newly learned so that it becomes one's own – ah, Vuillard.

More destructive are the narrow theories forced on unfolding clinical material by those who are insistently devoted to parochial schools of analysis.

I suspect all clinicians have heard at times from representatives of *every* analytic school reports of clinical work that did not sound and feel individual or fresh. After the first several minutes of listening in such instances, the final formulations that are about to unfold can be predicted with distressing success. Sadly, even the wording of interpretations can at such times be foretold. The listener may hear important analytic ideas exposed and clinically confirmed, but the material reminds one of the lawyer who starts his trial summary by saying, "And these, ladies and gentlemen of the jury, are the conclusions on which I base my facts."

Under such circumstances, surprise never seems present. The absence of the presenting analyst's being confused or bewildered (the natural state in the uncertainty of trying to figure out what has been kept unknown) goes missing, the analyst seeming never to be confronted by something totally unexpected. As Gardner put it, "It's a long way to heaven; and in analysis as elsewhere it is mainly a matter of meanwhiles" (1983, p. 34).

There is no royal road to exposure of the unconscious in clinical work; perhaps that is why it is called "work." Psychoanalytic theory drawn from generations of individual clinical analyses provides valuable clues for *possible* implications of new observations and for *possible* directions toward new progress. It cannot substitute for figuring things out afresh. Psychoanalytic inquiry is not a scavenger hunt in which the analyst searches to find the desired list of explanations thought to be provided by a favored theory.

All this and Freud too

Freud was aware of this when he stated,

> It is not enough, therefore, for a physician to know a few of the findings of psychoanalysis; he must have familiarized himself with its technique if he wishes his medical procedure to be guided by a psychoanalytic point of view. This technique cannot be learned from books, and it certainly cannot be discovered independently without great sacrifices of time, labor, and success.
>
> (1910, p. 226)

Freud was greatly confident of his clinical discoveries about the psyche, basing that confidence on the experience of relentless inquiry and repeatedly ready to alter prior convictions as the result of newer experiences. Reviewing psychoanalytic possibilities near the end of his life, Freud commented on both the value of theoretical inferences from experience and the limits inherent in even a disciplined attention to theoretical understanding. "We know," he wrote, "that the first step towards attaining intellectual mastery of our environment is to discover generalizations, rules and laws which bring order into chaos. *In doing this we simplify the world of phenomena; but we cannot avoid falsifying it*" (1937, p. 228; emphasis added). With his customary wit, Freud went on to say, "every step forward is only half as big as it looks at first."

Like Vuillard, Freud similarly preferred to "own up to my shortcomings [rather] than pretend to an understanding that I don't really possess" (Russell 1971, p. 20). What is valid and most useful is what we assimilate, not merely imitate.

References

Freud, S. (1910). "Wild" psychoanalysis. *S.E.*, 11:219–227.
Freud, S. (1937). Analysis terminable and interminable. *S.E.*, 23:209–253.
Gardner, M.R. (1983). *Self Inquiry*. Boston, MA: Little, Brown.
Russell, J. (1971). *Edouard Vuillard 1868–1940*. London: Thames and Hudson.

Part II

The psychoanalytic situation

Chapter 3

The analyst's witnessing and otherness

As Hanly (1990, p. 382) noted, "At the core of the being of each person there is a solitude in which he is related to himself ... The ground of genuine analytic work in the analyst is his attitude of respect for this solitude." Years ago, when I was a beginning candidate struggling to get patients into analysis, striving to keep patients in analysis, trying to learn what analyzing is, a dear supervisor gave me advice that has stood me in good stead ever since. Tell the patients something they can use and they will come back to get more. Interpreting, both of resistances and of emerging unconscious fantasies and even of the conflicts alive behind the two, continues to be at the heart of analyses that succeed.

In recent years, however, I have become increasingly struck by the great value of another less obvious function. Late as I was to notice it, the more I have attended to it the more I am impressed by its crucial significance. It is the action of the analyst as a witness, one who recognizes and grasps the emotional import of the patient's self-exploration in the immediacy of the moment, yet who stays in attendance without imposing his own supposed wisdom – at least not verbally. There are both times and levels where it is fitting for the analyst to be in part emotionally apart from the patient. Witnessing is but one of those ways and, I believe, a special one. This silent but active presence, this respectful attention on the analyst's part, this silence of engaged nonintrusiveness rather than of abstinence, complements the analyst's interpretive functions. The two, interpreting and witnessing, go hand in hand, each facilitating the other.

We have long been familiar with related yet different analytic functions. Witnessing by the analyst may have its origins in the analyst's empathic responsiveness or offering a holding environment, but it is an analytic function changed by maturation beyond those roots. Instead, it reflects advancing self–other differentiation, the patient's growing individuation and self-definition, even while taking place within the intersubjective clinical field. Indeed, growing self-definition and growing regard for the other's otherness are intrinsically unitary. Thus, the presence of analytic witnessing, often most clear in the termination phase of an analysis, brings into the open the connection between *self*-definition and the fabric of human *inter*connections.

Perhaps this will become clearer if I retrace steps from near the beginning of my thinking about witnessing, starting with an unhappy clinical moment when usual regard for interpretation was not immediately central. That day a bright and pleasant young woman in her late twenties came for her analytic session directly from what she had expected to be a routine appointment with her gynecologist. Unexpectedly and dreadfully, that appointment had turned out to be anything but routine. Terrible pathology had been discovered, a disorder that fortunately was curable but that unfortunately required a hysterectomy.

My patient, understandably, was horrified by the sudden stunning sentence of never being able to give birth to her own child. I could empathize and I could sympathize with her reactions to this grievous news – but only to a degree. In that tragic moment I was keenly aware that I was alongside her but not at one with her. No matter how one might view our engagement and speak of our intersubjective connection, we were together but our togetherness was like that of two people, one of whom was navigating dangerous rapids and one of whom cared deeply but stood with feet safely on the river bank. Tragic trauma exposed our essential otherness.

That young woman was courageous in the openness with which she faced her news. At that moment she had no interest in comments I might make that supposedly would sound supportive but implicitly would serve to show I was good and on her side, not to be blamed as part of evil fate. And she had no interest just then in ideas I might add linking her thoughts to pains or fantasies from other times. However, already knowing I was not indifferent, it did seem to matter to her that I stay by, understanding some of what she struggled with yet appreciating her essential aloneness dealing with a crisis in *her* body, in *her* life.

The riddle for me during the years since that hour is what it was that I was doing with that patient that she found helpful. From one angle, the moment was an ordinary critical moment in a person's life that stood on its own in a way it would have had we been two people together for reasons other than ongoing analytic work. Yet the perspective brought into view by the lightning flash of that experience raised in my mind the possibility that something akin to what then occurred might also be important within the analytic process itself, something beyond my providing a holding presence or empathic resonance.

For most of our psychoanalytic century we have tried to tease out the many subtle processes alive in clinical work behind the manifest scene of patient associations and analyst interpretations. All are cogent, but in that hour with my patient something else came clear. It mattered to my patient that I serve as an other, one whom she could see as hearing and grasping the anguish she was going through and who recognized the crucial import of her inner struggle, one who understood and *witnessed* her anguish and her efforts to digest her emotional trauma. It was important to her that I see her as a separate real person, one alone suffering a private pain that would alter her life.

Rather than dismiss this as simply a current trauma intruding on an analysis, with continued attention to such moments I have come to see my functioning as a witness to the patient's analytic introspective struggles themselves as a covert but intrinsic part of the analytic process, a function once recognized that can even serve as a subtle guide to how an analysis itself is progressing.

Bits and pieces of what an analyst does can be done for a patient by someone else, like a good friend. One can gain fragments of insight from the words of passersby, as one can from experience of successful art. But it takes the uniqueness of the analytic situation to integrate those bits and pieces into a process that extends one's struggle toward insight beyond levels of ordinary conscious access. So, too, is there a particularity of this task of witnessing that calls for an analyst. While friends serve such a function from time to time, the uncommon appreciation of powerful meanings that arise from the deep can generally best be obtained from someone who has traveled a significant part of the way along with a person to those depths. Whatever its extra-analytic place, witnessing is a vital psychoanalytic function.

Definition

Reviewing the nature of the psychoanalytic process and the patient's testimony, Felman and Laub (1992, p. 15) noted that Freud created "the *psychoanalytic dialogue*, an unprecedented kind of dialogue in which the doctor's testimony does not substitute itself for the patient's testimony, but *resonates with it*, because, as Freud discovers, *it takes two to witness the unconscious*." The possibilities and limits of self-analysis are for another time, but a century of clinical experience has taught us to appreciate the clinical process in which it takes two to witness the unconscious.

One clarification is necessary. The patient's unfolding testimony bears witness to truths not yet known consciously. My intent now is to focus on the analyst's participation in observing the patient's evolving testimony, and especially on that part that strengthens the patient by recognizing the patient's mastery of solo flights, as it were. This is not a question of the analyst's subsequent telling or testifying to others. Psychoanalysis is a process of shared exploration, not one of the analyst's divine revelations; for a patient's testimony to come to life, a comprehending witness is needed. A catalyst to a patient's capacity to know and to define himself as a unique one among others, witnessing makes personal testimony possible and meaningful.

Being witnessed is more than being pleased at being admired. It may at first seem this is no more than an analyst's empathic response, acknowledging the patient's emotion as a mother might mirror an infant, helping the patient learn to contain impulses, to recognize feelings, to master by naming. Kohut's empathy and Bion's containing are undoubtedly related to witnessing. But witnessing refers to mature derivatives of those forces, to forces farther along on the developmental line of relational capacities.

A time comes when warm empathy is not empathic, when anxiety-limiting containing inhibits rather than facilitates growth. We know it is the case when we hear a child's plaintive cry, "If you don't mind, Mother, I would rather do it myself." We know it similarly with patients who may not yet be free enough to cry the same when, as Sacha Nacht (1965) described, an analyst interprets a patient's change of subjects as resistance instead of appreciating that the patient has moved on to new areas while it is the analyst who must hang back.

Also, witnessing is more than simple validation or affirmation. At moments of pain as one deals forthrightly with personal responsibility for one's role in what had been painful to oneself or others, at those moments it matters that another know, that another understand, that another have some appreciation of the implications. Recognition, not exoneration, is what is then called for. At such moments, tempting though they be, expressions of affirmation would betray the genuineness of mutual recognition. Psychoanalysis works to maximize openness to personal truths more than to comfort. We strive to analyze pain, not anesthetize.

By "witnessing" I refer to an analyst's activity: the analyst's functioning as a patient's other who maintains an actively observing presence, who recognizes and grasps the emotional activity in the mind of the patient at work, and who is himself recognized by the patient as a distinctly separate person in his own right, not merely as a transferential object. Witnessing as a psychoanalytic function refers to the analyst's grasping and respecting the patient's meanings and the meaningfulness of those meanings from a position of separated otherness. Recognition of autonomy and respect for otherness are central to witnessing. Realization of one's self as unique and distinct from the actuality of an important other's equally unique self is significant for both of the clinical partners and the growth of that realization in an analysis evidences profound maturational changes in the analytic relationship.

Attention to this essential otherness of patient and analyst does not imply a return to the old argument of a supposed distinction between transference and real relationships. No moment of mental life exists removed from unconscious import. However, what here is crucial is the overall integrated moment of all levels come together in experienced actuality, an integration that recognizes the separateness of the patient as a full unique individual in his own right. The analyst's witnessing accompanies and follows exposure of unconscious forces; appreciation of unconscious forces and their power makes possible and enriches subsequent mutual awareness of otherness. Nothing in this concept dilutes or minimizes the relentless search to expose and explore the patient's unconscious forces. Indeed, increasing presence of witnessing is a consequence of just such prior analytic work.

Thus, while the analyst's capacity to witness as a caring other may grow out of the analyst's providing a holding presence, it goes beyond that in a relationally specific way.

Witnessing may develop from holding but it implies letting go, it implies respecting the patient's essential aloneness.

Witnessing develops from roots of interpreting as well as from holding, with the two, witnessing and interpreting, having a circular relationship. Interpretations make possible sufficient self–other distinction so as to permit the analyst to serve more fully as a witnessing other. And understandings from a witnessing position make possible openings to further understanding. Still, overlapping and circular though their relationship may be, interpretation and witnessing are not the same. Even though what is heard in witnessing may later come to an analyst's mind for use in interpretations, silent witnessing serves its own vital developmental role for the patient, a point to which I shall return.

Though the clinical field is always dyadic, the presence of recognized witnessing evidences that self-definition and self–other distinction have significantly progressed. As a result, with roots in separation–individuation and self-definition, the process of witnessing becomes most apparent the closer an analysis nears termination, the time for dissolution of the clinical engagement. It should be no surprise. Just as maintenance of personal integrity is the developmental task demanded by aging, waning powers, and approaching death, so in a termination phase is the maintenance of a firm respect for self and otherness demanded in the face of loss of the shared clinical universe.

Illustration

For illustration, let us consider work with a man whose analysis was close to its termination.

"If you have tears, prepare to shed them now." Those were the words that came to my mind as once more this troubled man came in for his session. I knew his entrance brought me anticipation of genuine sadness. We would not be facing the guilty grief provoked by someone depressed, but rather the sorrow elicited as with honesty this man continued to realize and face implications of his own earlier cruelty and pain.

We had worked hard through years of frustration and ever-worsening symptoms as his entrenched oppositionalism led him to hear any of my words, no matter how sensitively respectful and accurate they might be, as invitations for him to submit, and thus as threats to his private sense of himself. Everything had been experienced by him as a hostile power struggle. Whatever I said that he might have used was felt by him to be a danger undermining his very being. He felt his existence as an individual depended on his ability to frustrate others while on the surface appearing to be accommodating.

Behind whatever he wanted in life and in analysis was his deep conviction that any seeming victory was actually personal defeat. If analysis helped him, it meant to him that I won and he lost. To him, his provoking the other to deprive him was adaptive. Through it he protected his feeling of himself as a real person, even as a person with power. So, apparent defeat was for him the secret victory of guarding himself as untouchable. Whatever the actual loss, seeming defeat to him was survival of his self.

Eventually, we learned that where an exasperated parent might say to a crying child, "I'll give you something to cry about," in his fantasies were two other secret phrases. The first was his private thought, "*I'll* give *you* something to give me something to cry about." And, we much later learned, when finally he managed to get himself punished, his other fantasied phrase toward his oppressor was

"Now I have you where I want you." His life seemed dedicated to his power to seduce an aggressor.

We spent anguished years struggling to where we could learn and speak of what I so briefly summarize. And through further long months shaped by his meanness, his subtle cruelty, we came to discover an even deeper organizing fantasy – one in which, after he elicited punishment, he thought to himself, "I'm sorry; I'm sorry; I'm sorry." Buried below his masochism and below his deeper sadism was his hidden fantasy of reunion with a good mother, a fantasy that explained in part how his sadism had come to feel to him adaptive.

Now, much later, we were at a different point with different understanding and, important to our notice here, with a different relationship between us. No longer were we locked in a war in which he was consumed by efforts to infer my desires so as to frustrate me while seeming to be cooperative. We were sufficiently beyond that point that now he was recognizing and realizing the truly sad price he and others who mattered to him had paid as a result of his style, of his character, which he now saw as tragic in its consequences, no matter its having felt partially inevitable. I say "partially inevitable" because, regardless of the experiences that had helped shape that pattern in him, he now seriously acknowledged personal responsibility for his own subtle sadism.

The work with this man offers a particularly apt instance for our attention because on the manifest level much of our engagement had *seemed* as if structured by his maintaining a sensitivity to my, indeed to everyone's, otherness and alienation. However, as we know, manifest behavior is not a direct reflection of underlying meanings. Exploration exposed the intense engagement with his perceived opponents lying behind his air of pseudo-separateness. His seeming isolation expressed a fake otherness manifesting an underlying self–other unity despite his presenting that unity in the guise of detachment. Even my responsive feeling of alienation represented the way we each were closely tied in a transference–countertransference process. Frustrated and distant as he kept me and as I felt for many years, we were both bound in that idiosyncratic way of being-at-one. Slow and painful, step-by-step analytic work had brought us to the point where behind that transferentially shaped engagement our true separateness and distinction were validly recognized, where I came to be known by him as an other in my own right, not merely as the immediate embodiment of his ghosts and those of my ghosts he could call forth.

What we were facing when I found myself anticipating a session of sadness was not a depressive blackness but the sadness that can accompany self-honesty. The prophet in Ecclesiastes tells us that he who increases knowledge increases sorrow, and the knowledge this man now tried to face with courage and honesty was genuinely sorrowful.

As he faced cruelties delivered as well as cruelties received, my place was that of an other who had traveled with him to arrive at this point, one who stayed alongside to hear him at work. I was in attendance not merely to listen but to hear as he struggled to acknowledge what he found inside himself. He had come far enough that he now had his own ability to know what rang true, yet *my* "getting the point" was important to him. If necessary, he now would have continued his introspective work on his own. Still, it seemed to matter that an other know. My place was beyond that of offering a holding environment; my place was alongside.

Facing personal horrors, he also came to learn of his personal strengths. He needed me then not as a buttressing support or as a confessor or as an interpreter. He needed me as a witness. My observing and understanding presence helped him define himself as someone in his own right who had a presence as one among others. He was prepared to stand alone in the spotlight of self-scrutiny, but he was not prepared to live alone in a world unknown by others – as, I believe, no one is so prepared or so able.

My going through the psychoanalytic engagement together with my patient, my performing all those supportive and interpretive services an analyst does to promote and deepen the work, all of that had been necessary to bring us to where we now were. But my presence as a sensitive respectful other who witnessed his growing self-analytic labors also was essential to his realization of himself as a unique one in a world filled with unique and interacting others. "Attention must be paid."

Witnessing and the analytic process

Having defined witnessing as a psychoanalytic function, I shall next try to locate the place of witnessing within the clinical process. Then, using witnessing as the point of departure, I shall briefly turn to some of the broader implications in terms of the connection between self-definition and otherness.

Where does witnessing fit in the relational dynamics of an analysis? When I noticed that I had begun my case description with my own thought of now having tears to shed, I was struck by my having started with a feeling of my own rather than with a usual patient description. This is not simply a sign of my personal self-centeredness. Reviewing my attention to witnessing with patients in general, I realize each has involved a *shift* in my sense of my patient's and my relationship. At those times I become conscious of serving as a witness for the patient, and such times come clear to me most often on retrospective reflection; I am aware of a shift away from our more common mixed levels of relationship. At these moments, wittingly or unwittingly, I have, more than usual, a sense of the patient's and my separateness.

At such times I feel myself fully engaged and the other person experienced as somehow more in his own right. It is not that I am unaware of the patient's turmoil eliciting reactions in me. Rather, it is as if I am not so involved as usual with sorting out for myself how my own engagements are part of the developing process. Despite the possible presence of other emotional reactions to the patient, at these moments I have a generally comfortable and often new awareness of the patient's intact otherness even as we are together. I am more aware of the patient's personal integrity.

The unconscious never loses its power. I do *not* suggest that my own unconscious sharing, reacting, and processing forces are in abeyance at these moments. Instead, I have the impression that whatever their power, they combine to integrate a sense of genuine respect for the patient as apart. Even while considering the nature of our interaction, for certainly witnessing is a form of interaction, I am aware in such moments that we are two distinct people, two alert and sensitive to each other but *two who are profoundly apart even while immediately mattering to one another.*

In recent years the patient–analyst relationship has moved to the center of our study of the clinical process. The intensification of witnessing relates to a vital shift in the progressing clinical relationship, to a shift based on separation, with separation a negation of fantasied or felt merger or union. As a result, an aspect of negation takes a place at the heart of analytic progress. Let us consider a schematized review.

In his plenary address, Friedman (1997, p. 22) noted that "analytic treatment comes about, in the first place, because of the analyst's attitudes." Most, if not all, of us would agree that one fundamental analyst attitude is that of inquiry, the desire to explore for the sake of understanding taking priority over either wishes to dominate or therapeutic zeal. I believe that even that seemingly most basic of the analyst's attitudes implies one lying yet even deeper, "*the analyst's profound and genuine respect for the authenticity of the patient's self as a unique other, an other's self as valid as the analyst's own*" (Poland 1996, p. 7; emphasis in original). Whatever the analyst's curiosity, true analytic exploration is unlikely to occur without that underlying regard on the analyst's part.

The patient, of course, is unlikely to start with a similar reciprocal attitude. Indeed, we structure the analytic situation to allow the patient's most private and primitive forces to gain a hearing; we act to facilitate the patient's regression. Every person, analysts included, balances compelling inner developmentally regressive urges toward merger and developmentally progressive forces toward separation and self-distinction. Here "regressive" and "progressive" refer to developmental levels of relatedness, not to levels of pathology. The pressure to lose the distinction of one's own boundaries is as central to love and creativity as it is to mental disorder. What is relevant now is that the conflict between these forces is present in the analyst as well as in the patient, though ideally with the analyst's having more openness to them and, consequently, more mastery.

In practice, the analyst's sense of separation that comes from the patient's regressing provokes a pressure to stay emotionally united with the patient, to go along. The analyst foregoes a bit of personal emotional self-differentiation in an effort to stay at one with the regressing patient. As Greenson (1960) put it, empathy arises in the face of felt separation.

However, unless undue personal conflicts intrude, the analyst's professionalism and self-protective instincts combine to pull him back from that seemingly shared regression. At some point in his parallel partial regression, the analyst feels, whether consciously or unconsciously, a signal of caution. He steps back from his own regression.

This partial detachment from prior emotional engagement is implicit in the manifest message of an analyst's interpretation. No matter its helpful or even kindly quality, an interpretation implies a powerful statement of negation and separation deeply structured within it, a negation central to the analytic process. This deeper message, which I believe the patient comes at least unconsciously to recognize, is the implication that says:

> No. I am not you, nor am I one of your ghosts. I am a different person from you, someone other than you or your inner ghosts. I am one who will work with you to explore your inner world, to find names for your ghosts, to help find words to say it by, words which can render fears and uncertainties namable and potentially understandable rather than hidden nameless terrors. Yet, as much as we may share this clinical universe, No, I am not your fantasy actualized. We are separate people with separate lives.

An interpretation moves the relationship from one of seeming union to one of separateness, where contact, separate people touching, replaces fusion.

Negation, we know, is essential to development, the very establishment of psychic reality itself thought to involve an act of negation. Freud (1915) hypothesized an analogue of internal negation in the mind's first recognition of itself: when first crystallized out of an amorphous affective universe, the psyche was defined by negation. If it is bad, it is outside; if it is good, it is inside, it is self. The mind is born into its sense of a self apart through this act of negation, of separation, indeed of repudiation.

Negation exposes and determines essential otherness, leading to what is perhaps the deepest effect of any interpretation. As Laplanche (1997) pointed out, this effect is more profound than is acknowledged by those who feel it is language that guarantees the otherness of the other. Otherness is deeper than verbal communication. It is dawning and growing respect for this essential not-me-ness of the analyst for the patient that helps move the patient along the relational developmental line.

As negation is present in the birth of the mind, so also is negation present in the developing capacity of a mind to hold an inner dialogue with itself. Negation is an important way one disowns an impulse so as to allow it into consciousness. "I would not dream of such a thing" negates the wish but, in so doing, allows prohibited ideas into open consideration. A value of negation lies in its ability to permit a mind to consider forbidden impulses and forbidden fantasies.

The analyst's naming and interpreting, as already noted, implies the "No" that acknowledges the patient's unique separateness. The analyst's witnessing serves as a dynamic actualization and as evidence of the patient's growing autonomy. If early holding and early empathy offer safety and receptivity, witnessing offers the same regard but *without* the promise of magical union. Instead, there is the acceptance of separate lives with separate patterns and separate growth potential. The analyst in both interpreting and in related witnessing provides in interaction a model of negating in the shared clinical experience, a process that then can be internalized by the patient, leading to increasing capacity for self-observation and self-analysis.

André Green (1993) persuasively demonstrated in his study on negation that negation can powerfully imply affirmation. As Loewald (1980, p. 297) also said, "detachment in its genuine form, far from excluding love, is based on it."

While recognition of separateness leads to an increased awareness of solidity of self, sadly, it also brings a loss to one's infantile sense of power. With poignancy Shengold (1991) wrote of one's movement through life from everything to nothing, from magical omnipotence to recognition of loss of power, from the oceanic oneness with mother and universe to separateness and ultimate death. Yet he noted that it is exactly such losses that make possible the development of an identity. Emphasizing the value of dignity and integrity within this context, he was nonetheless direct in describing the inevitable movement from the magic of infancy to the losses culminated by the loss of life itself. Like the prophet who linked knowledge to sorrow, Shengold (p. 9) trenchantly added, "Every step away from the primal *everything* toward the establishment of an identity must be paid for since it involves a loss." The movement of a successful analysis is away from actualization of transferential unions toward separate intactness of distinct people in shared but separate collaboration, all taking place in "intimate separation" (Stone 1961, p. 91).

Analytically, "We shall not cease from exploration / And the end of our exploring / Will be to arrive where we started / And know the place for the first time" (Eliot 1971, p. 145). We have said that a very deep analytic attitude that was a basis of the analyst's work was that analyst attitude of respectful separateness. Yet in the course of the work that attitude becomes at times obscured, only to be discovered with new eyes through the collaborative ins and outs of analytic progress. This is in part why each patient analysis necessarily implies at least a partial further working through of the analyst's own growth.

Now each partner can see the other a bit more genuinely, with the self and the other each now recognized a bit more accurately for who each is. In a clinical analysis such steps most often move on almost microscopic levels, bit by bit, as the relationship ratchets up from a more transferential to a more open and less distorted engagement. But the move from something akin to living in a shared dream to that of recognizing the life of the dream forces, while respecting the essential separateness of the two persons, is sad even as it is both liberating and satisfying.

Self-definition and otherness

Let us step back from the clinical phenomenon and consider just two of the many broader implications of witnessing, the issues of self-definition and the import of otherness. Competing imperatives from the individual and from the group have been driving forces in history. The concern for intersubjectivity now commanding center stage in psychoanalysis is our own inevitable portion of the zeitgeist as we try to privilege both an individual's unique intrapsychic forces and the intersubjective community within which an individual becomes and exists.

It has long seemed to me that clinical analysis is the laboratory section of the course in which philosophy is the lecture section. Theoretical psychoanalytic questions are in their heart philosophical, questions of what is a self, what is an interpersonal unity, and how do intrapsychic and interpersonal relate.

Addressing the tension between the individual and the group, Isaiah Berlin (1958, p. 23) recognized the ironic presence of the group in the fertilization and birth of the individual. "They understand me, as I understand them; and this understanding creates within me the sense of being somebody in the world." The sense of "they" is part and parcel of the sense of "me," and the sense of "me" is part and parcel of the sense of "they." *Their* understanding has a hand in *my* sense of being.

Intersubjectivity

How are we to integrate our sense of no man's being an island, our concern for intersubjectivity, with our sensitivity to each man's being an island, our valuing of the individual? Also, are not separate people, cognizant of their separateness, even so still part of the same intersubjective field? A very brief consideration of differing relational points of view may help clarify such confusion.

For most of our history, whenever we spoke of any clinical engagement, our ideas were based on the principle of a subject–object split. Even attention to interaction and enactments implies such a split, referring as those words do to the interaction between two separate "subjects." "Intersubjectivity" used when we speak this way, that is, to speak of an engagement, refers to the communicative emotional flow between two different parties. This usage of "intersubjectivity" can be contrasted with the use of the same word to refer to a unified field. In this alternative usage, "intersubjectivity" views the clinical universe as an intact whole, one in which experience is generated and created by the engaged pair as an essential unity.

This second usage of "intersubjectivity" is based on the view that an individual never really exists outside an interpersonal human context. If this understanding does not arise from Heidegger's thought, it is at least rooted in the same philosophical understanding as is his. For it was Heidegger who most powerfully exposed fallacies in thinking based on a subject–object split. He saw a person as a being-in-the-world, living in an experientially unified universe that does not have the spaces between which our perceptions and dichotomizing minds create. Heidegger undid the subject–object dichotomy and provided a way to conceive of how a clinical engagement could valuably be viewed as an original construction. The dyad, a unified whole not as a symbiotic or psychotic state but as an essential quality of being, was mapped by Heidegger, perhaps the major philosophical conceptual author of this modern meaning of intersubjectivity.

Confusion can be cleared, unwitting inferential and conceptual shifts can be avoided, if we remember the difference between these two meanings and if we also stay respectful of the need for multiple points of view. We now are in a position to identify the *relational point of view* as involving three possibilities, one consisting of our necessary, traditional, intrapsychic one-person psychology and the other two consisting of two-person psychologies, one of which involves the emotional interaction of two *separate* subjects and the other of which involves the *unified* dyad.

> Indeed, it may be more logical not to divide relational points of view into three categories of one-person, two-person, and unitary dyad. Rather, the relational views can be seen from either person-separate or person-unified considerations, with the person-separate then examined from one-person and two-person angles.
>
> (Poland 1996, p. 266)

This is cogent if we are to understand how patient–analyst separateness can be true at the same time that continued existence of the intersubjective field remains true. It is important to distinguish the intersubjectivity of interaction, subject–object separation, from the intersubjectivity of the dyad, unified human field. The troublesome use of the same word for the different meanings does complicate our understanding. Certainly, everything so far said about the growing self-definition of the patient carrying with it recognition of essential separateness can also be viewed from the person-united dyadic position. However, *the presence of a dyadic viewpoint does not negate the vastly significant developmental shift in self–other distinction that can be seen from the one-person and interactive two-person viewpoints.*

The other and self-definition

We come back to our central concern, that of the place of an analyst's witnessing presence, a presence no longer simply actualizing the containing or holding human environment but now a presence as a separate and equal other who remains respectfully alongside of rather than supporting or surrounding the patient.

It has been noted that two sets of aims shape an individual's interactions, those aims "to attain a sense of self as separate" and those "to enhance attachments" (Bass & Blatt 1996, p. 270). If that is so, aims for separation and aims for attachment both manifest themselves within the transference. However, the clinical engagement that would gratify the transferential fantasies of separateness is *not* what the analyst's witnessing manifests. It is the analyst's respectful regard for the patient's own struggle to recognize and master transferential forces, whether their content deals with separateness or fusion, that facilitates the patient's authentic development and new capacities to recognize both self and other.

This brings us to the relationship between self-definition and interpersonal engagement. Recognition and mastery of transferential forces does not leave a mental vacuum in its place. The enrichment of personal identity that the mastery through insight brings forth is directly linked to the growing sense of the other as a distinct and autonomous person. *The growth of a true self is intrinsically part of growing respect for the other; growing respect for the other is intrinsically part of the growth of a true self. The capacity to appreciate self and the capacity to appreciate the otherness of the other do not simply go hand in hand; they are mutually interdependent and mutually enriching, all part of the same unitary phenomenon of growth.* Self-definition and awareness of otherness are a unitary phenomenon seen from different angles.

The attention to the place of the analyst's witnessing that we have discovered in our clinical laboratory parallels advances in thinking among our philosopher friends. Just as our own early attention to clinical phenomenology paralleled the thinking of Husserl, and just as our more recent attention to intersubjectivity paralleled the thinking of Heidegger, so now our concern with the limits of intersubjectivity, with the need to leave space for surprise between people and for individual definition, parallels the work of Emmanuel Levinas.

Heidegger showed that consciousness was rooted in a deeper level of being, of being-there, that came before knowing or mentally representing. Like our own constructivists, he emphasized the essential interwovenness of human experience.

Levinas, who had been a student of both Husserl and Heidegger, came to see behind the self that was an interwoven part of a unified world a more basic model of the self as always opening in awareness of otherness, an irreducible aspect of being. For him, one's very sense of being is always shaped by the surprise of otherness.

As for our own developmentalists, so too for Levinas, the face of an other person concretizes the essence of otherness, with the face specifically referring to an actual other person's regarding, looking at, and seeing one. In this context language is the manifestation of another person's speaking, a never fully knowable other's addressing one. "In this sense, the other comes toward me as a total stranger and from a dimension that surpasses me" (Peperzak 1993, p. 20). This sense of essential otherness is, I believe, the quality I referred to in clinical work as the negation buried in every interpretation, the surprising and crucial reminder that the two clinical partners are different people even as they share the clinical universe.

This is not the place for a substantial investigation of Levinas's thinking. However, one other major conclusion he drew is immediately relevant. For Levinas, the intrinsic link of recognition of an other to existence and to definition of a self means that an ethical relationship is central to self-definition.

Do we not now find ourselves back in familiar psychoanalytic territory? While we have in part been concerned with what has been called a decentered self (see Loewenstein 1994), generally, when speaking of a self we have always thought of a self's cohesiveness, of an ego's integrity. It cannot be chance that the same word, "integrity," refers to the intactness of a character structure and to the ethical consistency with which a person faces the world of others. Beyond matters of the superego, there are essential ethical implications of the ego's recognition of otherness as a core component of self-definition and integrity of self. In the sense of Shengold's summary of life's journey from everything to nothing, one becomes somebody by the way one regards and respects others even in the face of the strangeness of imperishable otherness.

Clinically, we aim toward the unconscious, sailing the edge of darkness where seas are blood-red more than wine-dark. To speak of the ethical implications of analysis is not to obscure or diminish attention to the forces of rage and lust. It is rather to remember that the analyst works in the service of the other, an essentially ethical task. Seeing and being seen – more specifically, regarding and being regarded – are essential building blocks of self-definition. The analyst's witnessing presence provides opportunity for the maturing of that self-definition within the clinical microcosm.

In closing

Witnessing implies caring yet letting go. If union and reunion, such emotionally appealing experiences, are the children of Eros, born in the heat of sexuality and swaddled in the warmth of love, then otherness may seem the descendent of Thanatos, chilled by the implications of separation, aloneness, and loss. Its relatives are indifference, alienation, and death. Can it be any wonder that we attend to it so reluctantly, often finding even the word "otherness" unpalatable, distasteful, not to our incorporating taste? From childhood on, we dread the feeling of "the cheese stands alone."

With successful growth, the early union manifest in the locked gaze of mother and infant gives way to a capacity for independent functioning, though one still warmed by a mother's receptive smile of recognition when the increasingly autonomous child comes back into view. The respectful regard of the analyst's witnessing implies acceptance of otherness. For otherness is not synonymous with alienation. Indeed, respect for otherness is the very opposite of indifference. The way a self relates to other selves in the face of acknowledged separate otherness ultimately may have most to do with defining what is integrated as a self, what is cohesive. It is acceptance, the persistence of Eros to care for the other even in the face of Thanatos, that allows each individual to be most fully human, to facilitate the growth and fullness of life of an other in that other's own way. The benefits of witnessing are thus reciprocal, enriching both patient and analyst.

None of this diminishes our central interpretive task of exposing and exploring unconscious meanings. An interpretation dissolves the merging implicit in transferential engagement; and the analyst's silent, respectful regard for the patient's autonomous self-analysis reinforces the patient's growing individuality. The analyst's witnessing, a profound nonverbal communication of recognition, is an essential catalyst to the patient's increasing self-realization, growing self-definition, learning what that personal self is like, and openness to appreciating the universe of unique others with equally valid differing selves – all in all, the patient's capacity for mature hate and mature love.

In witnessing, the analyst is at once both *a part of* what is unfolding and *apart from* the patient's unique singularity. In witnessing, we acknowledge the genuineness of what we grasp of the other while at the same moment acknowledging that we can never *fully* know or grasp what is essential in our patient's otherness. The part of a self that is, as Proust put it, "real and incommunicable ... otherwise than by means of art" (1981, pp. 409–410) becomes partially knowable through the high art of psychoanalysis – knowable but only partially knowable because of our essential otherness, the knowing and the not fully knowing both manifest in the analyst's witnessing.

References

Bass, R. & Blatt, S. (1996). Attachment and separateness in the experience of symbiotic relatedness. *Psychoanalytic Quarterly*, 65:711–746.

Berlin, I. (1958). Two concepts of liberty. In *Four Essays on Liberty*. Oxford: Oxford University Press, 1969.

Eliot, T.S. (1971). *Four Quartets* in *The Complete Poems and Plays 1909–1950*. New York: Harcourt, Brace & World.

Felman, S. & Laub, D. (1992). *Testimony: Crises of Witnessing in Literature, Psychoanalysis, and History*. New York: Routledge.

Freud, S. (1915). Instincts and their vicissitudes. *S.E.*, 14:109–140.

Friedman, L. (1997). Ferrum, ignis, and medicina: Return to the crucible. *Journal of the American Psychoanalytic Association*, 45:21–45.

Green, A. (1993). *On Private Madness*. Madison, CT: International Universities Press.

Greenson, R. (1960). Empathy and its vicissitudes. *International Journal of Psychoanalysis*, 41:418–424.

Hanly, C. (1990). The concept of truth in psychoanalysis. *International Journal of Psychoanalysis*, 71:375–383.

Laplanche, J. (1997). The theory of seduction and the problem of the other. *International Journal of Psychoanalysis*, 78:653–666.

Loewald, H. (1980). *Papers on Psychoanalysis*. New Haven, CT: Yale University Press.

Loewenstein, E. (1994). Dissolving the myth of the unified self: The fate of the subject in Freudian analysis. *Psychoanalytic Quarterly*, 63:715–732.

Nacht, S. (1965). Interference between transference and countertransference. In *Drives, Affects, Behavior, Vol. II*, ed. M. Schur. New York: International Universities Press, pp. 315–322.

Peperzak, A. (1993). *To the Other: An Introduction to the Philosophy of Emmanuel Levinas*. West Lafayette, IN: Purdue University Press.

Poland, W. (1996). *Melting the Darkness: The Dyad and Principles of Clinical Practice*. Northvale, NJ: Jason Aronson.

Proust, M. (1981). *The Guermantes Way*. In *Remembrance of Things Past, Vol. II*, trans. C.K.S. Montcrieff & T. Kilmartin. New York: Random House.

Shengold, L. (1991). *Father, Don't You See I'm Burning: Reflections on Sex, Narcissism, Symbolism, and Murder: From Everything to Nothing*. New Haven, CT: Yale University Press.

Stone, L. (1961). *The Psychoanalytic Situation: An Examination of Its Development and Essential Nature*. New York: International Universities Press.

Chapter 4

Outsiderness in human nature

A woman: severely suppressed in childhood and never fully knowing the right to a mind of her own, she was always suspicious facing the world at large. She had survived growing up by living as if in the underground, and it took years of arduous analytic work before she could begin to consider risking open engagement with a world that loomed always dangerous. At last, long last, she came cautiously to risk more openness. Her words were wary: "All right. I'll look at reality – but only as a tourist."

Happily, even a tourist can settle, assimilate, and move from immigrant status to full citizenship. One man in his time not only plays but also contains many parts, parts that are simultaneously true even though contradictory, parts that keep alive varied senses of self and diverse ways of being. Cautious concern can continue alongside or behind comfort. An infant can feel at once both magically powerful and terrifyingly helpless. A child can feel at once secure in the warmth of family love and frighteningly vulnerable to the unpredictability of power. An adult can feel confident approaching the world at large and at the same time know that his or her very sense of being was shaped by the strangeness of the universe into which he or she came into being.

Born into a warmly welcoming world, we can feel natural, at home. However, feeling natural and feeling indecisively naturalized can exist side by side.

The sense of strangeness is, of course, a dimension apart from whether one is troubled or not troubled. Here is another woman:

Because of distance, my bond with my dear friend, a respected Israeli colleague, is sustained on an epistolary basis. We are able to meet face to face only infrequently, most often at international meetings. The last time I saw her was at a biennial congress of the International Psychoanalytical Association where, a featured speaker, she received an award for her special expertise. She and I guard time to be together on such occasions despite the pressure coming from the many others who wish to spend time with her, a demand apparent in the frequency of my having to wait by the side as she is stopped and warmly greeted as she walks through the halls of the meeting venue.

So perhaps I should have been surprised by what she wrote in her first letter after that congress: "Big congresses have a depressing effect on me. Maybe it is the crowd, maybe the two-minute encounters followed by more similar encounters. I get exhausted and feel empty."

Describing the barrenness of feeling detached, she wrote that the recognition she receives nourishes her on one level but, paradoxically, adds to her sense of a lack of real or deep connection, her feeling herself actually to be an outsider at the very moment of being honored, indeed at the peak of appearing to be an insider. She had also felt touched, and I know her capacity to feel contentedly warmed by recognition. Perhaps the problem was with the frequent repetition of brief connections that provoked the haunting feeling that persisted behind her being moved. As I said, perhaps I should have been surprised by her letter, but I was not, and not only because I already knew her well.

The timid, frightened loner and the esteemed analyst have in common an uncomfortable inner sense of feeling themselves outsiders in their worlds. Clearly, the two representing extremes of conventional success in life stand only as illustrations, not proof, of the ubiquity of outsiderness. It seems likely that within the range of what might be called "average expectable adulthood," each person has had to confront the sense of strangeness or detachment, whether consciously or unconsciously.

Yet we cannot forget that manifest feeling and behavior can never alone reveal the uniquely individual import of what covertly lies behind them. Certainly, my patient and my colleague-friend whom I have described have vastly different constitutions and dynamic experiences behind their somewhat similar states of feeling. Nonetheless, the regularity with which one finds outsider feelings once one begins to recognize them suggests that such states ought not to be considered mere abnormalities or eccentricities. Rather than idiosyncratic distortions, these are more likely qualities innate to the human condition, whatever the varied ways they unfold in individual lives. The sense of outsiderness is likely essential in human nature.

Definition

Where is the darkness when the sun is shining? Where is outsiderness when we feel on top of life? The significance of outsiderness may not be totally absent while life feels good.

Outsiderness speaks to a sense of discordance, a lack of harmony between one's sense of self and the world of others. It implies a feeling that one does not fully and naturally fit in. The shadow of a false self (Winnicott 1955) can lurk not only behind the enhanced self of manic grandiosity but also behind substantially integrated feelings of mastery and success. In a way, even as we *are*, so are we always a bit *in process*, still *becoming*. It may be that the best way to think of an integrated personality is akin to that of a quiet hurricane, one that is still astir even as it has a center that will hold. No matter the high level of maturity, for anyone open and growing, security and even identity are not "once and for all." "Once and for all" implies the stasis of death.

To speak of someone as an outsider is to speak from the vantage point either of a member of the group or that of a detached, more academic or objective observer. *Outsider* describes a person who either is not a member of a group or at best is a misfit, an inadequately assimilated member of a group.

In contrast, outsiderness is an aspect of subjectivity, one that speaks to one's own sense of self as importantly apart from the immediate world of others. Indeed, for an individual it might be considered to be not only a sense of self as strange to the outside world, once a sense of self is relatively formed, but also an important aspect of a nascent sense of self on a primordial level of development, a hurdle for which each individual must devise a unique resolution.

Thus, *outsiderness*, as I use the term, is a quality of self-definition, part of one's sense of self whether that sense is conscious or unconscious. Therefore, it is not to be equated with the much broader and important concept of *otherness*, a subject perhaps most profoundly considered by the French analysts, significantly but not only by Lacan.

The matter of otherness came late to analytic attention, discoveries of depth psychology having been found so engaging that their exploration long preoccupied analytic minds. That understandable but regrettable error certainly was influenced by Freud, who early on wrote, "The sexual instinct and the sexual object are merely soldered together" (1905, p. 148). While there can be no drive without an object nor an object without a drive, appreciation of the significance of the other and of object relatedness was long delayed, relationalism and intersubjectivity coming fairly late to intensive analytic attention.

Otherness is a broad concept, one that includes the sense of distinction between self and nonself. It has so central a presence in the functioning of the human mind as to be relevant to all psychic activity. *Outsiderness*, by comparison, is much more narrow and specific, an aspect of personal strangeness ever there in an individual's sense of self.

The link between outsiderness and otherness and its implications have perhaps been explored in greatest depth by Lacan and Laplanche, who made clear the inescapable insufficiency of a developing infant's effort to please the mother (or other significant other), since the mother's unconscious is itself unknowable even to the mother herself.

No matter the level of seductiveness, the child can never fully satisfy desires that are unknown to the mother herself. As a consequence, the essential otherness of the world always implies some lingering qualities of imperfection in the child's growing sense of self. The result is that, however successful one is in defining oneself, to oneself as well as to others, vulnerability to the painful feeling of outsiderness, to the sense of a self-definition that is incomplete, always remains.

Appearance across life stages

If this is an inherent part of human experience, it likely will show its effects across all the stages of life. Despite the security that comes with good mothering, we are all born into a world where everyone else is there ahead of us, where we start with others who all know more than we do how the world works, what things mean. At the start, despite infantile grandiosity, everyone else is actually bigger and more powerful. Benefiting from warm welcome as we need and must, still we enter life as outsiders. Indeed, part of the pleasure that accompanies growth likely includes relief from prior feelings of lack, even if those feelings have not risen to the level of consciousness.

The effects of vulnerability to feeling oneself an outsider are present not merely in infancy but throughout life. To illustrate the relevance of this issue throughout life, I offer a passing sampling, conscious that the place of outsiderness merits deeper exploration of its relevance to each phase of the life cycle, such as sketched by Erikson (1959).

Not only does a newborn arrive into a universe filled with those already present and already knowing more, but as Montagna (Personal communication, 2011) noted, whatever its welcome, the new baby necessarily provokes turbulence in what had been the previous relationship of the parents. No matter how desired the new baby is, its very appearance inescapably disturbs the world it newly enters, its arrival powerfully altering whatever had been the equilibrium of those already there. The smile on a mother's face when a baby or child enters the room is enriching as well as comforting to the child, yet it can hardly fully and permanently erase any awareness that the same child's declaring its self and its presence at times means it dares disturb the universe.

Thus, it is not surprising that Millay (1954) would write that "The pictures painted on the inner eyelids of infants just before they sleep, / Are not pastel" (pp. 548–549). Although the neonate may coo with idyllic contentment at the breast, it shows a dramatic startle reflex when shocked. Whatever the security provided by good mothering, whatever the physical holding and emotional containing provided, still the newborn reacts to surprise with an alarm manifested by pulling back.

The Moro or startle reflex, a baby's basic reaction to unexpected stimuli, has the quality of the infant's withdrawal from the world with which it was in connection in the moment before the shock. Its nature is of the full body jumping back with arms extended, movements that look like letting go in terror, not of holding on. Were the provoking stimulus merely one that seemed strange, the child's curiosity might at times lead it to investigate. However, with the Moro reflex the manifest appearance is of an infant's retreat from a universe in which the child feels it does not safely belong.

The sense of disconnection, the feeling of not fitting in, can appear throughout life. Often, behind the angry sense of rejection felt by an oedipal child when excluded by the parental pair lies a deep conviction that such exclusion is based on the child's own unworthiness. Even without that, mastery of oedipal urges requires the growing child and adolescent to accept an insufficiency in belonging to the original family, resulting in the need to create a family where one's own place is unquestionable. Indeed, that may be one source feeding the apparently otherwise appropriate parental attitude of the statement to one's own child, "*We are the parents here – we set the rules.*"

Another instance: the uncertain discomfort one feels about oneself when not fully part of others is present in the childhood game in which all compete to avoid being the one left standing in the middle of a group while the rest sing, "And the cheese stands alone." Games like that and like musical chairs serve to help the child master feelings of personal diminishment resulting from loss and exclusion, exposing the commonality of such experiences for everyone.

The move from childhood to adolescence often reopens the discomforts of feeling self-consciously estranged from the world at large. For many, the vulnerability of outsiderness makes the move from primary to middle school one of the more threatening transitions in life, for many children one more fraught with danger than the move from home to kindergarten or that from local school to going away to college. This is so because the often shocking bodily changes of puberty and alterations in the inner world coincide with the need to change outer worlds. Just as one's body is in the process of changing, one moves from the relative security of attained seniority in the world of primary school to a new universe, one in sexual turmoil, where others already there seem to know their way around, and the newcomer is uncertain of success in joining in. From accomplished insider, one abruptly feels oneself a lesser outsider.

Resolving such vulnerability of the sense of self is a major task of adolescence, when the urge toward conformity demanded by peer pressure bespeaks the strength of the urge not only to fit in, but importantly to be seen as fitting in. "To thine own self be true," a father's advice to his son, addresses the adolescent's risk of compromising qualities essential to the child's self for the sake of acceptance by others, in the hope of diminishing the pain of outsiderness.

Such stress is often more settled in adulthood, yet it can easily be stirred afresh by changing career and family circumstances. It is evident in the shame and tendency to hide oneself felt by those struck by unemployment. Even in good times, the discomfort of feeling oneself an outsider is reawakened when earlier struggles are recalled to life by their fresh appearance in one's growing child.

The actualities and losses of aging call to the fore earlier concerns over outsiderness as the older person increasingly must deal with a world less and less his or her own. The elderly must handle more than the loneliness that comes from loss of friends and family, of the world in which they have lived. One must also develop ways to continue to feel individually meaningful in the world of others, even as one often finds oneself feeling increasingly invisible and irrelevant, at times like an intruder in the ever-changing, brave new world of youth.

One's sense of self as an outsider, a stranger, is an inescapable part of human life, a discomfort lurking in the background that cannot be banished by proclamation. It is elemental even as it is overdetermined.

Clinical illustration

Let us turn to a clinical instance, this time a man – let us call him Tom – an analysand who by all conventional standards is an outstanding success. Financially secure and highly regarded in his professional career, Tom, and along with him his family, are integrated into the world and well esteemed. Yet what unfolded behind the ennui that brought him to analysis is his back-of-the-mind sense of outsiderness. (That had not been his word, but it was what he repeatedly described, clearly and from many angles.) As Tom said, "I am not a natural at anything, and everything I've done has been with the feeling that I have had to figure everything out. Then I enjoy what I do, but I always feel that actually I have faked it. Even when I do something original, I feel I am imitating."

The complex, specific dynamics behind his pervasive sense of disconnection are unique to him, as they must be. However, the disquiet of feeling strange and uncertain even while feeling pleased by success is not exceptional.

Retiring from a successful professional career, Tom accepted a governmental position at a level that required senate confirmation. While political turmoil kept in limbo others awaiting confirmation, Tom's pleasant and agreeable demeanor, together with his public detachment from political controversies, allowed his nomination to pass. Once more he flourished, then retired a second time when there was a change of administration.

After a period of relaxation, he next accepted a senior position at an international firm, one in which he was put in charge of developing new ventures in remote parts of Asia. Tom at first was extremely anxious about working in strange lands, in places where he knew not the people he would now confront, not their cultures and not their languages. However, to his great surprise, something remarkable ensued. Having already done much introspective analytic work, he found the new worlds not to embody his expected terrors but to offer new experiences of delight. He had already known what it was like to enter strange professional territories and appear to succeed, even though he felt himself acting roles rather than engaging. Now, and – to his mind – for the first time, he was spontaneous in engagement. His center could hold well enough for him to tolerate vulnerability, not to have to smother it with forceful accomplishment.

Thus, Tom was astonished to hear himself say, "I'm a stranger. Nothing can be expected of me. So it's all right to let myself just be myself." The need to justify himself or to prove himself faded. With his fear of other people's eyes no longer dominant, he felt safe enough to be himself, indeed to trust that there was a self that would hold however he seemed to fit in or not fit in with others. Despite the lack of language and familiarity – perhaps possibly even because of those lacks – he found himself happy as he walked the streets of small towns, happier than he had felt in his hometown or the various cities in which he had lived. He took pleasure in developing simple conversational facility and individual closeness. With people he newly met, he made friendships that had a spontaneous openness and warmth that had only rarely occurred back home. As he put it, "Since no one expects me to be a native, I can let myself feel natural." To himself, he was like an illegal immigrant to the world, but one now accepted and naturalized.

Crucial questions are how did this unfold in the progress of the analysis, and where was I while all this was going on? Specifically, how did the issue of outsiderness appear in my own experience of engaging with this patient?

The answers to these questions are interwoven in a way that does not lend itself easily to a linear description. Tom, it turned out, had lived throughout his life in what might be called two different modes. The predominant one had been that of someone convinced he was physically fragile, someone who had repeatedly been taken to doctors and put to bed by a mother who saw any signs of excitement as evidence of serious illness. Actually strong and quite robust, even often energetic, he had been seen by his mother as ever at risk of imminent, catastrophic danger. He was not allowed to participate in normal physical activities, not allowed to play rough. He spent days in bed at the slightest hint of what might possibly be thought of as symptoms.

Tom recalls his uncertainty and feeling of strangeness when he started school and says he was described as having a school phobia. His mother, never distant, got a job at the school so she could be closely available to him – to his consternation, even changing to employment at the high school when he progressed to that level.

One outcome of this was Tom's deep conviction that he might come apart, that he could not trust his body, that he might not even wake up in the morning because of forgetting to breathe while asleep. He became phobic and terrified.

Yet there was another side to Tom as he was growing up. He was strong, robust, and properly acknowledged as being intellectually gifted. Without thinking of it consciously, even while frightened and constricted, he managed to live a parallel life, one in which he was vigorously active. He had close friends throughout school and was at times the leader in adolescent group pranks. He developed a full sexual life with his girlfriend in high school and maintained an energetic sexual life with a new girlfriend through his college years.

The family's life had been kept narrow, living as they did in a small, rural, middle-American town and avoiding travel other than visits to relatives. They spent three long days driving for such trips because of the mother's absolute fear of flying.

As he became a young adult, one who shared the terrors with which he had been raised, Tom – or what might be thought of as the other part of Tom – felt himself suffocating. He was determined not to let himself go under, so he forced himself into a self-conceived program of facing his anxieties. He searched and found the shortest airplane trip available, one of only 45 minutes, and despite real terror, took that flight.

For a long time he remained primarily constricted, willing to forego valued employment positions if they required plane travel, yet he also continued to find ways to extend his limitations. Always extending his range of travel was only one example.

What I, and later we, came to consider the two separate lives and qualities of life that Tom lived were currently evident at home. He felt a keen guardedness in terms of emotional intimacy with his rigidly proper wife, yet he was nonetheless able to have a partially constricted but active sexual engagement with her.

With Tom's style of engaging life as if on two different tracks, and without that being clear during our early years together – certainly, at least, before that was finally recognizable by me – it was difficult to understand what was going on in the analysis. As I will describe, for a very long time it seemed as if we were going through the motions of analytic work, yet I had the sense of emotional detachment between us. Some of the advances, such as his venturing to Asia, could be seen as signs of analytic progress, but I had no way of being able to tell how much the analysis had been relevant – or indeed, as I later realized, whether instead of making analytic progress Tom had simply been extending his traditional counter-phobic activity as a means of survival, of keeping himself alive.

That was how it was until something shifted, something I was first aware of in myself, something that then was shared with Tom and that then led to a striking shift that both of us felt. It was in that last period that our relationship, his relationship to his mother, and the sense of two separate Toms could all come together well enough so that we could engage them "once more, with feeling."

To look at the shift, I turn to how I experienced this from behind the couch.

As I describe when considering the analyst's fears, my sense of pleasure when starting any analytic venture with someone new is always touched by a tinge of fear, my awareness that wherever the new work goes will be bound to include areas where I myself do not want to go, and that whatever will come up to trouble and frighten me will never be what I might predict at the start. It will come, instead, unexpectedly, as if from around the corner. And this is so because no matter how secure I might feel during the consultation, this new patient will lead me into his or her private world, a world bound to be new, foreign, and strange to me. The initial consultation is conducted in my setting: my office and an analytic situation I actively structure. Yet that start will lead away from such safety and into new and mysterious territories.

While such a tinge of fear was present when I started meeting with Tom, it soon faded, quickly replaced by a sense of comfort and ease on my part. That quick fading of personal caution turned out to be a subtle but crucial cue, one that I did not pick up at the time, significant because it was my experience of how my patient characteristically handled his own profound outsiderness by not threatening the other.

As I said, Tom was very successful in the conventional world, but it was not because he fit in so well. Rather, it was because of not feeling himself to fit in, which had led to his learning how to use his many gifts to put others at ease, rather than alerting them to his not actually being a genuine member of their world.

My discovering this did not come from some single incident – not from a dream, not from slips, and not even from associations, at least not from any that I was consciously aware of picking up. Rather, it came from a slowly developing sense that an analysis that seemed comfortable and proper to me was in fact not going anywhere.

A few years passed, years in which we heard and discussed episodes current in Tom's life, connections to early childhood experiences and fantasies, even feelings about me that appeared to be valid bits of the transference now alive. We went on as successful analyses seem to go on, except nothing of significant importance changed in either his inner or outer lives.

In the face of my gradually increasing frustration (and parallel to his uncomplaining frustration), I found myself forming a new image of our work together, or more precisely, a vague sense of being that turned into a feeling state that eventually crystallized as an image. In me, it seemed to come from my interest in watching old movies. When the movie goes well, I am fully caught up in participating in the story. However, there are times when the story drags and I become distracted by the process of filmmaking itself.

One particular piece of that process usually commands my attention, perhaps because of echoes of childhood motion sickness. In such scenes, characters are talking as they sit in a moving car, sometimes driving through city streets, sometimes driving through the countryside. At those moments, for me the spell is broken by my keen, distracting consciousness that the characters and car are in fact *not* moving, that the appearance of their supposed movement is provided by images of passing landscape projected behind them. The spell is broken and I become totally distracted from the story line as I am preoccupied by my awareness of artifice, that the car is actually standing still while the landscape is made to look as if it is passing.

Thus I came to see that the analysis itself felt as if either the patient were moving ahead while the analytic experience seemed stationary, or else the analysis were advancing as analyses are supposed to, yet the patient remained unchanging. It was when I stepped back from my clinical engagement of dancing with the patient that I realized we were dancing in place. Something was not moving. Something was not truly connected.

It was this new recognition on my part that led me to listen to, and in truth even to listen for, elements of strangeness behind the content of whatever was coming up with the patient. I did not offer Tom some shaped formulation about his outsiderness, for indeed at the time my vague feeling did not even have that much shape in my own mind. I did, however, open new aspects of curiosity, ones I had missed before.

Where I had previously felt us to be deeply engaged, I now had a recognition that that conviction was not true, that we had had an illusion of full engagement while some artifice was at hand. I now had a dawning sense that my impression that we were going through the motions of moving through the landscape of his emotions did not fully ring true, but rather that he was "moving" with me, the observer, while himself remaining outside his own real emotional landscape. I could not yet know where the disconnection was: between him and his inner world, or between him and me, or between him and me as a reflection of the underlying split between him and his inner world. Somehow, he was outside his own emotional universe as I watched. And somehow, I had been participating in that structure.

I began to notice and to ask Tom about his privately feeling "outside." He responded intensely, as if a missing link had been found. He became more eager to come to sessions and was more actively curious about what came to his own mind, as if he was learning something new about himself that he could use for the first time. As I showed more interest in the state of strangeness itself, the profound significance of his sense of outsiderness opened up and followed along with that.

Where little had changed before, with this new area now seen and spoken of, put into words, it was as if everything seemed to change. Tom, formerly attentive but not feeling deeply engaged, showed a new enthusiasm for the work. To his mind, the analytic endeavor had finally moved from being yet one more apparent conventional success, even as it felt insignificant. Analysis now felt of use, a benefit he soaked up as if it were water falling on a dry sponge. "How could these last six months," he asked, "be so much more useful than all those years before? I was afraid that this analysis – like my whole life – would not make any difference."

The opening up that ensued brought clarity to both the dynamics of our clinical engagement and, importantly, to his understanding of his own development. For instance, the anxiety he felt when having to present formal reports to his company's board of directors (or, in his prior position, to present to high-level government officials) had often been conceptualized in familiar terms, those of seniority and juniority, of ambivalence and vulnerability, of conflicts over surpassing his father.

The entire world of his mother's pervasive and severe phobic involvement with him, of terrors of separation and abandonment, only then truly opened, responding to my alertness to separateness and feelings of being apart, an outsider. The terrors of the landscape of the world into which Tom had come into being, the essential scenery to which he never felt truly attached, even as he felt himself fully defined by it, were then accessible for analyzing.

The separateness of the Tom who was the shaky child of a terrified, severely phobic mother and the Tom who was a rambunctious lad full of vigor, the separateness of the analytic talk and the analytic emotional engagement, the separateness of my sense of feeling detached and my feeling engaged even when feeling at sea – all these became woven together as whole cloth rather than distinct strands, during this process of, in the meanwhile of, increasing recognition of the effects of outsiderness. As Gardner (1983) so eloquently put it, "It's a long way to heaven; and in analysis as elsewhere it is mainly a matter of meanwhiles" (p. 34).

My experiencing outsiderness in the analytic work and my coming to recognize and appreciate the import of outsiderness are likely to have been both inevitable and necessary for this analysis to succeed.

Analytic process as specimen

Let us step back from this specific case to consider that, just as the analytic situation can tell us something about outsiderness, so, too, can outsiderness tell us something of importance about the analytic process. Let us take a brief overview of clinical experience to examine some implications of outsiderness.

While early in its history, psychoanalysis first focused almost exclusively on the depth psychology of the patient, attention gradually turned to consideration of the analytic process itself. Freud, Robert Fliess, Helene Deutsch, and Max

Gitelson were early pioneers in this work, but each analytic school added its own contributions to our understanding. Some, like Racker and Ogden among the Kleinians, Jacobs among the conflict psychologists, and Greenberg among the relationalists, made particularly powerful contributions that have had great impact across our pluralistic field. In my personal development, the thinking of Loewald, Gardner, McLaughlin, Jacobs, L. Friedman, Boesky, and Chused has been especially significant. Broadly across our landscape, the last half century has proven to be an outstandingly rich period for the study of the dynamics and implications of the clinical engagement.

To reflect on the place of outsiderness in this process, I shall focus on a simplified and necessarily partial but essential aspect.

As the would-be collaborative partners consisting of the patient – someone with a difficulty – and the analyst approach each other and enter the analytic relationship, they come from within conventional roles of society: patient and doctor/therapist. However, the underlying analytic process is premised on a shift from what is conventional to the emphatically unconventional process of openness beyond usual taboos, an intimacy structured for expression, exposure, and exploration. In this new world of the analytic situation, each partner approaches the other as a stranger. Each feels vulnerable by virtue of being alien to the other's inner world of expectation and meanings. This is so even for the analyst, despite the fallback safety of professional identity.

Each participant starts as an outsider to the universe of private meanings of the other. Just as the patient confronts the vulnerability of strangeness and ignorance by utilizing the habits of character, so the analyst runs the great risk of using analytic theory to diminish the essential discomfort of the analyst's own vulnerable ignorance regarding the patient's emotional world. Yet in the presence of the analyst's faith in the analytic process and the patient's faith in being able to take enough risk so as to perhaps receive help, the two join together and begin to create a unique clinical couple. They share the effort to move from strangeness to familiarity, from parallel outsiderness to a mutual and growing, shared *insiderness*.

Let us narrow our attention to the analyst's engagement, the part that from our own experiences we can know best. Wishing to observe and hear the patient's story, and wanting to do so not merely in a purely intellectual way, the analyst opens herself or himself empathically to the pull of the patient, identifying with the patient and the patient's ghosts. The emotional power of what the patient says inevitably goes beyond the words told, with the telling always invoking enacting. As a result, the cockpit of the analytic office does indeed come to hold the vasty fields of France, to use a Shakespearean phrase. In fact, Shakespeare himself was at times remarkably like a modern analyst, at least regarding starting and ending a play. At times he began and finished plays in his own voice, that outside the circumscribed world of the story of the play itself, acknowledging the actuality of the theater before turning to the illusion of the drama. It is like an analyst's knowing he is an analyst, that the patient is someone with an unhappiness coming for help, when the two first meet in consultation – all before those actualities are allowed to become more hazy so that the world of transference and dream can come alive.

For a case in point, let us turn to the beginning of *Henry V* (1599), when Shakespeare has an actor look at the theater (this O construction) and wonder whether the tiny center cockpit of the Globe Theater can really be turned into the "vasty fields of France" (Chorus, 11). Quickly, the play moves from reality to illusion, from that acknowledged reflection on the uncertain possibilities of bringing an imagined inner world to life, and becomes the very world of the fields of France and Agincourt.

Henry V is a relatively early play. The circle of entering and departing the inner world is completed in the late play *The Tempest* (1611), a play about the renunciation of power that seems to express Shakespeare's own imminent retirement, his giving up his power to conjure new worlds, just as Prospero foregoes his power to enchant in the play. Here the prologue from *Henry V* is matched appropriately by an epilogue. With the story of the play complete, Shakespeare has an actor come forward and, speaking as both character and actor, ask for applause, saying, "Now my charms are all o'erthrown, / And what strength I have's mine own; / Which is most faint" (Epilogue, 1–3). What more beautiful statement might there be for an analyst's implicitly saying, "I'm only me, not your transference ghosts"? From outside to inside, and back to outside again.

It is unlikely that any authentic, meaningful opening up and change can occur without the patient's story coming to life, and without the analyst's partaking, at least partially, in the experience of the patient's tale. Yet if the analyst becomes so taken in by the pull of the transference and lets go of self-differentiation enough to feel part of the dream, sooner or later, both the analyst's self-protective instinct and professionalism lead to a pulling back, to detachment and observation rather than merely enacting. It is a process precisely described by Symington (1983) as an "analyst's act of freedom," and it is crucial to analytic progress.

As a result, whatever the analyst then says, from the most trivial clarification to the most profound interpretation, whatever the content of the words, a crucial message buried deep in the structure of the very making of the statement is one that states,

> *No*, I am *not* you, nor am I one of your ghosts, but as separate people we can speak of what is involved. No, I am not part of your dream, but as a person who cares for what you are doing but who is separate, I can help you find the words to say it.

When spoken with genuinely deep respect, that "No, I am not you" carries with it the importantly significant embedded recognition that "And *you* are someone, too" – the "too" implying someone separate yet of equal substance and equal value.

The empathic move toward understanding by joining in with the other involves a pull toward merger of self and other. In contrast, any comment, statement, or interpretation that moves beyond enactment represents a move to a different level of connectedness, one that replaces merger with contact. Union is supplanted by an attitude of mutually respectful recognition of essential separateness; now contact, connection through touching of two separate people, takes the former place of fusion.

In summary, in our laboratory of clinical analysis, both partners confront pressures to join in emotional union. At least in part, neither wishes to be cast entirely as the other's other. Nor does either want to fully lose his or her self within the other. From the uncomfortable separateness of mutual outsiders, each tries to find enough common union to feel central to the newly formed couple. Yet failure to go beyond such an enacted mutual reassuring society is a *folie à deux*, one that ironically implies the loss of the valid unique individuality of each.

My earlier discussion of outsiderness as appearing afresh at every stage of life must not be misunderstood to suggest that there is not a capacity for mastery at each stage. That outsiderness returns in varied forms does not mean that it cannot be tamed at each point. For that possibility of going beyond outsiderness is precisely what we see in and learn from the clinical analytic process. Despite the popularity of the phrase, nothing ever gets "analyzed out." Mastery implies taming, not banishment, of a vulnerability.

Let us look more narrowly at the taming of outsiderness in the analytic process. Individuation is as essential a part of a person's life and growth as is sharing, and there is always potential tension behind the balance of the two. Certainly, there are times of great sharing, emotional high points of people coming together. That is so in lovemaking, and it is so in shared intense aesthetic experiences. Yet all good things come to an end, and the end of such high union is separation. However, the presence of profound regard of one partner for the other can leave that other feeling enriched even while experiencing loss in the process of separation. As that is so in life in general, so is it also within the analytic process.

Outsiderness in human nature

While coming together and joining are vital aspects of clinical partnership, the losses that come with subsequent separation, with individuating and distinguishing oneself from the other, are equally vital to mastery. The uncomfortable uncertainty of outsiderness with which the clinical partners first approach each other can be followed by their becoming a new clinical couple. When the analysis goes well, that compels new separations by the partners, the analyst's "acts of freedom" and the patient's individuating. However, this new separateness, unlike that at the start, brings the capacity for greater solidity of both one's sense of self and one's respectful regard for the other. At the point of separation with termination of a successful analysis, one's separateness is substantially out from under the cloud of feelings of outsiderness.

In the analytic process, it is the analyst's deep respect for the individual uniqueness of the patient in the face of personal differences that is the essential element aiding the patient to solidify self-respect and go beyond the fragility of outsiderness. This respect – not only for the patient as he or she currently is, conflicts and constrictions included, but also for the patient's untapped potential for unique development (Loewald 1960) – is the most important factor in facilitating the patient's movement beyond the fear and shame associated with outsiderness. When successful, the outcome for the patient is not the pseudo-security of grandiosity or other neurotic defensiveness, but it is the solidity of self among others despite the constraints of human weakness and fragilities.

One's crystallization of a sense of self and one's respectful regard for others are mutually interdependent and mutually reinforcing. Successful analytic engagement and later open disengagement do not erase outsiderness but do diminish the fear of it.

Curiosity

There is one further factor in this course of outsiderness as part of clinical analytic progress that demands additional mention. It is the matter of curiosity.

Curiosity, the desire to learn and understand, is a central driving means of growth, of adapting in the face of what feel like the helplessness and ignorance that accompany the sense of outsiderness. Curiosity offers an alternative to depressed resignation. The greater the sense of strangeness, the sharper can be the curiosity, the desire to learn and grasp what is going on in and with the world. Curiosity arises as part of a life force central to the self-preservative instincts for survival and mastery, the *élan vital* of growth.

In clinical work, curiosity is nourished by identification with the analyst's interpretive attitude, the analyst's own curiosity evident in the analyst's underlying conviction that not only beyond whatever is manifest do hidden meanings still lie, but also that it is valuable and worthwhile to seek those unrecognized meanings. Indeed, along with the analyst's respect, that interpretive attitude on the analyst's part might be more crucial to the patient's liberation and growth than are manifest interpretations, important though the latter be. When rooted in respect for differences of self and other, curiosity is a fundamental force that makes mastery of outsiderness possible. Clinical analysis could not succeed were that not so.

Outsiderness and context

Attention to outsiderness brings to the fore a specific aspect of experience often unrecognized. Nonetheless, once addressed, this, like any concept, must be placed back into context so as not to obscure conflicting experiences and views. Outsiderness must be appreciated in context, in its relationship to all the varied competing and even conflicting drives and forces that contribute to, shape, and make up a life. Nothing said about the role of outsiderness exists apart from those multiple influences.

For instance, one can feel *a part of* the common human fabric, and at the same time feel oneself to exist within one's own experience *apart from* the common human fabric. One can feel oneself a highly valued insider, even as one simultaneously feels oneself an outsider, not part of the current group of others. That simultaneity of contrasting feelings was, for instance, clear with my foreign friend and colleague described earlier.

Negotiating the balance between separateness and commonality appears to be an endless task, one for which a single individual can develop several simultaneous – even if conflicting – solutions. Outsiderness exists, but it exists as a significant and foundational thread in the broad tapestry of the human mind. Its presence does not undo or negate all those varied forces that appear to dispel it. Similarly, our attention to its significance does not undo or negate those same other forces.

In closing

Outsiderness is a fact of life, intrinsic to one's coming into the world as a new intruder, even if that world feels mostly accepting. Although not discussed in terms of outsiderness, the subjective feeling of alienation has long been a part of analytic theorizing.

Freud (1915) observed that "loving and hating taken together are the opposite of the condition of unconcern or indifference" (p. 133). Unconcern and indifference imply detachment, the absence of connection. That may be why it has been easier for psychoanalysis to attend to aggression than to outsiderness, for the latter is the experiential manifestation of lack of connection, much more threatening even than the horrors of aggression. In some ways, being undone feels more devastating than being badly and painfully done to. Recognition of the experience of outsiderness can be comforting and lead to growth, while helplessness in the context of outsiderness can seem devastating.

Appreciation of outsiderness highlights another way of seeing the early psychological position described by Freud (1915) as "purified pleasure ego" (p. 136) and by Klein as the paranoid position. A significant portion of aggression toward others and the outside world may well rest on projection as a repudiation of one's own sense of outsiderness. "*I'm* not the outsider; *you* are." Alienation of the other is a fundamental form of repudiating and scapegoating one's own non-integrated feelings of outsiderness. Similarly, fear of the other as strange may include a disowning and projecting of one's fear of experiencing oneself as unacceptably strange in the world.

"Only as a tourist." Even though all of us must form a sense of ourselves in a world of otherness – an outer world essentially new and strange to us, however warm and great its welcome – happily, most of us grow into a sense of mostly feeling at home in the world. That is so *mostly* but never fully or finally. One is never immune to a time when "things fall apart; the centre cannot hold" (Yeats 1919, p. 184), when one's sense of self is freshly threatened, when the painful uncertainty and vulnerability of outsiderness can return.

Recognizing that, and therefore distrusting smug self-satisfaction, in my reply to my successful friend and colleague's letter telling of her outsiderness, I see that I wrote, "For myself I have never wanted to refer a possible patient to someone who is an analyst who never shows evidence of that uncomfortable sense of otherness leaking out."

Psychoanalysis can help and help significantly, but it cannot offer immunity. An analyst's capacity to help depends on a caring curiosity that is itself founded on recognition and appreciation of one's own outsiderness, that is respectful of the patient's separate sense of strangeness. Analysts at work need both to recognize their emotional similarities with their patients and also to keep in mind their differences. Thus each of them, analyst and patient, as much as they strive to be close to and know each other, can only do so validly if they come together in a way that protects and respects the ultimate chasm of separateness on the edge of which all of us live.

References

Erikson, E.H. (1959). *Identity and the Life Cycle*. New York: International Universities Press.

Freud, S. (1905). Three essays on the theory of sexuality. *S.E.*, 7.

Freud, S. (1915). Instincts and their vicissitudes. *S.E.*, 14.

Gardner, R. (1983). *Self Inquiry*. Boston, MA/Toronto, ON: Little, Brown & Co.

Loewald, H. (1960). On the therapeutic action of psycho-analysis. *International Journal of Psychoanalysis*, 41:16–33.

Millay, E.S.V. (1954). Intense and terrible, I think, must be the loneliness. In *Collected Poems of Edna St. Vincent Millay*, ed. N. Millay. New York: HarperCollins, 1990.

Montagna, P. (2011). Personal communication.

Shakespeare, W. (1599). *Henry V.* Oxford, UK: Oxford University Press, 2008.

Shakespeare, W. (1611). *The Tempest*. In *The Comedies of William Shakespeare*. New York: Modern Library, 1994.

Symington, N. (1983). The analyst's act of freedom as agent of therapeutic change. *International Review of Psychoanalysis*, 10:283–291.

Winnicott, D.W. (1955). Metapsychological and clinical aspects of regression within the psychoanalytic set-up. *International Journal of Psychoanalysis*, 36:16–26.

Yeats, W.B. (1919). The second coming. In *The Collected Poems of W.B. Yeats*. New York: Macmillan, 1956.

Chapter 5

The interpretive attitude

A dedicated painter paints, it has been said, in order to learn how to paint. Similarly, a serious psychoanalyst analyzes in order to learn how to analyze. However, while painters of widely discrepant schools can for the most part agree as to what is a painting, the same cannot be said for agreement among psychoanalysts as to what is an analysis.

Close consideration of debates about the fine points of psychoanalytic technique suggests that what shapes analytic work are not simply those details of technique but are the attitudes behind them with which the analyst approaches the patient and the work. What is the analyst trying to accomplish? Method matters, but it is the analyst's back-of-the-mind attitude that shapes the effect of any technical system. Technique addresses *how* we get to where we are going, not *where* it is we hope to get. Technique is attitude actualized.

The psychoanalytic attitude is at root one of professional responsibility in the service of another person's mental freeing up and growing. What makes such an attitude specifically psychoanalytic rather than simply therapeutic is the analyst's organizing principle that intrinsic to the patient's personal problems are powerful inner forces of which the patient is unconscious. Deep respect for the personal validity and unique individuality of the patient plus regard for the significance of what is hidden and can only be inferred as seen through derivative effects are both essential to a psychoanalytic attitude.

That psychoanalytic attitude is communicated. Patients have more strengths than merely those caught in their transference conflicts, and they use those strengths to read the analyst's mind as empathically as does the analyst's mind working in the other direction. Behind any manifest statement the analyst makes lie the unspoken messages of what the analyst thinks matters more and what matters less. The patient hears and reads those deeper messages.

Shifting estimations of interpretation

Study of the psychoanalytic process over recent decades has led to remarkable advances in understanding, exposing previously underappreciated aspects of the shared interaction of the two clinical partners. As that understanding has grown, the entire psychoanalytic enterprise has seemed to shift. Although insight as a principal clinical goal and interpretation as the analyst's primary technique for achieving that goal were the hallmarks of psychoanalysis in its first half century, in much of modern analytic discourse their place has diminished, at times to the point of disappearance. While maintaining respect for the significance of analytic interaction, it is appropriate to reevaluate the dwindling prominence of insight and interpretation.

At the start of our history, Freud moved to extend the radical genius of his self-analysis to a stunning exploration of unconscious forces in patients, thereby defining psychoanalysis as a process dedicated to exploring the meanings and forces behind disorders, to extending consequent insights as deeply as possible. A patient's freedom from symptoms and inhibitions was thought to come from mastery through insight, with the analyst's understanding making possible interpretations that were crucial to the patient's attaining new insights. Early psychoanalytic discoveries were so exciting that enthusiasm for new insights into unconscious activities stimulated a fervor that crossed national and linguistic boundaries.

Unfortunately, although enthusiasm and discipline often flirt, they do not always marry. Fervor for finding ever deeper discoveries too often led to pronouncements based more on an analyst's capacity for imagination than on clinical evidence. The birth of healthy depth analysis was soon followed by the arrival of its deformed sibling, wild analysis. As a consequence, just as in our early history liberation from symptoms and constrictions was the result of successful analyses, so were disappointment, disillusionment, and rage the outcome of wild analyses. (An ironical modern twist in shifting fashions merits notice. In our early days analysts seemed too ready to accept wild analysis as if it were truly deep. Today, many analysts seem just as ready to dismiss deep analysis as if it could only be wild.)

Whether coming from undue optimism, from the limitations of early technique, or from the effect of wild analytic excesses, the unreliability of analytic cures ushered in concern for what it is that actually does account for change when clinical analyses succeed. That question has continued at the forefront of our concerns.

Strachey (1934) addressed the problem when he brought to the fore the patient's experience and internalization of the analyst's nonjudgmental attitude. He stopped short of fully opening either the analyst's emotional engagement or the patient's adopting the analyst's approach of exploratory curiosity. His emphasis on the superego amelioration that resulted from the two-person psychoanalytic interaction maintained its place within the still accepted central importance of interpretation and insight.

Ensuing attention turned increasingly to previously unrecognized noninterpretive factors in effecting change. Analysts' views differed and continue to differ. Politics, by definition, is the combination of conflicts of people and policy; so crucial theoretical dilemmas soon became complicated by political struggles, a turn of events that seems as inevitable as it is regrettable.

In such a charged setting and with distressing oversimplification, Freud and Ferenczi have been posited as the leaders and precursors of two supposedly fully separate understandings about clinical change and about what analytic techniques lead to that change. Freud is purported to be the model for the value of pure insight developed through the analyst's remote detachment, and Ferenczi the model for change as deriving from the open and active affective encounter of the clinical partners. While there are genuine and consequential differences between the two, Freud's deep emotional engagement with his patients and Ferenczi's interest in insight are complications often brushed aside by those who prefer the comfort of clear polemical splits to the complexities of diverse factors.

While some continue to see insight as the keystone of psychoanalysis and interpretation as the primary psychoanalytic tool, others disagree. For many, insight is seen in a narrow partial meaning, derided as if it were no more than cognitive intellectualization. For them, the place of insight has shrunk to being merely the result of psychic change, removed of power to allow a person to effect further growth and change. As part of this trend, interpretation has been downgraded from its formerly preeminent position to being at best merely one mutative factor among many.

Indeed, in some contemporary circles interpretation is dealt with as if it were part of the sins of the fathers, an inheritance to be rejected as out of place in our enlightened modernity. Interpretation is judged not only immaterial to bringing about change, it is found even worse, an imposition on the patient that destructively imposes an analyst's authority over that of the patient. Paradoxically, some who hold this view most dearly simultaneously argue against the appropriateness of the analyst's concerns for neutrality!

Another diminution of the classical appreciation of insight to which interpretations aim comes in the argument for the irrelevance of genetic reconstruction or the recovery of repressed memories. Fonagy (1999, p. 215), for instance, states, "Some still appear to believe that the recovery of memory is part of the therapeutic action of the treatment. There is no evidence for this and in my view to cling to this idea is damaging to the field."

With current unconscious processes attributed to very early preverbal memories, memories seen as procedural and pre-discursive, there is said to be no point in trying to lift repression. It is as if exposure of consciously discrete memories with specific images were the sole function of interpretation. Indeed, searching for very early roots is called "damaging." In contrast, I wish to argue that appreciation of such very early phenomena calls for an expansion of the concept of interpretation, not its elimination. Increased conscious clarity of the experience of early feeling states is as valid and useful a form of memory recovery as is the derepression of later events.

Certainly, the recovery of discrete memories is, more often than not, replaced by reconstruction of the past based on experiences within the immediacy of the emotional present. The past is more often recognized by reconstruction from immediate emotional experiences than by dramatic derepressions. Correcting prior magical valuation of manifest interpretations does not require and should not lead to repudiating the interpretive attitude.

Although by its very nature insight is always partial and incomplete, introspection toward emotionally rich self-knowledge is intrinsic to the entire psychoanalytic endeavor. Our concern here is to focus more specifically on the analyst's role in the development of psychic change and in particular on the place of interpretation within that role.

Without providing an exhaustive list, let us first acknowledge some of the significant psychoanalytic operations that have been teased out as essential parts in the mixture of functions of an analyst at work. In helping to structure a psychoanalytic situation, the analyst provides a holding environment, an empathic ambiance, and a capacity to contain the anxieties and conflicts taken in from a patient's emotional projections.

The analyst respects, listens, hears, regards, and witnesses. The analyst stands as guardian of the analytic work and protector of the patient's interests while the patient sets aside some normal waking executive mental functions. The analyst, with the assistance of private self-analysis, acts to be available to the patient as a new object for both continued and new mental development. (All of these functions overlap, yet they are not the same.)

The analyst tries to help the patient overhear himself, the analyst doing what Bloom (1994, p. 70) noted that Shakespeare was the first to have his characters do. This metaphor from literary criticism comes close to traditional views of interpretation, but it does not extend to the analyst's telling the patient previously unrecognized messages heard in associations or understood from transferential evocations. While it need not include the analyst's bringing forth possible linkages not previously recognized, this concern for one's overhearing oneself implies the analyst's helping a patient learn to attend to the patient's own associative and emotional patterns.

This brief list is certainly not comprehensive. Yet vital as all of these functions are, interpretation is not evident among them. As we study the dyadic engagement of patient and analyst and explore the emotional interactions, we have tended to leave behind what earlier was central. Interpretation has often been left aside as if it were antique and arcane, irrelevant, harmful, and imperialistic. Along with the devaluation of specific interpretations, the analyst's maintaining a background investigative and interpretive attitude also at times is lost.

Declarative interpretations and the interpretive attitude

The loss of appreciation for interpretation is surprising in a field conceived by discovery of the power of the latent forces hidden behind the manifest. Decreasing attention to *explicit* interpretations has brought with it a devaluing of an approach interpretive in nature, the unspoken but communicated basic attitude that privileges searching for unknown and as yet undiscovered meanings. This *interpretive attitude* is one that not only searches for new levels of meanings but, crucially, profoundly values that search.

An interpretation enriches on two levels. One is the manifest content that opens the possibility of new understandings. The other is that of the new experiential moment, adding its own value of the search for new growth through continued introspection. The shared dyadic introspection increases the possibilities of the patient's increasing self-analytic skills.

"While there is no such thing as *full* understanding, whatever the levels attained, essential to the idea of meaning is the implication of connection, of linkage between separate levels, both those within a person and those between persons" (Poland 1996, p. 267). The content of an interpretation and the process of the enacted and experienced analytic attitude resonate, reinforcing each other. Indeed, considering the inevitable tentativeness of any particular interpretation, it is likely that it is the attitude of exploring for new understandings that itself becomes the most important factor for opening future growth.

The word "interpretation" has lately seemed to lose its specificity. It is used at times to describe an analyst's statements that more precisely could be called clarifications or confrontations or even descriptions. These valuable interventions do make something explicit, but they do so without extending into new linkages. An example, for instance, might be an analyst's commenting that a patient is avoiding an obvious topic. Although that is loosely called an interpretation of resistance, it is descriptive, falling short of being interpretive by failing to link the observation to any new aspect. That is less so, however, if the interpretive attitude is also present, the attitude emphasizing that there is more to be searched for. Then, the resistance interpretation communicates respectful curiosity for the reasons necessitating the avoidance. Even a seeming non-interpretation can have interpretive value in communicating an interpretive attitude.

Let us call the specific statement of a manifest extension of linkages a *declarative interpretation*. For an analyst's statement to merit being called a declarative interpretation, it must tell the patient something not already consciously known even if that new knowledge is chiefly one of bringing together differing aspects of meanings in a connection not previously recognized by the patient.

Individual interpretations are inevitably partial, addressing only a narrow aspect of what potentially could be elaborated, yet they can be powerful in their cumulative effect. Despite the tentative and fragmentary nature of any specific interpretation, we can conceive of a more total overarching model. It would be one that links the dynamics of the dyadic engagement ("Why now?") with the genetics of their development ("How come?").

Debate over manifest interpretations has obscured the importance of the interpretive attitude: one naturally is taken by the foreground before being able to observe what lies in the background. Perhaps it is inevitable that renewed appreciation of an analyst's interpretive attitude now arises in part as a reaction to recent emphasis on non-interpretive functions, for the very attitude of caring curiosity may well be what gives most depth to the other functions.

Interpretation implies exploration as well as explanation, interpretations containing questions as well as answers. Declarative interpretations and the interpretive attitude both work to extend the attitude of exploring for understanding from the interactive level of the clinical partnership to the patient's own inner mental functioning. It is so that "the analyst's contribution is more crucially one of exploration than of revelation" (Poland 1996, p. 81). Yet it is simultaneously so that the analyst's organizing attitude of holding exploration of unconscious forces dear can itself be taken in by the patient. "Being at-one-with in authentic understanding – while two are engaged together in ruthlessly honest searching – can be internalized as a model for valuing introspection and insight as important parts of the ego ideal" (*ibid.*, p. 80).

The first of these quotations emphasizes the value of the exploratory process over explanations revealed as if from on high. The second suggests that both the value of insight plus the introspective techniques for achieving that insight can be learned from the shared analytic investigative experience. The exploratory rather than revelatory approach succeeds only if it derives from the premise that there is more to be learned, that there are deeper connections and meanings to be found. Psychoanalysis is a form of inquiry, not indoctrination (Reed 1987); and that approach of inquiry is what is vitally present in the analyst's interpretive attitude.

As the analytic process unfolds, the analyst at times hears meanings before the patient can, notices patterns before the patient sees them. Abstinence from undue transference gratification does not call for withholding what could contribute to the shared task, including deep connections as they come clear from clinical emotional immediacy. When an analyst knows something a patient can use, it is appropriate to tell the patient so.

Several factors matter in what the analyst tells the patient. One is that such statements ring true as they arise from the affective experience of the clinical moment (accounting for the possibilities of deep interpretation) rather than as they come from an analyst's preferred theory or view of life (accounting for wild analysis).

Another essential is the analyst's modest appreciation that any interpretation is a trial interpretation. No matter how close an interpretive comment comes to the mark, it must always be translated by the patient into the patient's own inner language and modified by the patient to accord with the patient's own inner experience. Modestly and respectfully handled, declarative interpretations are necessary and valuable means by which an analyst contributes to a patient's analytic work. An interpretation can speak *about* a pre-discursive part of the patient while speaking *to* the adult part. The analyst listens to the archaic, but speaks to the mature.

The background *interpretive attitude* lends richness not only to declarative interpretations but to all other analytic functions by setting those functions within an ever open-minded exploratory context. Although unspoken, this attitude is communicated to the patient. Unconscious communication, to which we have been so attentive in our studies of empathy, travels in both directions. Just as we value the analyst's understanding as it comes from experiencing a patient's transferential evocations, so is it proper to respect the patient's taking in the powerful transmission of the analyst's interpretive attitude that lies behind the analyst's explicit statements.

Procedural and declarative memories

At first glance, this pairing of functions of declarative interpretations and interpretive attitude seems strikingly similar to another pair of functions now widely studied, the division of memory into declarative and procedural memories. However, so direct a matching would be misleading.

The burgeoning study of differing forms of memory has grown significantly within clinical analysis itself from thinking offered by the Sandlers (Sandler & Sandler 1984, 1987), in which they distinguished the past (infantile) unconscious from the present unconscious. The past unconscious is said to include those very early experiences that color the life of an individual but that have their impact before the mind supposedly has developed a capacity for symbolic representation. The present unconscious, in contrast, is said to include those aspects that have mental representation and can be worked with explicitly from within the transference.

These distinct areas of mental functioning come close to the two primary categories defined by recent studies of memory, those of procedural and declarative memory. In reference to the former the Sandlers state, "To the inner world which we attribute to the past unconscious we have to allocate highly developed interactions with the internal representatives of childhood figures" (Sandler & Sandler 1987, p. 334). If early experiences are pre-symbolic, then they seem to be part of procedural memory and untouchable by declarative interpretations.

However, the fact that an area developed "pre-symbolically" and "pre-verbally" does not mean that such early functions cannot later be brought under consideration by symbolic and verbal functions. Earliest experiences leave their record in attitudes, emotional postures, the ways one approaches, shapes, and sees the world. A psychoanalysis can work toward defining a pattern of character functioning and can help a person master previously constricted patterns by reconstructing the circumstances under which they grew. If the earliest memories are registered in ways not symbolic, are their reconstructions then any less valid in being confirmed by their leading to emotional procedural shifts rather than the appearance of verbal tales of specific memories?

Any transference exploration and resolution is possible because the mature strengths of the analyzing partners can be brought to bear on the experiences that had originally developed when the analysand was less mature and had developmentally early mental powers. There must be a difference between putting into words what occurred when words were not available and putting into words what occurred when speech was present. But that does not imply the irrelevance of using words for what originally seemed amorphous and undefinable.

Every verbal understanding and interpretation is a translation of an inner emotional experience, and to translate is always in part to betray. Yet despite those limitations, being able to put experiences and feelings into words, having the words to say it by, powerfully strengthens one. Rather than being damaging, the search for memories is a great source of analytic strength, even when that search is carried out significantly by examination of what unfolds within the dyadic interchange.

Indeed, even the distinction between past unconscious and present unconscious and that between procedural and declarative memories may not be as simple as such a comfortable dichotomy suggests. Not only can the past unconscious and procedural memories both be brought under study, but also even the most supposedly mature present unconscious and declarative memories have their own powerful connections to and roots in forces from before verbal levels. Of the two types of memories, it is likely that you can't ever have one without the other. The mind does not exist and work in theoretical boxes.

A particular risk of theories, invaluable as they are, is their effect of turning attention toward important areas at the price of turning it away from other important areas. Turning an analyst's mind away from the curiosity of a search for formative experiences is an unfortunate misuse of a theory about memory. Indeed, a great value of studies both from direct child observation and from neuroscientific studies of procedural memory is specifically the contrary, their enriching an analyst's capacity for grasping the possibilities of early experiences, even when those experiences had arisen during what appears to be pre-symbolic periods of life.

We cannot say that the fact that an experience occurred at the earliest time of life meant that it had not had a mental representation. In our inadequacies, we tend to apply distorting adultomorphic words and concepts to those early experiences. Yet it may be better to use our insufficient words and concepts, trying ever to improve them, than to say that it is damaging even to try to recover early experiences.

Even in areas of the highest levels of functioning, patients have to translate back into their own inner universe of meanings whatever it is that the analyst says. Clinical experience suggests that they can do so even on more archaic levels when the analyst succeeds in approaching those deepest inner experiences.

The need for an analyst to have judicious modesty using declarative interpretations does not suggest the interpretive attitude ought to be abandoned. *The analyst's attitude of working with analytic curiosity towards understanding and insight is the essential factor that shapes the psychoanalytic situation and makes possible the psychoanalytic value both of non-interpretive non-insight-oriented activities and of formal declarative interpretations.*

Why not simply call this the psychoanalytic attitude? While that name would fit, it would obscure something important. What distinguishes psychoanalytic from other helpful emotional, educational, or therapeutic endeavors is concern for hidden inner meanings and forces, bringing the detoxification that can come from their exposure.

Freud's motto for his technique may have been, as he said it was, "More darkness," but its aim was always to carry more light to those areas of darkness. The primary clinical goal may be helping a patient's life to be better and helping a patient feel better, but clinical psychoanalysis works by inquiry toward that goal.

One can only explore if one believes there is something of value yet to be found, that there is more that profitably can yet be learned. The analyst's interpretive attitude provides the ambiance that shapes the clinical work in that direction, implying the constant presence of newly open possibilities of understanding and growth no matter the forces of the patient's mind that are at hand.

Clinical illustration

The power of the analyst's interpretive attitude to help open constrictions and the benefits of reconstructing early experiences are both long familiar to most practitioners. Here, I shall offer a brief vignette, for which I am grateful to Katherine Burton, merely as a suggestive illustration of some of the experiences I have in mind.

My intent with the first is to demonstrate that both analyst and patient can emerge from a protracted enactment with more knowledge of themselves and with changed behavior, with this coming less from specific interpretations than from the freedom to engage afresh after the enactment is placed under the aegis of a renewed interpretive attitude.

Despite being modestly successful in his profession, Mr. L. sought treatment because he felt he never achieved the true success his talents deserved. Although married, he held himself remote from his wife both emotionally and sexually, obtaining his greatest sense of personal and sexual fulfillment from engagement with dominatrices hired anonymously via the internet. Feeling unfulfilled, he approached his work with his gifted woman analyst with the same air of cynicism that he had about his career and his marriage.

During the early months of the analysis Mr. L. talked about his life and his analysis in tones of detached disdain. Gradually he structured an analytic relationship in which he felt a constant struggle (initially more implicit than explicit) over power and domination. The more he became engaged with analysis and analyst, the more he warded off anything the analyst said. The alternative was his feeling belittled and undone by this newest aggressive woman who he felt held true power.

As the work progressed, Mr. L. at first continued to meet with female dominatrices. However, as the two clinical partners identified the unfolding pattern of engagement, Mr. L. began homosexual cruising, something he had never before done. The routine was consistent: the search for a man who seemed strong, one whom he could fellate and then flee.

The analyst accepted this behavior as expressive of unfolding feelings and fantasies rather than as misbehavior, yet also questioning the relationship of this behavior to the patient's growing intimacy with the analyst. Conflicts over gender and sexuality came more clearly to the fore and were explored. The flurry of cruising then faded and disappeared, replaced by increased turmoil within the analysis itself.

Mr. L. became ever more contentious. Nothing that the analyst said was right to Mr. L. From time to time he hinted at his improved relationship with his wife and his career, but he would deny these if the analyst included them in focus. It was as if change had to be denied to their shared notice as Mr. L. intensified his repudiation of the analyst.

Increasingly depreciated, the analyst underwent a gradual shift in a way likely known by all practitioners. Whatever she said or did not say was wrong to Mr. L. As evidenced by the life changes reported, even though disavowed, this was not a negative therapeutic reaction. The more Mr. L. improved in important aspects of his life, the more he devalued his analyst.

The analyst approached the defensive nature of what was happening; she addressed the immediacy of the transference engagement; she ventured to make helpful remarks about possible origins of this process. Whatever she said had the same result: she was said to be self-interested and impotent. She tried to connect Mr. L's responses to feelings he had about her, to feelings he had about himself, to actualities about herself that he had validly picked up, to the ghosts within him, to what was developing between them. Mr. L. was unrelentingly dismissive.

Feeling ever more uncertain about herself and becoming desperate about the analysis, the analyst gradually pulled back emotionally. She turned to self-analysis to help resolve the impasse; but regardless of the efforts she made, the pattern persisted.

At some point, however, without fully withdrawing, the analyst stepped back from the engagement in a way that was different from before. At that moment she discovered a newly gained or newly regained (she couldn't be certain which) sense of not having her integrity at stake within the engagement. She still cared greatly about the work and about the meanings of the emotional interchange, but now without the prior push for self-justification.

During the period of this impasse, the analyst's words had come less and less to inform the patient and more and more to pressure him. The parallel with the patient's dominatrices seemed clear as the analyst retrieved herself from the sway of this shared engagement, but similar formulations had remained useless until something had changed in her and the time was ripe. Only then was she able to reclaim her interpretive posture that had diminished before the growing power of the strong domination–submission conflicts alive in the encounter. That posture could be regained because of the persistence of her interpretive attitude. The interpretive attitude had kept its power even when both spoken dyadic and private self-analytic declarative interpretations were undone.

In short, as Mr. L. had become more negative, the analyst had reacted with increasing force. Then her messages were heard not as useful defense interpretations about the patient's avoiding open intimacy but as pressure that the patient *should* be intimate. Slowly, declarative interpretations degenerated into enactments in the guise of interpretation, with the process salvaged and utilized analytically only when the analyst's interpretive attitude could again hold sway.

What is most important to glean from this garden variety vignette is the connection between active interpretations and the interpretive attitude. Declarative interpretations are shaped and driven by the power of the analyst's underlying interpretive attitude. While both declarative and non-declarative aspects are vulnerable in the intense heat of an actual analysis, it is the analyst's commitment to the basic interpretive attitude that allows progress to proceed.

The place of interpretation and the past

It is unquestionable that there are qualitative differences between the internalization of experiences that occur while a developing child is extremely immature and those that take place when the mind has grown, when there is the power of object constancy and when symbolic representation can come under the influence of verbal skills. The child *is* father of the man, but both child parts and adult parts are present and active during a clinical analysis. Different aspects predominate at different moments, so the concept of transference regression lives on despite its diminution in current analytic theoretical fashions. While the analyst comes to experience the entire range, the analyst, as already noted, also knows the wisdom of speaking *of* the archaic but *to* the mature.

Fonagy is in at least partial agreement, feeling that since relevant early experiences will have occurred too early in a patient's life to be consciously remembered, "the only way we can know what goes on in our patient's mind, what might have happened to them, is how they are with us in the transference" (1999, p. 217). Such forces are suitable not only for hearing but also for telling They are as helpful for the patient's learning to overhear the patient's self as are autobiographical tales. *Valid regard for the patient's ways of relating as manifesting what we may interpret as evidence of procedural memories offers us the possibility of examining those processes for their informative value, approaching them with the same interpretive attitude that we carry to the content of more mature associations.*

Indeed, Fonagy cites Betty Joseph to the effect that interpretations dealing only with associations would touch only the adult part of the personality. In doing so, Joseph implies the breadth needed for a true interpretive attitude. Fonagy also describes a preference for understanding "in terms of the total interpersonal situation the patient creates in the transference with the analyst" (Fonagy 1999, p. 217). To do this fully would be to subsume procedural memories under the same interpretive attitude as later transferences. Understanding of a situation cannot be "total" if it removes aspects of the patient's experienced past from the analyst's curiosity and active seeking, removing them from observation, from exploration, and from readiness to discuss.

The view that the "recovery of memory is an inappropriate goal" (*ibid.*, p. 220) at worst or an "epiphenomenon" (p. 218) at best would turn analysts' minds away from that most psychoanalytic of implicit questions, the time-honored question about what unfolds in either the words or the music, the question "How come?" "How did it come to be that ...?" implies both past and interpretive possibilities. Without such critical questions, psychoanalysis would be desperately diminished.

Childhood diaries and letters can be of historical importance, but taken as such they exist outside the experience of the transferential engagement, outside the analyst's and patient's psychic processes. In contrast, the patient's enacted procedural memories emerge within the analytic situation and thus are "grist for the mill." Here, Fonagy agrees, saying "Therapeutic work needs to focus on helping the individual identify regular patterns of behaviour and phantasy based on childhood fantasy and experience, for which autobiographical memory can provide no explanation" (*ibid.*, p. 220). We are in accord that rich interpretive possibilities extend beyond accessible cognitive memories. Recovery of affective memories from earliest periods can be experienced on emotional levels even as later language is applied to give the patients the words to say it by. All memories can be spoken of no matter their original representation and respectful of their developmental vicissitudes.

Speaking to the mature part of a patient's mind does not exclude the power of those communications to resonate on all levels. It is so that the words with which an analyst tries to approach a patient's feelings and thoughts or fantasies and experiences can only be "approximate objectifications" of their nature (Arlow 1979, p. 381). Experience teaches us that the unconscious power of "procedural" forces can be tamed by the new-grown strength of a patient's personal insights.

Fonagy states that "modern emphasis on the therapeutic relationship as the primary motor of therapeutic reaction, for which we are indebted to Winnicott (1956) and Loewald (1960)" has not "succeeded in eliminating the emphasis on the recovery of childhood experiences" (Fonagy 1999, p. 215). Close attention shows that despite his reference to Loewald, Loewald's concern for dyadic interactions did not extend to wanting to eliminate what came before. Loewald wrote that

> the analyst, through the objective interpretation of transference distortions, increasingly becomes available to the patient as a new object. And this is not primarily in the sense of an object not previously met, but the newness consists in the patient's rediscovery of the early paths of the development of object-relations.
>
> (Loewald 1980, pp. 228–229)

To speak of "the patient's rediscovery of the early paths" rejects the artificiality of positing a dichotomy between exploration of the past and the significance of the object-related present.

The interpretive attitude is central to the analytic process, of which it is part, while any declarative interpretation is a specific product of that process. That process of an interpretive attitude is at first carried out by the analyst for the patient, but ultimately it is taken over by the patient. This is probably why, when asked after their analyses, patients so rarely can say what they learned but definitely feel they have changed, usually citing what we call "self-analytic" functions, developed for themselves functions we provided originally.

In closing

Clinical experience has clearly revealed that the evolving clinical engagement is the primary field for carrying out analytic inquiry and is a primary source for developing new understandings. Working within this context, the analyst's interpretive attitude is not an intellectualized detective search to uncover and unlock archaic historical events whose dramatic recovery will then magically lead to freedom from conflict. It is, rather, an approach of open-minded curiosity (Chodorow 2000) based on the certainty that unseen implications, hidden meanings, lie behind manifest symptoms. It is the attitude that exploration based on respectful but unconstrained inquiry has the power of enriching and freeing the patient.

Through the ongoing work based on such an attitude, analyst and patient are partners in a joint endeavor. The analyst works to facilitate the greatest possible expression and opening of the patient's private ways of relating, what in earlier days was spoken of as facilitating the regression. Technical skill and art are demanded for the analyst to draw attention to the patient's patterns in a manner that identifies them without implying that they are unreal and without aborting their further opening.

The analyst's freedom to speak of what occurs is put to its greatest use in declarative interpretations. Behind those interpretations and making them possible lies the analyst's basic stance, one that responds to the patient's evocations and provocations with respectful curiosity rather than with conventional reactions.

In a successful analysis, the patient increasingly identifies with the analyst's attitude of psychoanalytic curiosity, of freedom to search for whatever hidden meanings can throw new light on present emotions and experiences. That curiosity about as yet unknown deeper explanations is what places the unrestricted interpretive attitude at the heart of the psychoanalytic approach.

References

Arlow, J.A. (1979). Metaphor and the psychoanalytic situation. *Psychoanalytic Quarterly*, 48:363–385.

Bloom, H. (1994). *The Western Canon: The Books and School of the Ages.* New York: Harcourt Brace.

Chodorow, N.J. (2000). Paradoxes of self-knowledge in psychoanalysis. Presented at the 5th Delphi International Psychoanalytic Symposium.

Fonagy, P. (1999). Memory and therapeutic action. *International Journal of Psychoanalysis*, 80:215–223.

Loewald, H.W. (1960). On the therapeutic action of psychoanalysis. *International Journal of Psychoanalysis*, 41:16–33.

Loewald, H.W. (1980). *Papers on Psychoanalysis.* New Haven, CT: Yale University Press.

Poland, W.S. (1996). *Melting the Darkness: The Dyad and Principles of Clinical Practice.* Northvale, NJ: Aronson.

Reed, G. (1987). Rules of clinical understanding in classical psychoanalysis and in self-psychology: A comparison. *Journal of the American Psychoanalytic Association*, 35:421–446.

Sandler, J., & Sandler, A.-M. (1984). The past unconscious, the present unconscious, and interpretation of the transference. *Psychoanalytic Inquiry*, 4:367–399.

Sandler, J., & Sandler, A.-M. (1987). The past unconscious, the present unconscious, and the vicissitudes of guilt. *International Journal of Psychoanalysis*, 68:331–341.

Strachey, J. (1934). The nature of the therapeutic action of psychoanalysis. *International Journal Psychoanalysis*, 15:127–158.

Winnicott, D.W. (1956). On transference. *International Journal of Psychoanalysis*, 37:386–388.

Chapter 6

The analyst's approach and the patient's psychic growth

Introduction

While it shares many therapeutic aspects with other clinical approaches in the broad range of psychotherapies, and does so beneficially, psychoanalysis has central qualities that define it, that set it apart as unique. Its core concern with seeking increased self-knowledge, self-mastery, and freedom for the patient by exposing and exploring those unconscious forces that lie hidden behind manifest functioning leads analysis to use a particular approach of emotionally engaged but disciplined inquiry by the analyst. It is a process that commands the analyst's mainly silent self analysis in the service of the patient's analytic work, a process the patient senses. As a result, psychoanalysis is defined by *how* an analyst explores, not by *what* the analyst then finds. And the patient learns that *how*.

Clinical illustration

A clinical moment: Ms. R. was a bright but severely guarded woman, one who had been raised in a family of great social privilege but who as an adult lived as if alienated from the world. For the first several years of our work together, she stayed emotionally distant as she tried to do what she believed was expected – that is, satisfy me by speaking of her current life and of her childhood, but do so in a way that hid any genuine feeling and guarded against personal engagement. She spoke to satisfy the other, not to express herself. Whenever I addressed what was actually developing between us, my invitation for her to speak openly of her experiences and feelings seemed only minimally accepted.

Yet slowly, a tiny step at a time, Ms. R. began to open. She could not complain, but we gradually learned how severely harsh her childhood had been: how she not only suffered physical abuse from her mother, but how much more harrowing had been her experience of what Shengold (1989) termed *soul murder*. She was told what she felt and told what she thought. Any sign of her having a thought of her own was not only squelched but taken as forbidden rebellion. At age six she could debone a fish flawlessly, but she did not know how to play. Her childhood seemed an endless effort to survive by avoiding notice while living in the underground.

At times I commented to Ms. R. about aspects of her style. For instance, when I realized how intensely observant she was despite her seeming detachment, how she seemed never to miss a trick, I mentioned a piece of film that *she* brought to *my* mind. It was the image of one little girl sitting among others in an early film by Margaret Mahler of mothers and children in a waiting room. Every time that child began to crawl, to move to explore as all the other children did, her mother picked her up and placed her back in her original spot, always forcing the child to stay still. After a while, the child stopped even trying to crawl. The film's narrator commented on the intense curiosity the child subsequently manifested. The little girl stayed still but never missed a thing, always taking in everything with her eyes.

I wondered about the usefulness of my telling the patient something so intellectual, but what I said did not seem academic to Ms. R. For her, I was helping make sense of a piece of her life, and doing so in a way that opened the possibility of connecting her style to developmental forces and experiences, even from early preverbal days.

Our work continued at the patient's cautious, glacial pace, only gradually building tentative trust. Then, other early experiences opened in a much less delicate way, indeed in a way that seemed to be exposed by a sadistic force coming from me.

One day during an otherwise ordinary session, there was a sudden loud explosion just outside my office window. Startled, Ms. R. burst out, "What was that?" Calmly and in a soft voice, I answered, "What was what?"

If we were both surprised by the noise and if I was surprised to hear what I said as not what I would expect myself to say, I was then further surprised by my patient's response. What I think I had had in mind when I made my odd remark was a sense of commonality between us, the feeling that we had come so far that she and I could share being frightened, yet we two could face that threat together, even with humor. Of course, I too had been startled, but then I thought I could be reassuringly playful, my words implying "You and I can together play in the face of such shock." But that was not how Ms. R. heard what I said, so I then followed *her* line of thought rather than my own.

I was surprised she had taken my joke, cruel as it might seem, as if it were a statement about reality. Naturally, I was also concerned about my own sadism. Yet Ms. R.'s instant concern was as if to re-right herself after being disoriented. She wanted urgently to get clear whether in fact there had been a noise, whether in fact she had heard what she did or whether she had imagined it – this despite the fact that, without doubt, there had been a shocking noise.

What then emerged was a universe of memories from which, we learned, Ms. R.'s developing sense of reality had been undermined by a mother who decided for her when she was hot and when she was cold, when she was alert and when she was sleepy, when she was hungry and when she was full. It was as if she had been raised always to disown her own perceptions but to accept reality as it was defined by the other.

Looking back at it, the interchange seems to have arisen out of a confluence of the undercurrent of sadism with which the patient was raised, the characteristic guilt feelings and more deeply buried sadism of the patient herself, and the reservoir of my own personal sadism called to life in our relationship. My recognition of this, together with my unspoken acknowledgment of the meanness of my remark, led us to explore how this rapid transaction captured experiences from the earliest periods in Ms. R.'s life. These were times in which what Ms. R. as a girl felt was never defined by how she experienced her bodily sensations, but by her conscious acceptance as true of whatever her mother had proclaimed those sensations to be. One association led to another as memories tumbled out.

In what had been years leading up to this incident, my attitude had always been one of curiosity about the implications of whatever appeared. That approach was also present here: I was of course keenly curious about my personal sources for speaking in a teasing way, as if uncaring cruelty were a fitting way to express shared vulnerability to helplessness. The specifics of what I learned of myself were not, I believe, something to burden the patient with. Nonetheless, that I shifted a bit in my stance to myself and our clinical engagement is something I believe the patient could and did infer. Indeed, I think such incidents were actually important elements that made possible the patient's growing trust in my *trying* to be honest and thus trust in our work together.

"In the service of the other" implies that priority is given to the other's need, not to one's own. It was tempting to explain to Ms. R. what I had had in mind with my comment, but it was clinically more appropriate to follow where *she* had turned in *her* understanding. If the patient moves on, I first try to follow where the patient has gone. Resistance cannot be defined as the patient's moving away from what the analyst expects to come next, from what the analyst has in mind.

This incident can illustrate some of what I wish to discuss. In the course of our earlier work, I had offered declarative interpretations of the connection between the patient's experiences and urges, my comments about the child constrained by her mother in Mahler's film an instance. Equally important, on the whole (and "on the whole" is as good as one can get), I had also tried to maintain an outlook of analytic curiosity. That included respectful openness to her – not dismissing her urges and fantasies and whatever they evoked and elicited in me as pathological, but rather valuing them as expressive and informative, using my own emotional reactions as also informative. Then, having taken what I heard and experienced as data for consideration (which does *not* mean taking my own emotional reactions as if they could be translated directly as informative about the patient), I remained curious about possible meanings.

While the content of the words I subsequently spoke resulted from that process, I believe the patient could and did observe and infer both the curiosity and work of self-taming that went into what I said. The long experience, slowly developed over our shared time together (which by now she had come to trust, at least in part), made her know I was working emotionally primarily in her service, and this allowed her to move on without having to first explore aspects of my sadism beyond whatever was transferentially cogent to her. It seemed that at least for that moment, we had done that enough so that she could maintain her own efforts at inquiry.

Origins of the psychoanalytic way of thinking

My premise is that what is specifically psychoanalytic in clinical work arises from the force of the analyst's curiosity tamed in the desire to utilize that curiosity primarily in the service of the patient. The analytic point of view, the result of that combination, includes not only declarative interpretations but also the essential background interpretive attitude, with both necessary to have a truly mutative benefit for the patient.

To see where we are, let us consider how we got here. Psychoanalysis, the revolutionary route to self-knowledge, grew out of the insights of a lonely genius struggling toward insight in "splendid isolation" (Masson 1985, p. 412). Even as Freud strove toward self-analysis, at the same time, he approached patients with the very mind-set that would prove successful with himself: an insatiable curiosity that kept him listening over and over and over to what each had to say, convinced that seemingly meaningless symptoms and associations had to mean something.

Freud's genius provided the awesome power that let him grasp the importance and meaning of what he was observing, but genius alone was not enough. It was Freud's indefatigable *curiosity*, his always searching for what might be hidden behind what was manifest, that was the force driving his unrelenting explorations, that pushed him to succeed. As Freud wrote to Fliess, "I am actually not at all a man of science ... I am by temperament nothing but a conquistador ... with all the curiosity, daring, and tenacity characteristic of a man of this sort" (Masson 1985, pp. 397–398). His push to mastery was driven by daringly tenacious curiosity.

It was that curiosity that preceded and made possible his many breakthroughs, whether regarding dreams, infantile sexuality, or any aspect of the power of the unconscious. Nothing was dismissed as meaningless. Everything that might arise in the mind of the person under consideration, whether himself or his patient, was valued as worthy of search.

At the same time, in his clinical work as in his self-analysis, Freud's respect for each patient's meaningfulness was manifest in his persistent search for forces at work hidden behind their mysterious difficulties. Curiosity was shaped by respect.

There is an inevitable tension built in between those two forces: curiosity to satisfy oneself and respectful regard for the needs of the other. With the luxury of retrospection, we now see that problems followed from Freud's failure, at first, to recognize the differences between self-analysis and clinical analysis. He was slow to realize the effect of his own presence and influence on patients, slower still to appreciate their influence on him. He was slow to acknowledge the role of transference, slower still to appreciate the power of countertransference. Yet ever open to new learning, bit by bit Freud's growing appreciation of those forces led him to spell out in his papers on technique the import of two person engagement, and thus the importance of neutrality, abstinence, and anonymity – not as goals, but as principles in the service of exploration.

The need to respect and accommodate the patient's individuality in refining analytic technique had not been as immediately evident as had been the driving force of curiosity. As we now know, the tensions between one-person and two-person psychologies, between what is intrapsychic and what is interpersonal, do not yield to easy resolution. Nonetheless, it was from the marriage of *curiosity* with *respect for the other* that clinical psychoanalysis was born.

Let us consider how far we have moved from those early beginnings. More than a century has passed since Freud first excitedly wrote Fliess of his personal discovery, the oedipal nature of his own fantasies, and in that dozen decades the world has vastly changed. With it, psychoanalysis has expanded explosively, growing from the insights of a lonely genius to the turbulence of so vast and diverse a field of learning that we now name it *pluralism*.

Growth has brought its own problems. With pluralism, parochialism has ensued. That is not surprising, for the variety of analytic points of view is great – beyond the containing capacity of any individual mind. Focus of attention on any single point of view necessarily implies a turning of attention away from the multiple contrasting and even conflicting views. The result is that concepts that have contributed to the development of new schools of thought at times, unfortunately, have also brought with them loyalties that constrict allegiances to limited points of view.

At our worst or our most anxious, we become defensively dogmatic and quarrelsome. Our disputes often then attach themselves to the most outward manifestations of the structure of our analytic work, as if the mechanics of the analytic instrument are more crucial than are the underlying aims for which those mechanics exist. Frequency of sessions, use of the couch, use of a telephone or of other new media of communication, handling of the analyst's self-exposure, relative neutrality or abstinence – all these and endless more become areas of dispute in which underlying principles are too easily obscured by battles over rules.

I do not suggest that matters of structure and of an analyst's style are without profound implications for the analytic process. While the analytic process is undoubtedly affected by its frame, it is not the mechanical machinery of physical space and time that determine whether analyzing is going on. Those aspects matter, but the analytic work is essentially determined by the nature of the relationship of the clinical partners in their emotional psychic space, by the aims the collaborative inquiry struggles to accomplish (Poland 1996, pp. 13–34).

It is necessary to transcend partisanship. We have been enriched by detailed clinical reports of so many analysts from so many analytic schools that one observation commands recognition: successful analytic work has been reported, and reported in detail, by members of all major schools of analytic thought. These many schools have enlarged psychoanalysis – but most valuably when their contributions have been added to our common treasure. Knowledge is cumulative.

Thus, it appears valid to accept successes reported by analysts adhering to the full range of modern analytic schools. That being so, what is likely is that powerful underlying forces essential to analytic inquiry matter more than do superficial differences. What are those forces that unfold in common in all successful analyses? Can it be that some matters can be dealt with privately by a patient so long as certain essential core issues are sufficiently dealt with by the analytic couple? And, if that is so, what are these issues?

We should not be surprised that our path has led us full circle back to our basic concept, the meaningfulness of hidden forces, now applied to ourselves, analysts at work. Our theme arises from recognition that debates of technique too often have been focused on manifest aspects, not the underlying meanings behind them. Technique is the analytic approach actualized, inexorably so since unconscious forces contribute to the shaping of manifest behavior of the analyst at work.

Appreciative of Schafer's (1983) early commanding study of the analytic attitude, a broad and deep survey of multiple aspects of analytic technique, I too have thought in terms of attitude. However, reflecting on the broad range of forces underlying that term of complex inner compromise, I came to conclude that for me the word *approach* works better. It is not that critical distinctions exist between the two words, but rather that there is a cluster of connotations each bears that accounts for my choice. Intended or not, to my ear, *attitude* has too static, too fixed a quality; it carries undertones of posture and stance. *Approach,* in contrast, feels as if it bears more of a sense of activity, of movement. It suggests attitude alive at work, sounding more close to a verb than merely a noun. It is to emphasize the *active* psychological engagement of the clinical partners, unconscious or conscious, nonverbal or verbal, that leads to my preference for the word *approach.*

The forces at hand in an analytic approach include the analyst's multiple and varied underlying motivations for practicing analysis, together with their taming – the analyst's professionalism informed by education, experience, and practice. This implies that what matters most from the analyst's side in what develops in an analysis are not simply the mechanics of manifest technique, but more likely their implications, the unspoken and also unconscious meanings that evidence the analyst's analytic approach – the mind-set, outlooks, and feelings, all of which are ways of thinking and engaging the world that the patient can and does read, even when the analyst's own mind may not be conscious of them.

The patient and the analyst's mind

Before proceeding further to define the analytic approach, it is first fitting to step back and address possible doubt, the question of how much difference what is in the back of the analyst's mind actually makes to the patient if left unspoken. Are not the analyst's manifest actions, what is said and done, really all that count? Is not the nature of disorder such that psychic conflict leaves the patient unable to read the analyst's mind with significant accuracy?

I think we have to answer both *yes* and *no.* Yes, it is so that psychic disorders lead the patient to find and see what he expects to see. On the other hand, no – that does not mean that this is *all* the patient can take in.

Our literature has paid so much attention to the analyst's empathy that it has tended to overlook the patient's similar reading of what lies behind what the analyst says. One noteworthy exception appears in Hoffman's outstanding survey of attitudes about the blank screen. In the course of his incisive and extensive study primarily addressing the so-called blank screen and countertransference, he also refers to

> what might be termed *the naive patient fallacy*, the notion that the patient, insofar as he is rational, takes the analyst's behavior at face value even while his own is continually scrutinized for most subtle indications of unspoken or unconscious meanings.
>
> (Hoffman 1983, p. 395; emphasis in original)

Our relative lack of focus on the patient's perceptive skills may be little more than a reflection of how often we analysts underestimate patients' psychic strengths. In support of the patient's ability to read us, I offer two points. One may be merely anecdotal; the other, however, results from substantial study throughout our history.

First, the anecdotal. Let us consider candidly our own coffee table conversations when they touch on our personal past analytic experiences. How often we hear about quirks, foibles, and inhibitions of our prior analysts. What might once have been complaints are softened by time to a tone of sympathetic acceptance, yet we hear that one analyst could not tolerate *this* subject; another, *that*. One could not hear *this* kind of viewpoint straight on; another, *that*.

At times one hears statements that go something like "He just could not hear me if I talked about such-and-such, but we were able to get around to it another way." Or "We never really discussed such-and-such, but somehow I was able to work it through on my own."

These commonplace remarks are not to be dismissed solely as remnants of unresolved transference. Instead, it is likely that in the wish to get help, the patient adjusts to the analyst's idiosyncrasies. Indeed, how else could patients manage to succeed analytically in a world of analysts with so widely ranging and even seemingly contradictory theoretical approaches and styles? We ourselves as patients give evidence of the ways a patient is attentive to and bends to the idiosyncrasies of any specific analyst.

That brings us to the second indication of the patient's concern for the analyst's way of thinking, one more than merely anecdotal. Even as we cherish putting things into words, our experience consistently teaches us the power of unconscious communication.

One of the most valuable lessons learned in analytic experience is that a child identifies with the unconscious conflicts of the parents. It is not what the parents explicitly battle over that has deepest impact, but it is precisely what the parents cannot and do not talk about that registers most deeply and often influences the child most. No one survives infancy successfully without learning the skill of reading between the lines as well as possible.

That is so for the vulnerable patient as it is for the vulnerable child. Wanting to understand the patient, the analyst is empathic. Is it plausible that the patient would be any *less* empathic than the analyst, considering that it is the patient's very life that is at stake in the analysis?

That the patient predominantly expresses transferential forces does not mean that other parts of the patient are not also silently at work. With the vastness of our attention to the analyst's empathy, how slight seems the attention given the patient's reading between the analyst's lines.

Just as the child must learn to navigate the language and styles and emotional fashions of the parents, so must a patient manage to navigate the inevitable preferences and constrictions of the analyst. In learning to know us, the patient manages to get done what work can be done within *our* limitations. Indeed, it is only by staying respectful of the patient's reading of the analyst's unspoken messages that an analyst can render useful the crucial task of *listening to listening* (Faimberg 1996).

The analytic approach

Let us return to the analytic approach, that product of curiosity united with and turned to the service of the analyst's respect for the introspective efforts of the patient.

The analyst's mind-set not only helps shape the atmosphere of the analytic situation, but itself becomes an essential part of the medium of the analytic work. Clinically, that the patient takes in observations of how the analyst handles conflicts that have been evoked by the patient's forces brought to life has by now become broadly accepted. As Racker (1957) succinctly put it, "Every possible psychological constellation in the patient also exists in the analyst, and the constellation that corresponds to the patient's is brought into play in the analyst" (p. 321).

Thus, not only does the patient benefit from the content of what the analyst says focused on the specific issue of the moment, the patient also has the benefit of observing, and observing repeatedly, the analyst's way of handling conflicts, the analyst's preferred ways of delaying impulsive discharge and instead turning inner conflict into data for consideration. The analyst's approach informs the patient *how* the analyst analyzes.

The issue is complex because, while central, insight is not the only goal of an analyst at work. Indeed, there are broad clinical goals that analysts and non-analytic therapists alike share – goals such as working toward the relief of pain, toward increased patient comfort and symptom relief. Furthermore, there are important clinical functions in analysis in addition to those of psychic investigation and exploration. Thus, to be clear on what psychoanalysis can uniquely offer, we must de ne what marks a process as distinctively *psychoanalytic*.

From painful experience, we have learned to be both cautious and reluctant before saying that something is *not analytic*. Too often, that has been a statement too easily used as a way of defending one analytic point of view by arrogantly dismissing another. Respecting the caveat against such self-serving arrogance, we are nonetheless left with the realization that, if we cannot say that something is *not* analytic, then we are unable to say that something else *is* analytic, and *analysis* is then left meaning nothing because it is used to cover everything.

Schneider (2012) has valuably clarified that *non-analytic* and *anti-analytic* are separate categories – that non-analytic absolutely need *not* mean anti-analytic – and even that inclusions of non-analytic functions are not only valuable, but indeed are essential elements in a psychoanalytic approach. Now we face having to try to sort out what defines that which is uniquely psychoanalytic from that which is not analytic, doing so while cautiously protecting the place of the many non-analytic functions that may be simultaneously valuable and even necessary to psychoanalysis, but that do not demarcate it.

What underlies an approach as specifically psychoanalytic rather than simply broadly therapeutic is the central concern for the power and import of unconscious forces at work. What is uniquely psychoanalytic in practice is the disciplined effort to expose, explore, and understand those forces, including, in the process, the pressures that have led to keeping those forces hidden. All this takes as its clinical goal the patient's resulting introspective capacity for self-mastery and consequent broadening of freedom of choice.

That disciplined use of the analyst's self in the clinical engagement in the service of – indeed, as mentioned above, as part of the medium for – the patient's emotionally engaged introspective exploration marks clinical analysis. The word *disciplined* necessarily includes the analyst's own private, active self-analysis as part of that clinical work – whether that self-analysis is processed consciously or unconsciously, and whether that self-analysis is made explicit or, wisely and more commonly, kept silent and implicit.

Present in all this is the struggle toward insight, toward emotional self-knowledge. We should not be surprised that insight results in an increased capacity for self-mastery, because the passion to explore grows directly out of a curiosity that is basic to human growth. It is part of one's instinct to mastery. For the analyst at work, the drive to understand and to know comes to clinical life in the service of another urge: the desire to cure, to help, to aid the other (motivations essential but not unique to psychoanalysis). I will add just a few words about each: *curiosity* and *therapeutic intent*.

The drive to know – essential to the analyst's curiosity – has, since the time of Freud, been widely studied, perhaps emphasized most by Bion. Putting that curiosity into the service of the patient, which is the analyst's psychoanalytic therapeutic intent, at times creates a conflict. This is likely what provoked Freud (1912) to offer the model of the surgeon for dealing with the need to elicit pain in the patient in the short term in the service of long-term benefit. The conflict is evident in Glover's (1927) identifying the analyst's fear of his own aggression as the source of "over-solicitousness about the patient's reactions" (p. 512).

The tension between the analyst's curiosity and wish to advance inquiry, on the one hand, and the analyst's staying sensitive to the patient, on the other hand, demands creativity on the analyst's part. This is a large part of what makes clinical work an art. Yet whatever the conflict, the value of clinical analysis derives from channeling the analyst's personal desire to know into the service of respect for the other in the other's own right. Indeed, as in my opening illustration, it is the patient's sensing and benefiting from all that goes on that allows true emotional progress to result.

Still, even when investigation and comfort seem balanced, other derivative tensions appear, tensions that at times have led to dismissal of the importance and value of interpretation. Interpretation, putting into words significant links between transference dynamics and genetic roots, at times seems in conflict with other, non-interpretive functions.

In helping to structure a psychoanalytic situation, the analyst provides a holding environment, an empathic ambiance, and a capacity to contain the anxieties and conflicts taken in from a patient's emotional projections. The analyst respects, listens, hears, regards, and witnesses. The analyst stands as guardian of the analytic work and protector of the patient's interests while the patient sets aside some normal waking executive mental functions. The analyst, with the assistance of private self-analysis, acts to be available to the patient as a new object for both continued and new mental development.

All of these matter. Nonetheless, the list, while not comprehensive, goes far beyond the charge of interpretation extending conscious understanding. Often these differing pressures seem at odds.

Difficulty in integrating these differences, reinforced by reaction to authoritarian and rigidly narrow views of analysis, has led at times to an overreaction, one that devalued and dismissed interpretation. In addition, appreciation of the place of nonverbal communication has ironically been itself misused to repudiate the importance of interpretation. If insight can result without the analyst having spoken an explicit interpretation, then interpretation must not be essential for psychic change and growth.

It was for those reasons that when I first addressed this subject, I wrote of an *interpretive* rather than an *analytic* attitude.

Decreasing attention to *explicit* interpretations has brought with it a devaluing of an *approach* that is interpretive in nature – the unspoken but nonetheless communicated basic attitude that privileges search for unknown and as yet undiscovered meanings. This *interpretive attitude* not only searches for ever new levels of meanings but also, crucially and profoundly, values that search.

A specific, manifest declarative interpretation is not only of worth, but is often essential to free up psychic forces fixed in a symptom or other frozen function. It is hard to conceive of successful psychoanalytic work in which explicit communication of declarative interpretations and implicit nonverbal communication of an interpretive analytic attitude have not both been active. While a declarative interpretation contributes significantly to a patient's introspective progress and resulting insight, it is the analyst's ever-present interpretive approach transmitted through the parallel and shared introspective experiences that is crucial to increasing the patient's self-analytic skills. The analytic approach is based on the conviction that unknown meanings lie behind manifest meanings, and that conviction is communicated as it is actualized in the analyst's engaged self-inquiry, silent though it be.

The centrality given to declarative interpretations early in analytic history is a natural consequence of our field's birth in a self-analysis. The effect was as if self-analytic insight could be transposed to the office, with the patient's ana-lytic understanding remaining that of an uncomplicated one-person psychology. Understandable excitement over early discoveries in depth psychology, as already noted, obscured or delayed recognition of the importance of the clinical engage-ment. The results were narratives of content that developed without appreciation of the interactive process alive behind the growth of those narratives. And as an added result, declarative interpretations seemed the sole heart of the cure.

Only with increasing appreciation of how the transference was actualized in the clinical engagement could the interpretive stance of the analyst come into focus. Recognition of the unconscious communication of that analytic interpre-tive point of view is vital to the patient's not only internalizing specific insights, but also becoming much more able to generalize self-knowledge, to take personal benefit from internalizing the skill of self-analysis.

By the patient's *generalizing self-knowledge*, I refer to what seems implicit in a patient's making use of an analyst despite the analyst's at times narrowness of approach. Once internalized, insight can spread. A common example is seen in the frequency with which a patient's fear of flying is tamed without explicit analytic focus on that specific symptom. Once conflicts over helplessness are exposed and explored, the fear of flying often significantly fades. It then seems reasonable to think that some central conflicts have been mastered sufficiently for the patient to be able to extend working through on his own, whether or not it is done consciously.

Indeed, Reid and Finesinger (1952) observed such an increase of self-knowledge outside conscious attention as the effect of *a spreading factor* quality by which insight extends itself. This intrapsychic aspect of a *spreading factor* is itself evident in the good analytic situation. A successful analytic situation is one in which the patient, able to intuit and infer the self-inquiry of the analyst's mind at work, can then extend personal analytic mastery to areas not brought explicitly into the clinical conversation. Much of this processing occurs outside the patient's own conscious attention.

In the illustration of my work with Ms. R., declarative interpretations (both dynamic and genetic) had been essential to the building up of sufficient trust for her to develop increasingly her own self-analytic facility. It was her internaliza-tion of an interpretive curiosity that made possible her introspective usage of my unusual intervention in the incident described. She was thus able to turn an inter-change into data profitable for introspection, indeed doing so more swiftly than had I. In psychologically important ways, the analyst is always behind the patient, always following, leading only in the manner of demonstrating how to explore, how to look.

The approach to the approach

Before concluding, let us consider just a moment how that *how-to-look* model of analytic work first gets established. It is a method set from the start.

Someone with a difficulty and someone offering professional help come together, moving toward each other and bearing the conventional roles of patient and doctor or therapist. Analysis, however, is premised on setting aside what is conventional for what is undeniably unconventional, aiming for exploration of what is private behind what seems public.

In entering this fresh relationship, *each* partner approaches the other as a stranger, an outsider to the other's personal universe, with *each* vulnerable by virtue of being alien to the other's inner world of meanings and expectation. This is so for the analyst as well as the patient, despite the availability for the analyst of the fallback sense of safety of having a professional identity – too often the fantasy of the analyst's being the one of the two who knows better how to live life, a fantasy patient and analyst may even share. Just as the patient utilizes neurosis to contain vulnerability, so can the analyst use professional position, and even more often misuse analytic theory, to decrease the feeling of vulnerability that comes from being ignorant of the other's, the patient's, emotional universe.

For the work to proceed, what is essential is that, instead of imagined safety by virtue of being the one who owns the room, the analyst accepts personal ignorance, tolerating associated helplessness in dedication to working in the service of the patient. With such commitment in place, that is, with the analyst's faith in the analytic process sufficient to let the analyst tolerate not knowing, and with the patient's willingness to take enough risk so as possibly to receive help, the two can join to create their new, singular, and profitable partnership.

Valid analytic exploratory work demands true inquiry by both partners. Only that can ultimately lead to unexpected learning, to discoveries and surprises, rather than to the *quod erat demonstrandum* satisfaction of finding preordained proofs.

In closing

Psychoanalysis is only one of many therapeutic approaches designed to relieve a patient's pain, to help a patient live a less symptomatic and less constricted life, but it is a unique one. Its singularity comes from its central appreciation for the vital significance of unconscious forces at work, with its structure shaped to facilitate the patient's use of the clinical engagement as the living medium for experiential inquiry into those forces.

The analyst's contributions to the shared task arise from a broad range of motivations, with curiosity, a crucial part of the mind's instinct to mastery, fueling the ongoing search for hidden meanings and unconscious roots. Balancing curiosity with respectfully purposeful concern for the patient is one of those areas where it is fitting to speak of the "art" of clinical work.

It is in navigating the area at the edge of darkness between the differing psychic realities of the analytic pair – and doing so for the primary purpose of the *patient's* analysis – that analytic exploration can lead to genuine insight. Yet it is not only from the manifest interchange between the analytic clinical partners that the patient becomes able to transcend symptoms and constrictions. Remarkably and momentously, beyond what is manifest in the clinical work, the patient's capacity for psychic growth is liberated and facilitated by the patient's learning how the analyst's mind works while it is also silently working psychoanalytically.

References

Faimberg, H. (1996). Listening to listening. *International Journal of Psychoanalysis*, 77:667–677.

Freud, S. (1912). Recommendations to physicians practicing psychoanalysis. *S.E.*, 12.

Glover, E. (1927). Lectures on technique in psychoanalysis. *International Journal of Psychoanalysis*, 8:486–520.

Hoffman, I.Z. (1983). The patient as interpreter of the analyst's experience. *Contemporary Psychoanalysis*, 19:389–422.

Masson, J.M., ed. (1985). *The Complete Letters of Sigmund Freud to Wilhelm Fliess, 1887–1904*. Cambridge, MA/London: Harvard University Press.

Poland, W. (1996). From analytic surface to analytic space. In *Melting the Darkness: The Dyad and Principles of Clinical Practice*. Northvale NJ: Jason Aronson.

Racker, H. (1957). The meanings and uses of countertransference. *Psychoanalytic Quarterly*, 26:303–357.

Reid, J. & Finesinger, J. (1952). The role of insight in psychotherapy. *American Journal of Psychiatry*, 108:726–734.

Schafer, R. (1983). *The Analytic Attitude*. New York: Basic Books.

Schneider, G. (2012). Tertium datur. Über die Zugehörigkeit des Nicht-Analytischen zum analytischen Prozess. In *Zur Negation der psychoanalytischen Hermeneutik*, ed. T. Storck. Giessen, Germany: Psychosozial-Verlag, pp. 73–102.

Shengold, L. (1989). *Soul Murder: The Effects of Childhood Abuse and Deprivation*. New York: Ballantine Books.

Chapter 7

The analyst's fears

There is no hope unmingled with fear.

Spinoza, *The Ethics*

The day of the supposedly ideal psychoanalyst working free of all emotion happily has passed, a victim of the irrepressibility of reality. Indeed, concern for the sweep of feelings to which psychoanalysts are vulnerable has moved on from consideration of eccentric and neurotic distortions (narrow countertransference) to general appreciation of the more full panoply of affects that contribute to the mind of the analyst at work (countertransference in its broad sense).

Yet, perhaps not surprisingly, the analyst's fears seem not to have attracted the full regard they merit. They have been examined, for the most part, either in terms of specific anxieties in reaction to aspects of the psychology of the patient or in terms of the analyst's dread and despair resulting from therapeutic zeal. These specific aspects are certainly crucial to psychoanalytic work. Nonetheless, reviewing my personal experiences convinces me of the need to extend study of the analyst's fears to a wider range.

However, before proceeding, I believe that our current analytic zeitgeist requires a first word acknowledging the context of this discussion. In the first third of our psychoanalytic century, discovery of the amazing world of the unconscious led us to focus our attention on the deeply hidden forces of the private mind. Inevitably, we came to wonder how it was we knew what it was that we interpreted, and we turned attention to exploring how the analyst's mind works as an essential force within the psychoanalytic process. This area has occupied much of our attention for the last third of a century.

Unfortunately, too often exploring new fields has pushed older concerns to the side, sometimes all the way into the wings. Any clinical psychoanalysis is basically the patient's show. To do what we must for the sake of the patient's analysis, we analysts must be alert to the active presence of our own inner forces and must work not to squelch but to understand and to tame those forces in the service of the other. It is necessary and right that we address that portion of our inner forces that we least like to address, fears and terrors we generally are polished enough to obscure even from ourselves. Yet as we do, it is prudent to remember that we do so for the sake of our broader goal, our basic professional clinical task of working *in the service of the other*. We look at ourselves so as better to see our patients.

Introduction

My interest is to open for consideration the broad arena of the analyst's fears and to show how fears arise within an analyst as they are brought forth from the patient, from the analyst himself, from the unfolding of the clinical engagement, from the nature of the analytic process itself, and even from the unavoidable realities of the broad human condition beyond the clinical work. Often, perhaps most often, fear in the analyst has its effect and is processed without ever surfacing to the level of conscious awareness. Frequently, the first hint of underlying fear is the clinician's sense of a troubled uncertainty, uncertainty about how the work is proceeding, uncertainty about what is going on.

Thus, on the basis of how it feels, it might seem logical to discuss uncertainty before fear. Uncertainty very often is the opening emotional edge of the analyst's awareness of underlying fear. Nonetheless, I shall try to go about these matters in the order in which the process develops, looking first at fears at work and only afterwards commenting in closing on the analyst's need for certainty and on the analyst's misuse of theory to try to construct a comforting certainty.

Fears do not differ from other of the analyst's feelings in two fundamental ways, their sources and the uses to which they are put. The analyst must sort out the varied roots of the feeling and then must figure out how to use what has been learned in the service of the analytic task. I shall try to address both, initially the sources looking at the breadth of factors that color the analyst's fears and then the steps involved in turning those feelings to clinical use.

First, however, it is important to recognize a central way that fear does differ from other feelings. In our very being, in our basic biology, we react to reject and repel whatever causes fear. I was reminded of that even as I sat to write. I am chagrined to recognize that although I have written about aspects of the analytic process and the analyst at work for well over 30 years, my looking directly at fear comes so very late, nearer the end rather than the start of my thinking. Chagrined, but not surprised: the delay is no accident.

We leap for joy, but we cringe from fear. Yet we know that cringing resistances not only hide but also signal what threatens to emerge. So it is worth the effort to look fear as much in the face as possible.

The most familiar times an analyst is confronted with uncertainty and fear are those that reflect crises of seemingly relentless resistance and despair in the clinical engagement. The sense of malignant hopelessness we speak of as a negative therapeutic reaction is our extreme model.

While that experience might be paradigmatic, we have to be alert to the many other roots of the analyst's sense of being lost and afraid. In addition to the impact of the patient's unfolding character on the analyst, there are unsettling factors intrinsic to the very process of analysis itself. There are, similarly, factors deriving from the analyst's own character, including not only neurotic aspects but also those unavoidable by virtue of the analyst's being human. As a result, factors extraneous to the patient, including those such as the analyst's age and own developmental stage of life at the time of the analysis, color what fears unfold.

To further complicate the picture, we also have to recognize that the movement between the analyst's mind and the analysis travels in both directions. Just as the analyst's psychology helps shape and color the unfolding clinical experience, so too does fear arising in an analysis affect the analyst's mood and even character.

Everything has unconscious significance, but not everything is neurotic. We have come to appreciate countertransference both in its narrow sense as eccentric distortion and in its broad sense as the analyst's mind at work. Now we are called to consider the impact of clinical fears on the analyst's character, not merely narrow eccentric reactions but results that contribute more broadly to the analyst's continuing character growth.

Clinical illustrations

For illustration of the range of the analyst's fears, let us turn to some examples.

I start with a dramatic extreme. We had worked for many years, this angry paranoid man and I, and during that time he changed, moving from playing his role as his family's designated crazy one to a way of life in which he merely seemed odd while still keeping his troublesome habit of speaking uncomfortable truths with unadorned directness. During our work he became able to question his paranoid ways of looking at the world, and with many years of hard analytic work he tamed his rage sufficiently to come to face his own longings and losses, desires and depression. It was, at last, as if we entered a time of rebuilding after a lifetime of destructive and degrading war.

Then, as if without warning, over the span of a few sessions his old anger returned, increased, boiled over, and exploded in rage at me. We had faced anger at me before, but this was different and more fierce. I do not know whether I had missed clues as to what was coming or whether some inner shift in him had been precipitous, but the suddenness and the power of his fury had me at first disoriented and disorganized, even before I recognized my feeling as terror.

In retrospect, it reminds me of a time that I saw a 3-year-old child scream, "NO! NO! NO!" at his 1½-year-old younger brother. The smaller child ran in terrified chaotic disorder, ever changing direction each time another "NO!" rang out. At that time, the horror of seeing such emotional disintegration took me over and I instantly stopped the older child. Now, before I could address what my patient was doing with me, the power of my patient's primitive rage resonated through me with just such a disorganizing impact. My own unvoiced early fears, especially fears of unbound primitive aggression, were brought to the surface of my awareness in a way that since earliest childhood I have rarely allowed while awake. It was as if in the clinical session I found myself abruptly in the middle of a childhood nightmare; and if my first sense was of feeling disorganized, my reflex reaction was to flee.

Of course I didn't simply flee, at least not physically. I cannot capture all of the details to know for certain how much I fled psychologically, but that clearly was my first short and sudden step. Then, in my urgency to reintegrate myself consciously, I thought at least momentarily that my patient was crazy. That way I distanced myself from frightening engagement with him by draping myself in a professional diagnostic robe. Such are the uses to which diagnostic thinking can be put.

However, while trying to reassure myself at the expense both of the patient and of our work may have been a first reaction, as soon as I had sufficient sense of myself to realize what I had done I was able to get back to work. I could appreciate that the terror the patient both bathed me in and had elicited from me came first from inside him, the patient. As in *The Red Badge of Courage*, it sometimes takes more than one go-around before one can hang in with a battle. This second time, recognition of the terror's having arisen from inside the patient was no longer my defensive shifting blame but was now an effort to follow the danger wherever it was.

Following the order of my reaction as consciously experienced, first came a sense of disoriented confusion, then a sense of conscious terror, then a primitive reaction to protect myself, and only then a remembrance not only of who I was but of why I was there, that is, an orienting and organizing call back to try to work for the sake of understanding.

Being in the service of the other can, of course, be used as a guise for a defensive or even for a sadistic enactment of power. But when not perverted, when genuine, it provides our primary orientation for turning experience of fear into the service of the clinical goal.

Terror feels amorphous, nameless, overwhelming, truly disorganizing. Fortunately, with this particular patient the crisis deflated sufficiently for us to regain working connection. We learned some of what had set off that profound regression, some of what was being worked through. But we did that without ever truly knowing all we would wish could have been learned about what was involved. And we did so with my experiencing enough of the horror to remind me of why I sometimes regret being in a line of work I otherwise love.

As we move on to tease out those hidden elements involved in order to understand the sources of fear and the ways we can make use of fear, we ought not to forget the difference between the ease of these reflections in the comfort of retrospection and the terror felt while we are lost and alone on the front lines of work.

Despite implicit complexities, that introductory vignette has an almost caricature simplicity in its demonstration of fear as developing in direct response to an eruption from something within the patient. More common are those slowly mounting difficulties that grow within the interactive engagement of the clinical pair. These periods of an analyst's growing apprehension and uncertainty usually start insidiously before being recognized as fear, as concern for the survival of the analysis, for the survival of the patient, or even for the survival of the analyst's own sense of self.

My second fragmentary illustration, a more familiar one, is of a sense of increasing dread working with someone not merely depressed but militantly hopeless. I think of a woman with whom I worked many years who, as I often thought of her, had inconsolable colic as an infant and whose life had gone downhill from there.

This woman sought help because of persistent unhappiness. Yet whatever developed in our work together that might have improved her feeling about herself and her potential led, instead, to greater despair. Despite my efforts to address what was taking place, even despite my efforts to be what might seem supportive, this woman only felt worse. Worse and ever worse, to the point of suggesting inevitable suicide. She never explicitly said I was responsible for her dreadful state, but I came to feel that accusation always implicitly present.

There were occasional moments when I could get her to consider what occurred between us, but they were infrequent. Once I described my sense of her having come to me to accompany her as she climbed a hill of understanding. I described my feeling that she would never allow me to be alongside her, that it was as if she slowed down when I sped up to catch up with her or else she sped up if I slowed down to what had been her pace. There were such times when our ideas could meet, but they were few.

More regularly, when I tried to explore what was taking place, her need to undermine doomed my efforts. I came to feel ever more hopeless and desperate, and I felt her death foreshadowed. Then, along with my fear for my patient, I began to imagine my own undoing as I would be destroyed publicly, picturing myself ruined, even subsequently sued so that not only my but even my children's futures would be devastated.

It is easy from this distance to speak of transference evoking despair; but it is important to remember that before such understanding is possible, the fear and despair themselves are genuinely felt. When we are working at our best, we may at times process such issues unconsciously. But fear is not a theoretical concept; it is something that lies cold at the bottom of the stomach. For long spells I found myself wanting to pull away as I approached our sessions.

Gradually, after a long period of my feeling uncertain about what was going on, uncertain of what to do, and frightened of the future, I came to find my own increasing unhappiness with this patient intolerable. The next step after feeling that this could not go on forever was my consciously reminding myself that she was she and that I was I, that we were in fact two separate people.

This realization brought with it another shift that at first surprised me. I found myself finally thinking, "If she dies, she dies." While I would be glad to be free of her if she died, I realized that if that were the case that I would feel deep sadness and regret, but I would not feel guilt. My life and my family would go on.

I do not know how much the resurgence of my restitutive powers was first colored by my own retaliatory sadism. When threatened, I can turn to fight as well as flight. Yet it was only when I had felt and dealt with my own despair that either I was able to speak to the patient in a way we both could hear or that sufficient shifts had taken place in both of us that we both were able to proceed. It has been said that the only person in an analysis that an analyst can analyze is himself. That may be more clever than true, but it certainly is true that the analyst's self-analysis is an intrinsic sine qua non of clinical analysis.

What I have described as if it were a single event was, instead, a repeated pattern of engaging, feeling lost, stepping back, and then re-engaging from a more separated rather than merged togetherness. Fourteen years of such work passed before this woman ever spoke openly of warmth and friendliness between us.

The last illustrations I offer are of two different patients, one a man whose father was dying during my patient's analysis and the other a woman who was herself discovered to have a cancer after we had set a termination date, a woman who died about two years later.

I select these two to make clear that even when working best, an analyst is not invulnerable to the perils of reality. Such actual dangers exist whether we choose to acknowledge them or not, and awareness of them can both interfere with and facilitate the work. An analyst's relentless private self-analytic honesty provides the greatest protection for continuation of the analytic task and the greatest defense against a pseudo-professional denial of danger.

Along with the analyst's underlying character, where the analyst is in his or her own developmental line also influences what is felt as frightening. And, conversely, what arises in an analysis that is frightening affects the analyst's character and handling of those personal crises against which no one is immune.

When I was a young analyst, concern for the demands and risks associated with sexuality commanded center stage. Now, at this later age, conflicts over loss of loved ones and of self seem more central. I try to adjust for my own concerns so as to be most true to where a patient is, but I can never do so with perfectionist calm or with psychoanalytic omnipotence.

How might this show up clinically? During a time when I was awaiting my own annual physical examination, a patient with whom I worked told of his father's having a cancer discovered during a routine examination. My patient was distressed and, medically knowledgeable, described in detail the likely course of the aggressive malignancy.

Those few days while I was waiting to learn test results of my own state of health, I dreaded sessions with this particular patient. I tried to maintain my professionalism, but those hours were more difficult for me and those nights were more sleepless than they would have been otherwise. On the other hand, when my own good test results returned comfort to my mind and left me more at ease with the patient, who can say what had been lost and what had been gained from my own terrors?

That last clinical vignette is a modest version of a more terrible experience in which a wonderful woman who was finishing difficult analytic work and who had set a termination date was herself discovered to have a horrible malignancy, one from which she died two years later. Proud of her analytic accomplishment, this woman decided to keep the termination date set, although she and I then continued intermittent contact, meeting for what turned out to be our last session two days before she died. Along with the grief I still feel from her death lies also a newly deeper sense of potential horror of loss that echoes through my work with other patients, that reverberates through my own life.

All of that brings me to one other experience that I want to acknowledge candidly as having a personal truth, one that I believe at least some others must share, yet one that I do not know and cannot say is universal. It has to do with my personal sense of increasing vulnerability to the contagion of fear. I believe that my clinical skill has for the most part increased with increasing years of practice. Yet, my growing experience and possibly growing skill have either led to or permitted me more openness to more deeply felt dread and sadness. Pleasures have also grown, even greater appreciation of the delight of very small pleasures, but the awareness of more freely feeling fear has brought a sense of poignancy that I did not know when I was younger.

I do not think these changes are simply the result of continued loosening of an obsessional character. That must be part of it, but it is not the most important part. Something about aging in a life immersed in other people's analyses has been incredibly enriching but has changed me so that I feel more open to anguish. I pose this as an observation that raises questions, not conclusions, about the occupational hazards of practicing analysis, of possible increasing vulnerability to the contagion of fears even as there is increased capacity to tolerate such feelings.

Dangers vary according to where one is in one's life span. Perils linked to earlier attachments take on new life based on new experience, and I know that the loss of my terminating patient who died has left a frightening effect that remains a part of me.

While my life, naturally, is idiosyncratic, each analyst must deal with such painful actualities, each in that one's equally unique way. My intention in choosing these vignettes has been to illustrate the broad range of fearful experiences.

Discussion

Traditionally, we make a neat distinction between fear and anxiety, using "fear" to refer to the sense of peril responding to clear external danger and "anxiety" to refer to emotional jeopardy responding to inner dangers. Such tidiness of definition betrays actuality. Our minds are unitary, whole cloth, and there is no outer danger without inner significance or inner conflict unrelated to human connectedness. Knowing that all mental phenomena are overdetermined, we have to beware using outer actuality to obscure inner difficulties and also have to avoid attending to inner difficulties to conceal recognition of outer danger.

Trying to conceive of how a sense of clinical danger resonates across all levels of emotional experience, we can place such processes into four overlapping clusters. They are (1) those responsive to specific countertransference fears provoked by a patient, (2) those related mainly to the analyst's own character idiosyncracies, (3) those intrinsic to the analytic process, and (4) those resulting from the human condition, from the analyst's vulnerability to the demands of reality and fate even when working best.

These categories overlap and interact, so we can never have a true dissection between them. Still, examining each category may help us minimize our using attention to one as a way of diverting attention from another. Let us look at the first two categories together.

1   *Countertransferential fears provoked by a patient* and
2   *Fears idiosyncratic to the analyst's character*

It is good to make things as simple as possible but not more simple, clarity carrying a high price when it makes things seem clearer than they actually are. Distinguishing fears provoked by a patient from those that result from the analyst's character is useful but often too simplistic. Before an analyst can say validly that an issue is "the patient's problem," the analyst must genuinely address the analyst's own emotional engagement.

Whether we call it trial identification or empathy, the analyst goes along with the patient's state, transiently vicariously grasping what the patient experiences. That partial and temporary identification carries its own anxiety, the at times discomforting loss of clarity about what is me and what is you that precedes sorting out and subsequent interpretation.

There is great benefit in Racker's (1968) distinguishing an analyst's concordant and complementary identifications. (The concordant are those where the analyst feels like the patient's own self, and the complementary those where the analyst identifies with the patient's objects.) Yet the more closely we look, the more we appreciate that even when the analyst seems to be functioning in one of those modes, on deeper levels there are always reversals in the interplay between the clinical partners.

Positions of subject and object subtly interchange. No matter how it seems on the surface, below the surface traffic is always two-way. However, so long as we remember this and with due modesty avoid simplistic proclamations, it is helpful to speak, even if tentatively and partially, of the patient's eliciting of an analyst's fears as separate from the more personal fears an analyst brings to the encounter.

My fear with my paranoid patient seemed substantially to be the pure notes of a reaction to outbursts of his untamed rage, even if it is doubtful that that could be the entire story.

The fears with which I struggled with the depressed and militantly negativistic woman, however, were more clearly a mutually composed symphony of difficulty, a symphony that the patient both composed and conducted but in which process I actively participated. Feeling pain, she came to me and gave me a task of helping her feel less pain. Then, she responded to my efforts as if anything I did only caused more pain. How could I not first doubt my usefulness and only later, dealing with my own emotional contribution, regain my professional balance?

I tried to care without getting caught up in my own therapeutic zeal, but that is easier said than done. Also, I came to resent her. She felt that nothing she was given was good, so what I had to offer was no good. At times I would feel resentment turning to sadistic rage, but that feeling does not rest so easily in me as perhaps it ideally should. My tendency was to feel guilty, and guilty not just because I was not a good enough doctor but because I also had to deal with my own reactive bubbling sadism.

I thought at times that this woman had come mainly to drive me crazy. At times I thought that her pained cries were siren calls to beckon me to my destruction while she stayed safely on the ragged rock of her unyielding character. But I knew her pain was genuine, that she was not comforted by wounding me. What arose in me was never simply a predictable or likely universal reaction to her provocations. It always was more a complex mixture of my partaking of all sides of the emotional battle.

My fears were revived from my large old private reservoir of fear by the way this woman related to me. However, my feelings were not simply reactions to her: my own resources took an active role contributing to and shaping my crescendo of despair and fear. My self-preservative instincts were necessary to reinforce and thereby save my professional therapeutic functioning. It at times seems to me that the degree of unwanted but necessary self analysis that a patient's analysis provokes in me is related to how far the patient's own analysis goes. (While that may at times seem so, from cooler detachment I doubt it is a general truth. Many analyses go well without such inordinate emotional labor on my part. None proceeds without some of such struggle, but happily such inordinate emotional effort is not routine.)

It is important to add that the uncomfortable and at times agonizing inner introspective strife in which I was engaged as part of this patient's analysis was not carried out by my discussing it with my patient. I did discuss whatever spilled over that came to our attention. Nonetheless, it seemed important that I resolve my own issues in myself, using them to facilitate but not to complicate the patient's work, not to burden it with my private labors.

3   *Fears intrinsic to the analytic process*

If one goes swimming, one gets wet. Fear is intrinsic to change, and there are fears an analyst is bound to feel because of the very nature of the analytic process. I am convinced that this is true even with those model analysts for whom such emotional dangers seem so successfully dealt with as to keep them on the whole outside the analyst's conscious awareness. I believe that those analysts who present successful analytic work where they never seem to have to deal with such fears consciously have managed to process such identifications and reactions unconsciously or preconsciously.

The analysis of a person is not that of a text, with the analyst attentive to the patient's associations while untouched by engagement and attachment. Powerful emotional communications go back and forth between patient and analyst whether they are admitted into notice or not. The analyst cares, and to care is to be vulnerable. The principle of neutrality matters precisely because the analyst cannot be emotionally unengaged.

The psychoanalytic process itself implies the analyst's experiencing two particular fears: (1) The analyst, having attached emotionally to the patient, must then go through the experience of loss of attachment. (2) Looked at from a different angle, the analyst, linked to the patient's observing ego, must face the power of resistance when struggling to bring the conflictual sphere under the sway of the observing sphere.

First, let us consider object attachment and loss. No matter how empathically linked the analyst wishes to be, at some point the analyst must detach from the patient's emotional pull. Not only in interpreting but ultimately in all ways that foster the patient's autonomy and lead to successful termination, the analyst must deal with feeling acted on and with feeling loss, feeling threatened by becoming bereft of an attachment with the patient, whether these threats unfold on hidden microscopic or on more gross macroscopic levels.

Second, let us consider structure and resistance. I have already mentioned the analyst's despair when therapeutic intention is insistently undermined by a patient's relentless negativism. In less dramatic form such problems appear in any analysis. Patients are in conflict, and conflict intrinsically implies resistance. Indeed, without the resistance evidencing such conflict, no analysis would be possible. No matter the analyst's ability to inhibit therapeutic ambition, a patient's mounting resistances to reflection at some points are bound to threaten the analyst's faith in the analytic process and sureness about professional self. My described experiences with one committed to undoing any analytic progress was extreme, but on a more subtle level an analyst is always confronted with doubts that threaten the soft voice of reason.

The comforting security that grows from clinical experience is not to be confused with defensive smugness that proclaims away the unease of doubt. The practice of psychoanalysis is not a spectator sport; and risk, feeling emotional danger, comes with the analytic territory.

4   *Fears related to the human condition*

In addition to the emotional bruising any psychoanalytic journey entails, the analyst must deal with that sleeping sense of danger which the vicissitudes of another's life are bound to awaken for someone closely involved.

Oliner (1996) has described how at times analysts use dedication to exploring the unconscious defensively so as to dilute or avoid acknowledging terrors arising from external reality. Analysts at times twist attention so as to focus only on inner meanings, trying to minimize emotional immersion in experiences of horror regarding massive trauma.

We spend years in intimate emotional engagement with each of our patients, and during those years those patients are bound to confront dangers and losses on all levels. In our private lives we have learned to use the theater in its many forms to provide ourselves safe opportunities to imagine and imaginatively live through all sorts of perils, knowing we can then leave a theater and go home in safety. After all, it was only a play. That is not the case with patients. They are real people. Unlike experience with the theater, we leave the analytic hour but the hour does not leave us.

The transference neurosis may come alive clinically like a dream of the patient's that we temporarily live through and share, but not all of the dangers that patients face are simply transferential. All carry transferential significance, but they are not *only* transferential. Patients remind us, and often when we are least prepared, of just those parts of life about which we least want to think. Training and even the best of all possible training analyses cannot and should not try to provide an analyst immunity from the emotional hazards of life, dangers involving separation anxiety and loss, involving fear of bodily damage and mutilation, involving dread of nonbeing, and so on.

Certainty and theory

I have addressed the analyst's fears without focusing on the analyst's uncertainty. Uncertainty, of course, is the essential state of the analyst at work. It is the hallmark of true inquiry as contrasted with indoctrination that is masked in the guise of psychoanalysis. When genuinely at work we live in a state akin to what Dickens (2003, chapter 72) called "a perfect bog of uncertainty." So our concern is not merely with uncertainty but with those times when uncertainty becomes troublesome or even painful for the analyst. For it is then that the analyst's position of informed ignorance, of knowing just enough so as to be curious about what more yet unknown meanings might be present, becomes marked by anxiety. Here, the anxiety is often a signal that something frightening, something threatening, is pushing to emerge.

Browsing in a bookstore recently, I met a woman with whom I had worked analytically 30 years ago. We greeted warmly, and she kindly filled me in a bit on how her life had unfolded since last we met. Then she asked whether I was still practicing analysis. "Yes," I heard myself spontaneously answer. "I'm going to keep doing it until I get it right."

I will not live long enough to get to that point, but that remark captures a feeling I have had since the day I began as a student in an analytic institute. In my mind were questions that shaped my thinking when I am with a patient and that remain active and unfinished to this day: What am I doing here? What is it I am trying to do? What should I be doing? I still lack an answer that feels sufficiently satisfying to me, yet I have come to be more comfortable with the constancy of uncertainty. To my surprise, I even have become distrustful when I find too much comfort, too much certainty. Too much certainty and I begin to wonder whether inquiry has been smothered by mutual reassurance.

Theory offers us a superstructure built through a century of experience, one that lets us hold in mind a broader range of possibilities than any single focused mind could ever contain. Theory reminds us to wonder and to ask about areas that might otherwise be beyond our regard. At its best, theory is organized knowledge based on generations of experience and thought. And knowledge is power.

But power can be used in many ways, and the power of knowledge can be used by the analyst for the defensive comfort of closure as well as for opening. Insistent knowing so as not to feel uncertain and afraid in uncharted territory is a misuse of theory. As Anna Freud pointed out, analytic technique was not devised for the defense of the analyst.

Yet as we try to stay alert to the misuse of theory as a way of warding off uncomfortable uncertainty, we must also stay alert to the countervailing risk. Misuse of theory does not negate theory's valid application. It certainly does not justify the self-serving know-nothingism that suggests that the limitations of theory and technical principles call for their abandonment rather than their refinement. In the face of the combined complexities and insufficiencies of our current theories, such nihilism gets a distressing foothold.

While not wanting to oversimplify, I believe that on a level deep within myself I analyze in part, as Flaubert wrote, to take revenge on reality, to try to prove to myself over and over and over and over that insight truly can gain some dominance over terror. Yet I learn repeatedly that fear can be tamed but never fully vanquished. So my career-long eagerness to have a new analytic patient is now accompanied by a hesitant fear, a small reluctance to start a new analysis. For as much as I want to do my work, as much as I enjoy doing my work, as much as I believe that the likelihood of success justifies the pains ahead, still there is something else I also know. And that is that whatever else happens, this new analysis is going to go into areas I don't want to enter, into fears I would rather keep hidden away. And I know that whatever they will be, they will not be what I could predict or even guess at the start. What will make me wish I were somewhere else will come unexpectedly, from around a corner. So no matter how much I love to practice analysis, no matter how much I cannot imagine doing other, I always approach analytic work with the edge of a shiver of fear.

References

Dickens, C. (2003). *Barnaby Rudge: A Tale of the Riots of Eighty*. London: Penguin Classics.
Oliner, M.M. (1996). External reality: The elusive dimension of psychoanalysis. *Psychoanalytic Quarterly*, 65:267–300.
Racker, H. (1968). *Transference and Countertransference*. New York: International Universities Press.

Part III

Challenges within the psychoanalytic process

Chapter 8

Problems in pluralism

Narcissism and curiosity

The staggering complexity of the workings of a person's mind is too great for an individual mind to grasp, so it seems proper as well as inevitable that generations of psychoanalytic study should now lead to our present state, one we speak of as pluralism. For us to attain the benefit of such wide-ranging diversity, for us to come closer to grasping the varied subtleties of what in life is unitary actuality, we need constantly to contextualize our separate observations and to integrate observations from differing vantage points. Open and respectful conversation is the essential path to cross-fertilization.

Sadly, despite clinical sensitivity when listening to patients, analysts have not fared well in hearing and talking to each other with respectful open-mindedness. How well do we learn from each other, how well do we talk, and how well do we listen? If we look at ourselves with candor, we see that we have limited cause for pride of success in this collegial task. Too often, like characters in an Edward Hopper painting, we occupy the same space but do not connect.

As clinicians we spend our lives struggling to hear our patients as they reluctantly reveal themselves. Clinically we learn to listen ever better, yet the contrast in our hearing one another is shocking. Happily, despite our difficulties, analytic thinking flourishes. New ideas bloom; our journals grow. Nonetheless, even as some cross-fertilization takes place among us, we see diversity bring with it Balkanization, division into smaller and even hostile sects.

New learning demands full discussion, a genuinely open debate we wish to both guard and facilitate. That we argue with passion is good, for our passion comes not merely from the vanity of vested interests but crucially from our caring deeply. Also, we know that caution in approaching new contributions is particularly prudent because of a problem unique to our field, that is, that our central focus is on unconscious forces, forces that stir unremitting resistance. Aware of the subtlety with which defenses can mask themselves and knowing the sophisticated skill of our minds, we appreciate the extra care called for when new ideas challenge prior analytic knowledge.

But caution and care are not the same as defensive distrust and dismissal of what is different, unfamiliar, or new. When we look at ourselves with candor, we see something beyond benevolent skepticism. Too often we see polemics and partisanship crowd out mutual respect, with ridicule even at times rearing its malignant specter.

Tension is inevitable for the growth of a science, just as it is for that of an individual, and such growing pains are to be welcomed. Open-minded controversy does not require endings in which everyone agrees. Premature closure hides what is still unknown, while respectful acceptance of continuing differences protects the path to further knowledge. Ideas must stand and fall on their merits, not on the prestige or power of their proponents. While some new ideas will not stand up to close examination, we must leave room for and welcome those that do have merit – even if they discomfort us by contradicting more familiar meritorious views we favor.

Full growth can only come from controversy that is both unobstructed and disciplined. "Unobstructed" means genuinely open; and "disciplined" demands rigor in conceptualization, regard for prior learning, and tolerance in the face of unyielding paradox. For years there were battles between analysts prioritizing drives and others prioritizing object relationships, with extremists on each side repudiating the other. Those extremists fought, as do extremists today, as if paradox meant an enemy were at hand rather than that a narrow theory was insufficient. When bias shapes conclusions, whether a bias favoring the new or the old, true growth is stunted.

Problems arise in part from success, with difficulties heightened by pluralism. Is there one psychoanalysis or many? Asked another way, can we continue to grow and venture beyond the boundaries of our accustomed ideas and still, as I believe we must, keep central as common to all of us the core concern for unconscious forces, the orientation that distinguishes what is uniquely psychoanalytic from that which is broadly psychological?

These questions will not be resolved by proclamations of open-mindedness if at the same time our dialogues degenerate into parallel monologues. Walls separating our enclaves will not fall before the trumpeting of good intentions.

The challenge now confronting us is to help define our behavioral battles so that with recognition we can proceed to explore their roots analytically rather than continue to enact them. With that in mind, I will sketch an overview of the patterns of our interactions, aiming to expose and explore their underlying dynamics.

As I sketch problems evident when we come together in groups, it is useful to keep in mind the underlying vicissitudes of demands for self-satisfaction and desires for exploring outward. Behind our convergences and divergences lies the restless marriage between narcissism and scientific curiosity. When our narcissism is secure or, even better, mature, we are free to venture farthest in our inquiries. When our narcissism is threatened, open-minded, outward-looking inquiry deteriorates into a politics of identity. In closing, I will return to this crucial issue, but let us now look at those conflicts that cloud collegiality.

Human structural limits

To do so, it is prudent to start by acknowledging limitations beyond our control that add to our dissatisfaction with others and, which we are less quick to admit, with ourselves. We strive for answers that always extend beyond our reach, for we are after all only human. We accept that we are not omnipotent, but we act as if we could – and indeed should – be omniscient, as if we could ever know all there is to be known, as if our theories could ever be unitary and sufficient. Our knowledge and our theories are remarkably good, but they always fall short, always constrained by the limits of our capacities.

For the world and its phenomena are too large, too varied, and too complex ever to be fully contained by individual human minds. We have no reason to believe we are the end of evolution. When we deny the constraints of our mental hardware, we forget that even when stealing the fire of the gods, still we are not gods. Our vanity is easily offended.

We face the complexities of the universe by cutting them down to size, creating conceptual categories that then lead us into paradoxes that are artifacts caused by the categorical nature of our human logic. To study the world we tease fragments out of their natural context and focus study on them. Our minds dichotomize, endlessly subdividing the categories we create. As a result, in developing science, our human way of organizing knowledge, we create maps that have artificial boundaries. Hazards ensue.

While focused attention is essential and fruitful, artificial fragmentation brings misleading side effects. In dissecting out that which we study, we isolate those excerpted pieces and thus create borders that do not exist in nature. Every time we turn our eyes toward something, we turn them away from something else. As a result, the question 'What have we left out?' must never be far from our minds. We may be able to think of only one approach or some few approaches at a time, but not to keep open alternative views collapses full inquiry into the parochialism of partial interests.

With no choice but to think of a piece at a time, we should be wary about taking possessive pride in personal positions, keeping "a lively appreciation of how people get stuck with a view because it has become their identity" (James 2007, p. 601). Rightfully proud of what we add to what was known before, we are reminded by history that it is also right to remember that others will come to change and add to what we contribute. As a Stoppard (1997, p. 53) character commented, "Every age thinks it's the modern age, but this one really is."

One antidote to such allegiance to fragments is to recontextualize what is newly learned, placing fresh observations back into the open field of accumulated experience. Such recontextualization is essential even as we recognize that the very acts of abstracting and then recontextualizing themselves alter actuality, as we have learned in clinical practice. Despite the appeal of parsimoniousness, single explanations rarely suffice. Occam's razor often cuts too close.

On guard against single views, so must we also be wary of the seduction of simplistic Hegelian dialectics, the idea that there is always a rising pattern in which a synthesis will grow from every thesis and antithesis. Contradictions are not merely to be tolerated. They merit appreciation. They must be protected, discomforting though they be.

Furthermore, knowledge is power, a reassuring antidote to the feeling of helplessness. When confused and overwhelmed, when our knowledge feels insufficient, we fend off the horror of helplessness by calling the world Chaos. However, the world is the world, and 'chaos' is not a description of the world but of our frightened failure to conceptualize it in a way congenial to our minds. The sense of chaos cannot be dispelled either by a favored single theory or by a promiscuity of interpretations with all taken to have equal value. Such is a perversion of the principle of multiple determination; evidence must always be weighed (C. Hanly, personal communication). Open-minded does not mean empty-headed. Evidence must always be weighed.

Respectful attention to the contrary ideas of others provides our greatest opportunity to correct the built-in limitations of our minds. That, however, demands a love of learning based on a solidity of self beyond the child's wish to be the favorite one.

Human frailties

Now, what of frailties that are amenable to mastery? How could we start with other than the issue most immediately apparent – competitiveness? Beginning with an analytic quest held in common, we soon act not as if we share the goal of extending knowledge but as if we are competitors in a battle to outpace each other. Questions of theory or technique are then felt not as useful but as attacks on personal status. Vanity, thy name is everyone.

Who among us would not be the conquistador the young Freud was? With maturity, the narcissistic center holds and the vanity of childhood dreams of glory gives way to the satisfaction of achieving real goals. Also, as we mature, so does our scientific field. While psychoanalysis continues to grow, new growth no longer has the wondrous revolutionary grandeur brought forth by our early pioneers. That grandeur may be part of what first attracted us to this field, but now our field is different in both quality and quantity. Freud opened to us a new ocean. Neither we nor our work are diminished by our exploring the multiple rivers that lead from that common sea.

When threatened competitively, our mastery of early narcissism regresses and too quickly we return to the hunger for pride of place. Every editor has painfully learned that even most senior contributors can quickly become childishly graceless when something in a manuscript is questioned.

Also I remind us of Wheelis's (1956, p. 172) observation that analysts "frequently describe one or another of their colleagues as rigid, dogmatic, and authoritarian; yet no analyst ever so describes himself. The inescapable inference is that some of us have taken refuge in dogma without knowing we have done so."

The painfully familiar "narcissism of minor differences" is so apparent and so everlasting that Freud (1918, 1921, 1930) returned to it repeatedly at different stages across his thinking. Indeed, knowing the regularity with which this self-love recurs, he remarked, "One is tempted to ascribe [to it] an elementary character" (1921, p. 102).

Of course, curiosity not fed by personal investment and desire for success would be a weak mover indeed. Personal ambition cannot be denied or willed away. Instead, narcissistic intensity needs taming, vanity needs to mature, if ambition is to contribute to progress. Mature love for the other, even for knowledge as an ideal other outside oneself, implies a maturity of narcissism, not its absence.

The task of exploring the sometimes converging and sometimes diverging pulls of inward vanity and outward curiosity is complicated by the unusual nature of our occupation. Even as clinical work is profoundly intimate, it is also profoundly lonely. At work we must limit our self-gratification as with each analysand in the privacy of sessions we are immersed in all emotions from apathy to ardor, moving from quiet gray to blood red and to black as we pass from session to session, from hour to hour, from day to day.

Major adjustment is needed for us to move from these intensely private moments at work back to the world at large. Just as our eyes have difficulty adjusting from dark to light, our sense of ourselves has similar difficulty adjusting to the shift from being in-the-office to being in-the-broad-world.

It is easy to forget to leave behind the asymmetry of the analytic partnership when we move from behind the couch, easy to fall back to that clinical asymmetry of the office when we feel challenged outside the office. In dialogues with our colleagues, discussions best held on level ground, we retreat too readily to the sense of superiority that can attach itself to an interpretive position.

Perhaps unaware how often he, too, fell short of this ideal, Freud (1914, p. 49) warned:

> Analysis is not suited ... for polemical use; it presupposes the consent of the person who is being analysed and a situation in which there is a superior and a subordinate. Anyone, therefore, who undertakes an analysis for polemical purposes must expect the person analysed to use analysis against him in turn, so that the discussion will reach a state which entirely excludes the possibility of convincing any third person.

The air of superiority spreads broadly. It is evident in collegial consultations when a supervisory tone replaces mutual respect (Gabbard, personal communication), and it appears in our literature when a writer's own thinking, presented in its greatest strength, is contrasted with contrary views presented in their weakest light. Our debates are rife with such straw men.

Unsure of ourselves, we demean the other. When thus defensively self-serving, we serve neither our science nor ourselves well.

Problems related to group dynamics

Acknowledgement of these, our individual foibles, leads us to look at their effects in our interpersonal realms. The movements of narcissistic self-satisfaction and of curious reaching out reflect the conflict between desires for individual self-distinction and those wanting acceptance and union. Each person wants to be uniquely separate and at the same time longs to belong, to have an identity known and recognized in connection with others. Inevitably, we face the problems of group dynamics.

Before narrowing attention onto psychoanalytic groups, it is necessary to acknowledge how our analytic groups are themselves influenced by the broad cultures from which they arise. As just one illustration, the colonial past has left a legacy of confidence of power and an air of moral superiority on the side of the former colonial powers and a legacy of defiant resentment of imposed power on the side of those whose worlds had been subordinated. This inescapably carries through to difficulties analysts from differing national cultures have in addressing each other with true equality. With such an historical background, an exchange of ideas can come to feel like a power struggle and an agreement can feel like a submission. Sadly, both prejudice and narcissistic wounds have very long half-lives.

Acknowledging this, let us turn to dynamics within the analytic universe. Ideas may be born in splendid isolation, but they need to be tested by others if they are to grow as more than private fantasies. To deepen our studies, we narrow attention to particular areas of interest, consequently removing ourselves from the open marketplace. Later taking our thinking back into the public arena, we find we have to explain how our thinking developed. It is then, unfortunately, easy to feel that being questioned is being attacked, to feel unappreciated and become guarded, finally too easy to retreat to personal provinces detached from common contact. Still thrilled by the excitement of discovery and appreciative of advances not yet broadly accepted, narcissism can overtake curiosity. In the name of the new but too often in the service of the self, we develop allegiances to our narrow views.

Problems of radical schools

I begin with the extreme of radical schools, where vanity overpowers open-minded curiosity. New learning modifies prior understanding as it is incorporated into the collective body of analytic knowledge, and a multiplicity of understandings replaces the clarity of an individual voice with the rich counterpoints of a choral symphony. Yet alongside new voices integrated into the common chorus are others who insist on standing apart, adamant that their solos stand supreme and displace the rest.

At times new ideas are truly revolutionary, resulting from radical new ways of looking and of thinking. As members of one of the great revolutionary movements of history, analysts have reason to value and to protect the possibility of the drastically different. But history repeatedly reveals revolutionary causes perverted for personal gain. It is specifically that to which I refer when speaking of radical schools.

By radical schools I do not refer to new or unusual ways of thinking but instead to those enthusiasts discontented with even close compatriots felt to compromise the exclusive supremacy of their new ideas. These are impassioned ideologues who insist that their views supersede all other analytic learning. Calling such groups "radical" does not disparage what they add but rather refers to the demand that such contributions replace other understandings. Even as contributions are enriching, demands for exclusivity are destructive. Old understandings are of course changed when new discoveries are brought to them, but 'radical' refers to insistence on primacy.

I offer illustrations as examples, sample specimens of a ubiquitous problem. For instance, ego psychology adds much to our understanding of the ways the unconscious is processed. "Radical ego psychology" would have clinicians always cling solely to the surface, attending only to how a patient's mind observes itself and never venturing to the depths. For instance, self psychology adds much to our understanding of the ways a person handles essential need for recognition and regulation of esteem. "Radical self psychology" would focus so totally on issues of attunement as never to attend to unconscious conflicts. For instance, attention to the here and now of transference interpretation greatly advances our clinical skills. What might be called "radical concern for the present" would repudiate concern for the past as damaging to our field.

The list goes on. These are the sort of people Machiavelli must have had in mind when he said that some people know everything, but that's all they know.

Splendid isolation can intensify a focus of attention to make possible ever deeper explorations and understandings. However, insularity, the failure to reconnect with broader knowledge, results in a nonsplendid hermetic isolation that turns schools into radical schools and turns radical schools into cults. At such times self-satisfaction smothers true curiosity. When narcissistic rigidity replaces open mindedness, such analysts become like the French revolutionaries of whom it was said that they built their prisons from the stones of the Bastille.

Freud (1910) knew how difficult is valid self-criticism, writing in a letter to Ferenczi, "Self-criticism is not a pleasant gift, but it is, next to my courage, the best thing in me." Openness to contrasting views not only does not betray viewpoints but actually helps one strengthen them.

Still, it is natural and helpful that we join together and form schools. Uncertain in the loneliness of creativity and vulnerable to the reactions of others, we turn to like-minded colleagues for support. Searching for help in developing our perspectives, we are susceptible to the criticism of extremists on one side and to the inspirational seduction of charismatic figures on the other. We need others to be trustworthy, respectfully honest, if they are to help our self-critical capacity grow, just as we are obliged to be respectful when questioning what we newly hear.

Even when schools are not radical, they necessarily take differing and at times opposing positions. Contradictions are neither to be denied nor forcibly integrated. Rather than accept that contrary viewpoints can validly stand alongside one's own, one is tempted to retreat to the safety of a private orthodoxy. Then partisan fights ensue, battles akin to those of chemists disputing whether it is hydrogen or oxygen that gives water its taste.

This too-familiar difficulty was explored by Gabbard's (2007) incisive critique of ideology as a retreat from the demands of the principle of overdetermination.

Since no single point of view can suffice for full understanding, forgetting that favored views are themselves abstracted from the wholeness of experience is a retreat from respect for multiple determination. Gabbard recognized the place of theory as metaphor in organizing thinking, but he also pointed out the limits of metaphors, making clear how their derivative theories inevitably break down. Defensive retreat to orthodoxy is rooted in the universal temptation to protect feelings of certainty and the personal identity dependent on that certainty.

Our history is heavy with theories hypertrophied from concepts based on experience into proud pronouncements of identity. We see it when a theory is presented as a flag to distinguish one group from another, when debate over observations is replaced by a politics of identity. For groups as well as for individuals, it is not the narcissism of identity that is destructive, but it is its immature form, where vulnerability of self-definition retreats from the capacity to love a shared ideal.

Development of separate schools can lead to difficulties that result (a) from parochialism, (b) from group dynamics and the structure of organizations, and (c) from the impact of new ideas and new groups on language. I will say just a few words about each.

Problems of parochialism

The anxious uncertainty intrinsic to creativity stimulates the pressure for team loyalty. As a result a new group, vulnerable to the reactions of traditional conservative forces, has the regressive tendency to fall back to that early developmental position in which good is seen as inside and bad as outside.

When a paper from within such a group is not accepted by an established journal, the inference is taken that the establishment is hostile and closed. New workers, huddling in felt isolation, speak mainly among themselves. To have freer outlet for their work, they establish their own journals, thereby further diminishing exposure of their thinking to the broad community. Next, within the new group younger colleagues see their own promotion enhanced by publishing in the group's own journal, with such local journals deemed more advantageous for in-group advancement.

Both the local groups and the broad community suffer as a result. Parochialism relieves the new group from fully considering conflicting ideas developed by others. And the analytic community at large is denied the benefits of the new work, the opportunity to reevaluate and update prior understandings. While some new journals weaken and die, others become established and eventually valued for the level of their standards and the richness of their contributions.

One result is the development of two tiers in our literature, the broad and the more focused, both needed and both valuable. What might be called house organs, like the *International Journal of Psychoanalysis*, the *Journal of the American Psychoanalytic Association*, and the on-line PEP website, try to provide a broad and fair hearing for all schools. Other journals, like *The Psychoanalytic Quarterly*, *Psychoanalytic Dialogues*, and *Contemporary Psychoanalysis* (along with a full range of others), provide avenues for closer expression of each point of view. (I assume a parallel development has occurred in other national languages.) Both levels are needed, with each level complementing the other.

Problems of organizations

Beyond journals, organizations themselves both facilitate communication and, unfortunately, compound problems of exclusivity and isolation.

The analytic establishment and the analytic movement are not the same. Both are vital, forming a symbiotic as well as a competing pair. The establishment is needed to organize efficient interchange, to remove training from the idiosyncrasies of an apprentice system, to maintain standards. It is conservative and is needed to be conservative. The analytic movement, in contrast, is unrestrained in its questioning all established ways of thinking and acting. It is subversive and is needed to be subversive.

The tension between establishment and movement is a sign of life, and analysis flourishes best when the two are in working balance. When either overwhelms the other, the entire field suffers. Excessive strength in the establishment leads to rigidity and a dearth of discovery. Excessive weakness in the establishment leads to license rather than liberty for the analytic movement, with laxity of intellectual discipline and wild analysis ensuing. Excessive weakness of the movement leads to conceptual stagnation and ultimately rigor mortis. New ideas move us forward, while testing of evidence protects us against wild analysis.

That tension between establishment and movement also colors how analysts approach each other. So it is not surprising to hear analysts say that at congresses and conventions they learn most not in meeting rooms but in hallways or over coffee tables. When colleagues from different schools talk informally, at times even feeling they do so surreptitiously, they have the sense of safety that makes open and free exchange possible.

An exemplary illustration was provided by Confrontations, a series of discussions over years ultimately published as *Cahiers Confrontation*. At a time when French analysis seemed splintered, analysts from different schools met independently and informally, at first as a small group in the organizing member's office. Free from the competitive pressures of their various societies, these meetings grew and developed into an increasingly open and fruitful exchange of ideas.

Similar results are seen in other groups when analysts from different societies meet informally to exchange ideas in a setting where neither personal status nor advancement nor potential referrals are at stake. People best hear the ideas of others and best expose their own uncertainties when no one with consequential power is present. With our clinical experience, we should not be surprised.

Rather than being threatened, wise organizations recognize that they strengthen themselves as well as psychoanalysis in general by facilitating the development of such private cross-cultural discussions away from the power structure of the organization itself. "In private" matters.

Problems of language

Words may be humanity's greatest yet most devilish invention. Indeed, language may be humanity's sorcerer's apprentice. Naming at times becomes a substitute for questioning, a place where the mind itself begins to doze. A name is not an explanation, yet the names we give processes and the theories constructed of those names at times extend far beyond the evidence from which they arose.

Our fragmentation into schools has a parallel problem in the deterioration of a common language into provincial dialects. We define ourselves by our language, and we do so defensively. I am reminded of an American friend who picked up a piece of cutlery and said, "It's funny. The French call this *un couteau*. The Germans call it *ein messer*. And we call it a knife – which it is!"

Knowing the multiple levels of translation needed to turn inner feelings into words and knowing the ever-changing nature of words, it is amazing that we communicate as well as we do. Indeed, the problem of language is present even when we think we are in a group speaking the same language. No two people truly speak the same language. Rather, they have enough commonality of denotation and connotation to succeed, on the whole surprisingly well, in sharing ideas. Well, but only "on the whole."

Miscommunication occurs even with words we think we hold in common. Words change with usage so that old words newly carry different implications. "Ego" seems so simple a word, present from early in our shared history. Yet when "ego" is used, some hear "second structural theory," some hear "self," some hear "vanity," some hear "mental executive functions." Words that in their youth have the strength of specificity weaken with age, often corrupting into polemical code words. With that complication present in shared words, how optimistic can we be when using words that name newly recognized phenomena?

Difficulty is compounded when we talk with colleagues outside close circles, even those within the same analytic society. Communication becomes yet more complicated when we speak with analysts rooted in other analytic cultures. Then, naïvely, we act as if we speak the same language because we sound as if we are using the same words.

Boesky (2008) has described the impossibility of finding a Rosetta stone for our Babel of pluralism. At times we use language to expose and at times to hide. At times we create new words to give newly recognized phenomena new names; at times we press into service old names for new ideas. In addition, at times we use different words for the same phenomenon, and at least equally troublesomely, at times we use the same word when we refer to a different set of forces with a different set of implications. Difficulties abound. The temptation to coin new words for theory is always risky, and one risk is that it hides an inability to be sufficiently clear about new thinking so as to be able to express it in ordinary language.

Narcissism and curiosity

What can we find in this survey of difficulties that we can use to enrich our continued growth? For, happily, our strengths outweigh our weaknesses, and

Freud (1914) knew what he was saying when he adopted as a motto for the psychoanalytic movement that of the city of Paris: *Fluctuat nec mergitur*. It is tossed by the waves, but it does not sink.

Our task as always is to expose and explore the hidden forces lying behind our difficulties, and the two ever present in this consideration have been narcissism and curiosity. Narcissism speaks of emotional investments aimed inward, while curiosity refers to those aimed outward, even when facing unconscious forces beyond one's conscious self. Narcissism and curiosity, inner and outer – like conjoined twins, the two always go in tandem even when in conflict.

Our study of narcissism – starting with Freud, highlighted by Kohut, and contributed to by all schools – is much too complex to be captured in a moment here. However, two points are relevant. The first is that of basic security, the need for a center that will hold if one is to be able to venture forth. When that center feels attacked, one defends it as a reflex: one can only be open to disagreement when one's essence does not feel threatened.

The second point is that narcissism has its own developmental course along a continuum from primitive and immature to mature. It has been said, for instance, that a parent feels a greater pain if a child is threatened than if the pain is aimed at the parent because of projected narcissism. That phrase misleads. More accurate would be to say that the parent has the capacity for love beyond the parent's immediate self. Mature narcissism serves the self by cherishing the other, by caring about others and about ideals beyond oneself. Basic security allows sufficient sense of self to make possible exploring beyond one's narrow self-concerns. As Lao Tzu said, being deeply loved by someone gives you strength, while loving someone deeply gives you courage.

Curiosity, too, has its own complex continuum of development. It is present in an infant's exploring his mother's breast and his own hand. So long as helplessness is not so overwhelming as to be disorganizing, a child reaches out to learn about the world. The child desires both to know and to have power over the world. Curiosity, with its awakened awareness of the distinction between self and other, invokes both questions: "Who am I?" and "What is it like to be someone else?"

With curiosity as it was with narcissism, all schools have added their own contributions, from Freud's attention to sexual curiosity and others' later thoughts about instincts for mastery on to current concepts about a drive toward knowledge. Now, however, we must respect our earlier caveat about simplistic dichotomization and avoid too tidy a distinction between narcissism and curiosity. For the child at the breast, like the analysand in analysis, there is a unity between seeking and satisfaction, between drive and defining experience. Self-concerns and experience of the other are unitary in the process of creating meaning. Satisfaction for one's own sake and reaching outward, curiosity about the world beyond oneself, can never be fully divided.

How does this apply to our problems with collegiality, and how does it apply to our desire both to share and to learn so that psychoanalysis is advanced? Mature narcissism's love of curiosity gives one entry into our universal conversation. Experience and maturity teach us that we are heard best when we ourselves can hear best. Indeed, it is as we can regard the other most openly that we become most fully defined as ourselves. As Shevrin (2000) so aptly put it, "If Descartes were alive today, he would say, 'I listen, therefore I am.'"

We also learn that we must live with irony, with the poignant awareness that growth implies loss. As the secure child grows more aware of the outer world, that knowledge brings awareness of finiteness, ultimately of mortality. But sufficient security allows acceptance, the self-respecting modesty based on a center that does hold. Recognition and regard, one's seeing oneself as seen and respected by another, are equally essential along with basic security, holding, and containment for narcissism to mature. Curiosity, desire to know and engage the world with willingness to risk uncertainty, can only grow solidly on the basis of this selfsame confidence.

Regardless of whether narcissism or curiosity dominates, the road from infantile to mature is never a royal road. It is one always marked by conflict, by potholes and detours. One's self is always shaped by the sense of strangeness of the universe into which one is born. The strangeness of otherness, even when softened by the confidence that comes with the security of early love, colors each aspect of one's finding one's place in the world, coloring the continuous interplay of self-definition and regard for otherness. Despite the defensive power of narcissism, despite infantile fantasies of omnipotence and would-be omniscience, the world – including the inner world – always surpasses one's own understanding and full mastery. Confidence empty of vulnerability is the confidence of ignorance. To explore is to take risks. To be open to one another, whatever the form of congress involved, is to be vulnerable.

Because no one can ever know all there is to know and because no word can ever be the last word, the courage of our convictions can never be more than the courage of our temporary convictions. The pride with which we at times present our theories suggests the fear of uncertainty and the anxiety of feeling lessened if we accept the influence of others. The very word "achievement" implies completion, yet we are not diminished when we acknowledge that our achievements always can refer only to what one knows so far. Science never simply is but is always becoming.

The feeling of "Eureka" in making an advance in science is as satisfying as is the sense of "Aha" in clinical analysis. Each gives cause for pride. Yet such moments are best followed by recognition that, wonderful as they are, they are never the end of understanding. New insight, like interpretation, is both a commemorative event and a new beginning. Each new advance strengthens the possibility of further advances – but only when the glow of success does not dazzle one into the fixity of conceit.

So, in closing, I offer only a signpost pointing to one path for future study. It is the study of those intrapsychic and interpersonal forces that interfere with the confidence to be vulnerable in the service of open-mindedness. When narcissism and exploratory curiosity together grow, when pleasure in generativity outweighs pride in prestige, then we and the field we love both do grow best. When that creative love of curiosity falters, whether in our science or in our clinical work, we have a signal to step back to explore the causes of such a change. Science and we thrive most richly when reciprocal teaching and reciprocal learning go genuinely hand in hand.

References

Boesky, D. (2008). *Psychoanalytic Disagreements in Context*. London: Aronson.

Freud, S. (1910). Letter from Sigmund Freud to Sándor Ferenczi, 17 October 1910. In *The Correspondence of Sigmund Freud and Sándor Ferenczi, Vol. I 1909–1914*, eds. E. Brabant, E. Falzeder, & P. Giampieri-Deutsch. Cambridge. MA: Belknap, 1994, p. 227.

Freud, S. (1914). On the history of the psycho-analytic movement. *S.E.* 14, 7–66.

Freud, S. (1918). The taboo of virginity. (Contributions to the psychology of love III.) *SE 11*, 193–208.

Freud, S. (1921). Group psychology and the analysis of the ego. *S.E.* 18, 65–143.

Freud, S. (1930). Civilization and its discontents. *S.E.* 21, 57–145.

Gabbard, G. (2007). "Bound in a nutshell": Thoughts on complexity, reductionism, and "infinite space." *Int J Psychoanal*, 88:559–74.

James, C. (2007). *Cultural Amnesia*. New York: Norton.

Shevrin, H. (2000). Unpublished discussion at Estates General, Paris.

Stoppard, T. (1997). *The Invention of Love*. New York: Grove Press.

Wheelis, A. (1956). The vocational hazards of psycho-analysis. *Int J Psychoanal*, 37:171–84.

Chapter 9

On immediacy

"Vivid contrast between past and present"

What gives immediacy to the immediate?

The Tempest, the last of his plays that Shakespeare wrote entirely alone, was the only one that respected the classical demand for unity of time: the time of the story unfolded in the drama is the same as the passage of time in the action on stage. Thus, scenes from the remote past could not be enacted but had to be recounted as a present telling in order to inform the audience of what had led to the current moment.

To accomplish this, Shakespeare had Prospero tell Miranda the history of their situation, simultaneously offering the explanation to the theater audience. This speech, starting with "My brother and thy uncle" (I. ii. 66), runs on for 40 lines, ending "Dost thou hear?" (I. ii. 106). Frye (1986) described a common reaction to the speech, calling this recounting of the somber tale of treachery "no really convincing general source" (p. 72). Indeed, Kermode (2000) was so strongly struck by Shakespeare's uncommon clumsiness in this speech that he conducted a linguistic analysis of it, trying to understand its "taut, compressed, anxious" quality, its "dissipated" and "relatively unimpressive" effect, its being "unnecessarily awkward" (p. 288).

What possible significance might there be in an exposition so awkward and unengaging near the start of so famously poetical a work? Offering his own answer, Kermode made a point fully as telling for us:

> What can be said of this performance is that by abolishing the great gap in time between the early events and the arrival of Prospero's enemies on his island Shakespeare has forfeited immediacy; there is no vivid contrast between past and present.
>
> (Kermode 2000, p. 289)

I take "vivid contrast" here to mean vital connection, relevant similarities and differences, not mere opposition. The word *immediacy* implies more than present tense. Rather, it suggests a present tense that carries emotional vividness. To be poignant, a stimulus must evoke, wittingly or not, emotional echoes of older depth. To convey immediacy, the present must bear more than recognition of the manifest here and now.

As one of many who have tried to reclaim the present in a psychoanalytic world dazzled by the past, I wrote:

> (1) that life exists in the present moment; (2) that like a crystalline drop of water mirroring the universe, the worlds of past and present, self and others, are made visible by exploring the reflections in the tiny and fragile drop of the immediacy of the moment; (3) that what we see when we look closely at those reflections are the lights of the present – the past does not merely repeat itself in the present, but the present creates our pictures of the past; and (4) lastly, that it is the emotional sensations experienced in the moment that shine the light that makes possible our seeing and knowing the inner universe of buried dynamics and of the past.
>
> (Poland 1996, p. 36)

Unfortunately, historical psychoanalytic tilting to the past in ways that undid the power of the present now too often sounds as if it has been replaced by a modern tilting to the present in ways that would undo or minimize the power of the past. Recent analytic attention has at times turned to views of co-construction and intersubjectivity in a manner that with distressing frequency seems to emphasize concern for the here-and-now present as if that here-and-now or experience-near quality could stand alone. Without the emotional power of unvoiced meanings and their context from the past, the here and now is merely the present tense, a more or less interesting passage of time and events, rather than the unspoken "vivid contrast between past and present" that gives emotional immediacy to any moment.

Immediacy speaks of the present, but with the intrinsic implication of a context of hidden affective meanings that transcend the manifest here and now; and those meanings are born out of urges, feelings, fantasies, and experiences alive from the past. Without due regard for those, attention to the here and now loses not only its poetry but also its immediacy, becoming as ineffective, dry, and academic as did Prospero's expository lecture.

References

Frye, N. (1986). *Northrop Frye on Shakespeare*. New Haven, CT: Yale University Press.

Kermode, F. (2000). *Shakespeare's Language*. New York: Farrar, Straus & Giroux.

Poland, W. (1996). *Melting the Darkness: The Dyad and Principles of Clinical Practice*. Northvale, NJ: Aronson.

Shakespeare, W. (1971). *The Tempest*. New York: Penguin Books.

Chapter 10

The limits of empathy

Moliere's physician, asked why opium caused sleep, answered that it was because opium contains "a dormitive principle." Naming, crucial for learning, at times becomes a place where the mind itself begins to doze. In the history of psychoanalysis, we have seen names that started as valuable contributions too often used to close off questioning. Defenses, resistance, projective identification, holding, and containing – each of these enriching concepts has been degraded by some into a shibboleth of parochial allegiance. Caution is needed when we are tempted to expand our concepts because, in the face of unending uncertainty, we are all vulnerable to compromising discipline in our longing for final answers.

Empathy, too, is a valuable concept that at times has been stretched beyond its natural shape to serve as a universal explanation. Let us first consider some misapplications of the concept and then, returning to empathy proper, begin to place the concept in the context of new developments in analytic thinking.

Misapplications of empathy

First, misapplications, those distortions that dilute the validity of the basic idea of empathy. Too often, we debate by misrepresenting opposing views, creating straw men easy to tear down. My attention to misuses of the concept of empathy is meant to clear away misrepresentations, to protect – not undermine – what is truly valid in the concept.

The word "empathy" was imported from aesthetics, where it is used to describe *a means of perception*. That question of *how* one perceives was of concern to analysts very early on. Freud and Deutsch had been keenly attuned to unconscious communication; Fliess and Gitelson spoke of trial identification; and Racker provided a major advance by examining the process closely. It was, of course, Kohut's 1959 paper that brought the word empathy to its analytic prominence. Previously, however, as empathy had named the way a person grasped the feelings carried by a work of art, so it had been used to identify a way an analyst grasps the feelings in the patient.

The Encarta online dictionary recognizes both that empathy is *a form of perception* and that it is vulnerable to distortions introduced by imagination. After defining empathy as "the ability to identify with and understand another person's feelings," the dictionary speaks of the origin of the word in aesthetics, "the attribution of feelings to an object, the transfer of your own feelings to an object such as a painting." empathy inexorably carries "attribution," distortions induced by the mind of the empathic person. No one can ever purely know what another experiences.

The first misuse of empathy was to elevate it from being simply *one of many* roads contributing to understanding to being *the* royal road, one substantially freed from the need to correct for the observer's attributing bias. Understanding another demands relentless self-analysis if one's empathizing imagination is to *approach* valid perception.

Kohut (1959) recognized this, having initially included personal introspection, self-analysis, when speaking of vicarious introspection. Yet, in practice, often that self-analytic discipline has been obscured as a tidal wave of enthusiasm for empathy swept over our field.

Empathy soon ballooned from being a form of perception into an explanation for all seasons. It has been seen lying at the heart of growth and development; its lack has been posited as the centerpiece of pathogenesis; and it has been put forward as the essence of what is mutative in the analytic process.

No longer limited to perception, empathy was assimilated into the greater territory of the empathic response, with reaction now added to perception. Indeed, in clumsy hands that stance was further degraded into a posture of all-accepting sweetness. This misuse of empathy sidesteps the observer's need for the uncomfortable work of self-analysis. One paradoxical result is an undermining of the patient's separateness and uniqueness.

By soldering response to perception, the analyst acts as if the patient were already understood rather than being ultimately, and only partially, understandable. Sympathy replaces true empathy.

One person never truly knows what the other feels. Yes, we all want to know that another person "gets it," but genuinely "getting it" recognizes the difference between the two parties. This is likely why Anna Freud (1981) distinguished understanding from insight. One can have an understanding of someone else, an appreciation of what is going on inside that person; but the depth of true emotional insight is something one can have only into oneself.

To move now from clinical practice to the arena of theory, empathy – or, more specifically, a deficit of empathy – has frequently been seen as the crucial source of psychopathology. Over and over, we have all heard the tendency to view the patient as innocent victim of insufficiently empathic mothering. The patient's conflicts, the patient's own aggression and sexuality, the patient's past and present organizing fantasies – all these too often have disappeared from consideration.

In addition, converting empathy from a form of perceiving into an interpersonal posture of warmth and goodness denies the many ways empathic perception can be used hatefully. The con man, the demagogue, the exploiter, and the sadist all function best when their empathic skills are sharp. Indeed, the effectiveness of a sadist's cruelty is directly related to the capacity for empathy, to the ability to sense what will hurt most. The successful sadist and the flourishing flimflam artist, quite as much as the successful psychoanalyst, achieve victories in direct proportion to their capacity for empathic attunement.

How one perceives and how one subsequently acts are linked but are not the same. Extending empathy beyond its clear relevance as a form of perception undermines the value of the concept.

Structural problems with the concept of empathy

Now, setting aside misapplications and returning to the value of empathy, let us consider its place in the light of recent shifts in analytic thinking. Changes in practice and theory both require clarification when placing empathy in the context of present-day analysis rather than that of 1959.

The word "empathy," as noted, was imported into our field from aesthetics, where it refers to an individual's feeling his way into an inanimate work of art. However, our clinical objects are living people, and feeling one's way into a text or painting lacks the vital back and forth flow that arises when two living people interact.

Analysis was born in Freud's revolutionary self-analysis. That uniquely internal exploration by Freud of his own mind led to a mode of clinical work where the patient's mind was at first similarly addressed as if it too stood singly on its own, that is, to the period of depth psychology characterized as "one-person analysis." Gradually and awkwardly, recognition of the presence of the analyst's mind in the clinical field resulted in an appreciation of "two-person psychology." It was in the earliest two-person psychology that empathy (or trial identification) fit most easily. Here, the way an analyst sensed what a patient felt accorded most closely with the aesthetic origins of empathy. It was in this early two-person context that Racker (1968) valuably defined the categories of concordant identification, where the analyst identifies part for part with the patient, and complementary identification, where the analyst identifies with the patient's objects.

Yet, inevitably, the plot thickened as we learned how wondrously fluid are subject and object within people's minds. Just as one can never be a clinical observer without participating in the interactive field, so too the position of empathic trial identification, whether supposedly concordant or complementary, could not be so simple and pure. Emotional traffic goes two ways, with concordant and complementary aspects inevitably both present at the same time on different levels, even though only one might seem apparent on the surface.

Furthermore, we learned that while empathy offered a form of perception, the analyst's very act of perceiving carries its own interactive effect. At the end of his life, Kohut (1982) acknowledged the problem in two statements he made looking back on his 1959 contribution. "As an information-collecting, data-gathering activity," he wrote, "empathy ... can be right or wrong, in the service of compassion or hostility, pursued slowly and ploddingly or 'intuitively,' that is, at great speed. In this sense empathy is never itself supportive or therapeutic" (p. 397).

However, he went on,

> I wish I could stop my discussion of empathy as a concrete force in human life at this point without having to make a further step which appears to contradict everything I have said so far, and which exposes me to the suspicion of abandoning scientific sobriety and entering the land of mysticism or of sentimentality. ... I must now, unfortunately, add that empathy *per se*, the mere presence of empathy, has also a beneficial, in a broad sense, a therapeutic effect.
>
> (Kohut 1982, p. 397)

What might have seemed sentimental becomes less so upon further examination. Ideas about holding, containing, and witnessing have all opened ways to understand how an analyst's act of perceiving in itself carries consequences for the other person. Apart from other analytic responses based on *what* is seen, the impact of *being* seen matters to the one so witnessed. The effect of being seen is not to be confused with the effect of an analyst's responses after having done that seeing. It is the impact of seeing in and of itself. In order to place this effect within our theory, it is necessary to step back from single points of view to combine observations from different angles.

Rapaport and Gill (1959) gave us the model for this in their description of multiple points of view. Now, consideration of object-relational points of view may offer an approach for addressing how perceiving can itself have an effect on another person apart from the effects of the analyst's active responses.

To repeat what I have said before, empathy implies separateness, one person's understanding of another. To speak of empathy is to imply the presence of two separate people. If we are to understand empathy, we need to return to our consideration of one-person and two-person viewpoints, and clarify them. This clarification has become necessary because, within two-person psychology, the word "intersubjectivity" has been used in conflicting ways.

The first way that intersubjectivity has been thought about is in terms of an interaction between two separate people. Transference and countertransference, conscious and unconscious interactive effects, one's evoking and eliciting responses in the other, projective identification, role-playing, and enactments have all been parts of the study of intersubjectivity involved when two people come together.

Yet a different view of intersubjectivity has been growing in both clinical and philosophical thought. This is not the intersubjectivity of two separate people who come together; rather, it is that of a singular composite emotional being, the couple. This unified couple has been spoken of as the dyad, the unified field of the engaged partners who co-create what unfolds in this collective yet singular entity. A ready model for this difference lies in the distinction between the mother and child pair as comprising two people and the mother–child unity as a being in its own right.

There is substantial debate about the legitimacy of such an idea of a dyadic unity. Many argue that each person remains a unique individual whatever the relationships that exist, while others emphasize that there is no such thing as a person outside the fabric of an interpersonal context. Whatever one's preference in this conflict, there is no doubt that the relationalists who focus on and privilege the dyadic unity of the clinical couple have raised observations that enrich us and questions that cannot be ignored.

We cannot discuss empathy without implying intersubjectivity, and we must face the fact that the word "intersubjectivity" is used both to imply separate people interacting and to imply people unified as a singular couple. In essence, with respect to our viewpoints of one-person and two-person psychologies, we now see that the two-person psychology must be subdivided into one view that respects the two persons as distinctly separate and another view, the dyadic, that considers the unified couple. Despite the ambiguity of using "intersubjectivity" to cover *both* meanings, there is a difference between the standpoints of the separate person and the unified dyad.

So where can empathy be placed in the context of contemporary understanding?

Empathy, which unfolded during the period that the "separate person" viewpoint held full sway, continues to be a valuable contribution in that context, a context in which Racker's elucidation of the varieties of trial identifications retains its significance.

Empathy, however, does not fit neatly into a view of the clinical couple as a dyad having its own unique life and language. Nonetheless, that dyadic vantage does offer promise for understanding such matters as the undemarcated flow of concordant and complementary identifications. Empathy is primarily a concept of great utility for an object-relational point of view based on the separateness of people, even if its limits do not extend to the perspective of the dyad.

In closing

Despite misuses and misapplications of the concept of empathy, and despite its not fitting well into all analytic points of view, the word and the process it names remain vital to psychoanalytic work and thought. Respecting its great value, we must in closing yet remember one further limit of the idea. As valuable as the concept of empathy is, it is not an irreducible basic concept. Empathy can be factored; it has roots.

Empathy, which refers to how one person perceives another when two separate people come together, can be valid only when founded on profound respect for otherness, the full respect of the observing person for the singularity and particularity of the other. Empathy can only approach knowing; it can never lead to full knowledge. For empathy to be valid, respect for the difference between self and otherness is essential. In clinical analysis, the basic principle from which *all* principles of technique – including empathy – derive is regard for otherness, the analyst's full respect for the authenticity of the patient's self as a unique other, as valid a self as the analyst's own, yet one that can never be fully knowable.

References

Freud, A. (1981). Insight – Its presence and absence as a factor in normal development. *The Psychoanalytic Study of the Child*, 36:241–249.

Kohut, H. (1959). Introspection, empathy, and psychoanalysis: An examination of the relationship between mode of observation and theory. *Journal of the American Psychoanalytic Association*, 7:459–483.

Kohut, H. (1982). Introspection, empathy, and the semi-circle of mental health. *International Journal of Psychoanalysis*, 63:395–407.

Racker, H. (1968). *Transference and Countertransference*. New York: International Universities Press.

Rapaport, D. & Gill, M. (1959). The point of view and assumptions of metapsychology. *International Journal of Psychoanalysis*, 40:153–162.

Chapter 11

Beyond bedrock

The trap of abandoning psychology

That one can go no further in a search for meaning does not imply that there is no further that can be gone. The biological basis of psychoanalysis does not provide a legitimate conceptual escape hatch when one reaches personal limitations in psychological inquiry.

Sometimes, we think that as far as our eye can see is the end of the road. As it is for us, so was it at times for Freud.

Psychoanalysts, in exploring unconscious forces within the mind, formulate interpretations tentatively, repeatedly recognizing the need to alter former conclusions that do not stand the test of new clinical experience. As a result, all interpretations are recognized to be trial interpretations.

However, such necessary flexibility and openness of mind reach their limit when a blind spot develops in the analyst's mind. Then, at times, external explanations are defensively brought into play. Often, an analyst ascribes the flaw to the patient, sometimes to the analytic process. And sometimes an analyst turns entirely outside the analytic universe to relieve the frustration due to some unrecognized anxiety arising within it.

An instance of such sidestepping of clinical engagement is seen when emerging aggression is obscured by an agreement between the analytic partners that "someone out there" – a boss or a parent or a sibling or anyone outside – is the "real" cause of the problem. A paranoid *folie à deux* relieves the clinical couple from facing what might be threatening.

Another such defensive process occurs on a theoretical level, albeit with clinical consequences, when an analyst pulls back even from recognizing that an unresolved issue is not yet sufficiently understood and instead concludes that what has appeared is simply not understandable. At that point, analytic inquiry ends, with nonanalytic factors offered to deflect frustration and uncertainty. Nothing can be analyzed if it is regarded as inherently inexplicable.

We see the presence of this strategic misunderstanding when an analyst proclaims that a seeming dead end is due not to the presence of as yet unrecognized psychological forces but to something biological, and thus outside the psychological realm. Such a movement away from the intersubjective psychic domain of analytic exploration invokes biology in *deus ex machina* fashion as an explanatory solution.

Conceptual universes have their own rules, and leaping from one universe of phenomena to another cannot validly erase difficulties. Such confusion of conceptual frameworks was captured well by the humorist who said of an event, "I can't remember whether it happened last Thursday or on the third floor."

Biology matters greatly to psychoanalysis, which is rooted in the biological, but it is not legitimate to use biological conceptualizations to extricate the analyst from a psychological impasse. An early instance of such an unwarranted maneuver in psychoanalysis may be found in a well-known statement made by Freud.

It was Freud's insistent curiosity about hidden meanings that made all of his subsequent historical discoveries possible. Before he developed his metapsychology, before he made his discoveries about infantile sexuality or dream psychology, before his full recognition of the central power of unconscious forces, the crucial and essential quality that shaped Freud's contributions was that he approached clinical work with a powerful curiosity about *meaning*. His drive to understand was most often combined with an equally strong commitment to relentless inquiry.

As a young clinician trying to establish a practice and to develop a career, confronted by the unyielding symptoms of seemingly intractable clinical problems, Freud *listened* to his patients over and over and over. Feeling that it all must mean something, he was tenacious in his search for hidden depths of motivation.

Yet there were moments when Freud drew back from his exploration, moments when he stopped in frustration. There was a time when, instead of saying, "at least now, here *I* can go no further," he said, "This is as far as can be gone." Finding himself unable to go further, he concluded that it was *the path* that ended. He spoke of hitting "bedrock" (Freud 1937, p. 252).

Before considering what was called "bedrock" on that well-known occasion, it is worth remembering that Freud himself warned against this very way of acting. To borrow another of his metaphors, when he claimed to have reached bedrock in the realm of biology, Freud forgot his own caveat that one must "not mistake the scaffolding for the building" (1900, p. 536) and we "must always be prepared to drop our conceptual scaffolding" when it is not sufficient for comprehending "unknown reality" (p. 610).

Let us look now at the specific example of premature mind-closing. Nearing the end of his life, pessimistic about a world on the edge of yet another war, about himself, and also about the limits of clinical analysis, Freud turned in "Analysis terminable and interminable" (1937) to survey those factors that interfere with therapeutic success.

In the short statement with which he closes that paper, we should note that he does not suggest that what he has in mind is *always* fatal to the successful termination of treatment, but his pessimism is clear when he addresses what comes "into especial prominence and give[s] the analyst an unusual amount of trouble" (1937, p. 250).

The themes that he believes lead to a clinical dead end are penis envy in the female and in the male a struggle against a passive feminine attitude toward another male. What the two have in common is said to be the "repudiation of femininity."

Earlier in his career Freud had spoken of how difficult it is for any analyst to go beyond the limits of his personal psychology in doing clinical work, but here he does not question that his conclusions might be shaped by unresolved issues of his own. Instead, he proclaims in his final paragraph:

> We often have the impression that with the wish for a penis and the masculine protest we have penetrated through all the psychological strata and have reached bedrock, and that thus our activities are at an end. This is probably true, since, for the psychical field, the biological field does in fact play the part of the underlying bedrock.
>
> (1937, p. 252)

A century of clinical experience has shown that the syndromes of female penis envy and of male equation of passivity before other men with castration do exist, but they have not been demonstrated to be either universal or irreducibly primary.

For instance, I have worked with a woman for whom both deep shame and profound guilt rather than gender turned out to be the focus of our analytic work. As those issues became less burdensome and with gender identity not at all part of the manifest content, this woman began to look more inviting, warmer, indeed sexually seductive – and to the surprise of us both she announced one day with a smile, "I feel feminine. For the first time, I feel feminine." With basic conflicts cleared, this woman's own inner femininity shone through.

It has been similar with men. The specific repudiation of femininity of which Freud spoke, a man's inability to tolerate passivity before another man, certainly does occur. Again in my experience, however, this trend has been matched by the equally frequent appearance of its contrary, a man's avoidance of taking a dominant position over another man, or what I call his "clinging to juniority." Of course, at times such clinging to juniority is a defensive reaction formation to underlying conflict over male-to-male passivity. But that is not always so. Many factors can lie behind such resistance to forthright self-definition, and psychoanalysis best succeeds and brings about the greatest opening of previous character constriction when individual particularity and uniqueness are valued over dictates of theoretical fashions. The *scaffolding* of theory must give way to the *building* of individual experience.

But just as we are at risk of closing off understanding by speaking of unalterable bedrock, so also we face the opposite danger – the risk of avoiding everything solid and throwing up so nebulous a scaffolding of theory that it has no specific shape, as if anything can then mean anything.

Such a hermeneutic mish-mash is like a concept from the theater, the so-called "six degrees of separation" by which any one person or thing can be linked to any other, no matter how circuitously. Such radical deconstruction pushes meaning through a food processor to yield a purée of possibilities, with useful understanding lost forever. The principle of overdetermination cannot mean that everything implies everything else. The question of what is enough, of where Occam's razor should cut, can be handled clinically according to the heuristic principle that what counts for the patient is a sufficiency of understanding to result in new freedom from prior constrictions.

Furthermore, dedication to open-mindedness is not a valid cover for an analyst's avoiding the need to make definitive interpretations as they are called for clinically. This seems to be what Freud (1912, p. 115) had in mind when he used the metaphor of the surgeon, advising that the analyst's sentiments not be allowed to stand in the way of appropriate interventions.

From the excessive optimism that everything is possible, we return to the equally excessive pessimism that there are no more unfolding possibilities, to our specific instance of where Freud stopped his investigations. For what is "bedrock" but a place where the search stops?

Impasses such as Freud faced are familiar to us in clinical experience – for instance, in negative therapeutic reactions with their contributions from both partners. Uncharacteristically, however, Freud did not keep open a consideration of possibly unrecognized forces either in his patients or in himself. Instead, he shifted phenomenological universes. He said that *here* the world of psychology ends, and *here* the world of biology begins.

I do not suggest our falling back to a Cartesian mind–body split. A person is entire, whole, and mind and body one. Research in the neurosciences offers great promise for increased theoretical understanding of the body's effect and influence on interiority and subjectivity. But respect for that essential unity means that in *our* effort at observation and study, we cannot hop from one scaffolding to another merely on the basis of personal comfort and congeniality. We cannot use the body as if it were a "get out of jail free" card to be played whenever we are faced with psychological frustration.

Psychoanalysis has always rooted psychology in the imperatives of biology, for instance, when Freud defined drives as the demands made by the body on the mind for work. But even when dealing with the body, the field of psychoanalysis is the functioning of the *psyche* – though this always involves the power and demands of the body, of others, of the culture, and so forth.

Finding himself unable to continue exploration, Freud said that it was biology that played the part of the bedrock. Observing this, I suggest that we analysts need signals by which we can be alert to our own blind spots, and that any shifting from the psychological to a nonpsychological realm always demands a second look, a frank reconsideration of how much such a move might be a clue to our possibly rationalizing the frustration of not yet being able to proceed farther with our own understanding.

It is such a spirit of self-questioning and inquiry in the clinical analytic laboratory that ultimately turns unprofitable bedrock into the richest pay dirt.

References

Freud, S. (1900). *The Interpretation of Dreams. S.E.*, vols. 4 and 5.
Freud, S. (1912). Recommendations to physicians practicing psychoanalysis. *S.E.*, 12:109–120.
Freud, S. (1937). Analysis terminable and interminable. *S.E.*, 23:216–253.

Chapter 12

Oedipal complexes, oedipal schema

Moving from his revolutionary self-analysis to his clinical psychoanalytic experience and considering both culture and myth, Freud took the oedipus complex to be central to human life. However, questioning that drastic inference has never disappeared from the front lines of analytic debate. Do oedipal issues stand at the heart of the psychoanalytic venture, defining an individual's character (as some believe), *or* (as others are convinced) does such a view wrongly exclude vast areas of human experience?

The controversy is centrally a problem of definition having to do with levels of abstraction, with the difference between unique phenomenological experiences and the theorizing generalizations drawn from and about them. Human experience is always specific, singular, particular, unique. Just as no two snowflakes are exactly alike, no two *anything* are exactly the same. Generalizations are essential to the recognition of patterns, yet no two instances can be identical.

The oedipus complex in individual lives differs from that spoken of by theory. While the specifics of any individual's oedipal constellations can deviate vastly from the abstracted norm, far from Psychology 101 simplistic models, essential aspects of that infinitely varied human life that we also call oedipal may nonetheless indeed be universal, even inevitable.

Freud's personal and clinical work led him to take one specific myth as a model metaphor for development. To the extent that the narrow tale of Oedipus fitted him and his experience, it is specific and appropriate. Nonetheless, the manifest myth that best captures one person's life and times may not be most apt as the metaphor for another person's life. Indeed, humanity has created many myths precisely because individual constellations of experience and psychology are numberless. The Persephone myth, incisively defined by Kulish and Holtzman (1998), fits some, as also does the tale of Achilles' humiliation as emphasized by Chodorow (n.d.), or the myth of Cain and Abel, and on and on and on. Beyond those legends readily familiar to us, there is a wide range of tales alien to our Western eyes, with each fitting the life stories of individuals in their respective cultures.

Nonetheless, there are issues innate to human life whatever the setting – issues of sexuality, aggression, and conflicts related to the distinction between generations. Each child entering the world must come to grips with the differences between the sexes and the riddle of where babies come from. Each child newly born must deal with smallness and helplessness in a world structured by bigger older people. Each child must deal with biological imperatives, not only those crucial sexual and aggressive drives but also inner forces pressing for mastery of self and world. It seems reasonable to infer that this mixture of love, hate, and cross-generational struggle is what Freud (1905) had in mind when he wrote, "every new arrival on this planet is faced with the task of mastering the oedipus complex" (p. 226n1).

To address these matters, Freud and his early followers used the model at hand that seemed to them to fit best, the oedipus myth. Similarly, it seems fair to say that most of those who now argue for the universality of oedipal issues are not ignorant of or indifferent to individual variability, to specificity, singularity, and particularity. Freud himself made the distinction, noting, "the simple oedipus complex is by no means its commonest form, but rather represents a simplification or schematization" (1923, p. 33) in the face of the variety of actual experience.

A price is paid for keeping the local name "oedipus complex" to refer to the universally inevitable but infinitely varied human struggles of every child newly born onto this planet. Had Freud called the theoretical complex by a different and more general name, perhaps we would not have these present disputes. But given the weight of historical usage accrued by the word "oedipal," it is unlikely we could now coin a new name for the theoretical level of inescapable forces. Clarity may be accomplished by borrowing from Freud's hint. We may achieve more light and less combative heat if we call the individual clinical instance an "*oedipal complex*" and refer to the broad organizing forces of psychic imperatives as the "*oedipal schema*," whatever individual shape those forces may take.

How we got here

While thinking of oedipal complexes and schemas, it is useful to turn for just a moment to the historical path by which these questions arose. We start, necessarily, with Sophocles, whose drama crystallized yet earlier myths into their now definitive form. The tale comes to us as a play, a story learned through firsthand emotions experienced in a theater. That is relevant when later we turn to Freudian understanding, which also places experiential engagement in the clinical theater as the medium of emotional learning.

Sophocles' drama presents the tragedy of human helplessness before the inexorable power of the gods. Oedipus acted in good faith, trying to sidestep a fate foretold. "Luckless Oedipus" (l. 1195) was "bred to misery" (l. 1182). At the end of *Oedipus Rex*, the self-blinded Oedipus says, "It was Apollo, friends, Apollo that brought this bitter bitterness, my sorrows to completion. / But the hand that struck me / was none but my own" (ll. 1329–1333). Oedipus describes his own deed but sees it as an enactment of the power of Apollo. It is that helplessness that then leads the Chorus to cry out to blinded Oedipus, "I pity you" (l. 1303). Even as we onlookers are horrified, we too feel grief-stricken for an Oedipus innocent at heart.

In keeping with Oedipus' line, "The hand that struck me was none but my own," Freud drew a radical conclusion. If weight is given to that line, then Sophoclean determinism bends toward Freudian partial free will, a will that has choices even as it is constrained by inevitabilities. If Oedipus' oedipal issues *were* his own, that is *inside* rather than *outside*, then there is space for personal agency alongside or even behind the powers of fate.

Freud realized that what is *inside* is nonetheless felt by each individual *as if it were outside*. Thus, Freud moved his reading of the powers shaping life not merely from outside to inside but, importantly, to an *inside experienced as outside oneself*. One is always in part a stranger to oneself.

With this, the possibility of therapeutic psychoanalysis was born, a new form of drama wherein one's own stories can be played out with play and player examined, all at the same time. The odeon became the couch.

Unfortunately, Freud also drew a line in the sand that created new battles. In his *Three Essays on the Theory of Sexuality*, he teased apart elements of drives, describing sources, aims, and objects. Noting that "the sexual instinct and the sexual object are merely soldered together" (1905, p. 148), he felt attention could most profitably be directed to sources and aims. Perhaps not realizing or intending the consequences, he seemed to imply that objects were less important an area of study.

How different might our field be today had Freud seen all three aspects of drives as being of equal importance. Focusing on the *sources* of drives, he turned his attention away from the power of the object world.

Simplistically, it could be said that the Sophoclean oedipus is a tale of humanity's struggle shaped by the power of outside others, the individual defined by the influence of intersubjective forces. Similarly, it could be said that the Freudian Oedipus is a tale of humanity's struggle shaped by the power of biology of the body, emphasizing drives as the demand of the body on the mind for work.

The Sophocles/Freud contrast of emphasis seems a battle over which comes first, the chicken of the interpersonal fabric or the egg of the individual. Even other current analytic controversies seemingly remote from oedipal questions stand in the shadow of the outside – inside distinction of Sophoclean and Freudian visions.

Yet it could only have been a matter of time before a synthesis was bound to appear, and this came in Loewald's fresh integration in his paper "The waning of the oedipus complex" (1979). Loewald used the word "waning" on two levels. First, he felt that oedipal issues are not a one-time thing with supposed resolution in childhood. Instead, he saw that these conflicts "repeatedly require ... some forms of mastery in the course of life" (p. 753). Second, he questioned the "decline of psychoanalytic interest in the oedipal phase and oedipal conflicts" (p. 753) as attention turned to preoedipal infant–mother issues.

Focusing on cross-generational aspects of oedipal conflicts, Loewald brought together drives and objects and inner representations, making clear the presence of all these factors in all levels of movement toward individuation and autonomy. Feeling that "oedipal attachments ... must ... be understood as new versions of the basic union-individuation dilemma" (1979, p. 775), Loewald concluded that "the different modes of ... [the oedipus complex's] waning and waxing during life stages give it renewed significance and weight, and that ... [this developmental movement] throws additional light on its centrality" (pp. 774–775).

Forces intrinsic to human development can have universal power even as they are ultimately expressed and experienced in infinitely varied idiosyncratic and unique ways in the immediacy of an individual life unfolding in a particular time and culture.

References

Chodorow, N. (n.d.). The riddle of masculinity: Faultlines and vulnerabilities. Unpublished manuscript.

Freud, S. (1905). *Three Essays on the Theory of Sexuality. S.E.*, 7:125–245.

Freud, S. (1923). *The Ego and the Id. S.E.*, 19:12–66.

Kulish, N. and Holtzman, D. (1998). Persephone: The loss of virginity and the female oedipal complex. *International Journal of Psychoanalysis*, 79:57–71.

Loewald, Hans. (1979). The waning of the oedipus complex. *Journal of the American Psychoanalytic Association*, 27:751–775.

Sophocles. (1970). *Oedipus the King*, tr. David Grene. In *Sophocles I*, ed. David Grene and Richmond Lattimore. Chicago, IL: University of Chicago Press.

Part IV

Beyond the clinical setting

Chapter 13

Reading fiction and the psychoanalytic experience

Proust on reading and on reading Proust

Introduction

Two hundred and fifty years ago, Samuel Johnson wrote in *The Rambler* an allegory on the vagaries suffered by Truth (Bate & Strauss 1969, p. 149). Truth, daughter of Jupiter and Wisdom, was sent to humanity as a gift from the gods; Falsehood came from below. However, confronted by Prejudice and Passions, wounded by Impudence and Sophistry and Vanity and Obstinacy, Truth felt unable to survive among mankind and fled back to the gods. Still, Johnson went on to write,

> Jupiter compassionated the world too much to grant [Truth] her request ... [so the] Muses wove ... a loose and changeable robe, like that in which Falsehood captivated her admirers; with this they invested Truth, and named her Fiction. She now went out again to conquer with more success; for when she demanded entrance of the Passions, they often mistook her for Falsehood, and delivered up their charge; but, when she had once taken possession, she was soon disrobed by Reason, and shone out, in her original form, with native effulgence and resistless dignity.
>
> (Bate & Strauss 1969, p. 152)

At times, Truth may be approached more readily when she arrives draped in the robes of Fiction.

We are much concerned in psychoanalysis with efforts to approach truth and with difficulties in those approaches, the problems of evidence inherent in knowing. Remaining properly alert to the seductive deceits of fiction, we, like Johnson, also recognize that fiction can offer paths to truths not otherwise readily approachable. Reading likely can never produce the depth of psychic change possible in clinical analysis, but analysts' sometimes proprietary sense of exclusivity for the power to effect change must yield to broad experience.

Psychoanalysis was born in Freud's revolutionary self-analysis. A clinician, Freud naturally turned most of his energies to extending what he learned into the therapeutic setting. Deeply civilized and profoundly curious, he felt that analytic investigation ought also to be extended to the study of culture.

Nonetheless, standing in the shadow of preoccupation with the clinical, analytic concern for the culture has never thrived. The past tilt in the investment of psycho-analytic energy away from applied analysis has corrected a bit as public support for analysis as a formal therapy has diminished. However, some of the burdens carried by applied analysis come from its own intrinsic nature.

Without addressing those in depth, one particular aspect demands acknowledgment. We have long been discontented with analytic readings of fiction because of our inability to engage a text and then observe its responses, the text's own ensuing associations. A text is mute in response to interpretation.

Balancing that, however, applied analysis has a compensatory advantage that is absent in examination of clinical interpretations. As idiosyncratic as differing readers' reactions may be, every reader has the opportunity to approach a text that remains unchanging. With time, readings and understandings of texts change, yet a published text is constant, ever available for all to study. In contrast, only the analyst present at any clinical moment can ever experience and truly know the substantive engagement with the patient during that moment.

There is one other advantage reading has over the clinical engagement, and it is one described in detail by Proust. A reader can feel greater safety suspending disbelief approaching a text at the start than can an analysand trying to suspend defense when first engaging a living analyst. The presence of a responsive other alerts resistance; the absence of such a living presence while reading can ease the sense of emotional engagement.

Proust serves as an exemplary illustration, but first it is proper to recognize that while the richness that Proust offers seems limitless, much that he has to teach has, since his time, already been widely studied. With studies of Proust as with the applied analysis of literature in general, attention focused first on a text itself and then later on the connection between a text and the author's life.

In recent decades, clinical psychoanalytic attention has focused more fully on the intersubjectivity of the engagement between analyst and patient. In like manner, literary studies over the past two decades have turned to the engagement of the reader and reading. Thus, modern developments in understanding of the analytic process follow a path parallel to that taken by reader response theory. Perhaps most central to this has been the work of Norman Holland. In *The Dynamics of Literary Response*, Holland (1968) examined the reading of texts in terms of a reader's introjection of fantasy and form, with the reader's subsequent addition of personal meaning. However, in his later *5 Readers Reading*, Holland (1975) turned to a more full appreciation of the interactive process between reader and text. Theories of reading and theories of the psychoanalytic process have progressed side by side.

When considering the work of the mind in reading fiction, it seems particularly appropriate to turn back to Proust, for Proust's consideration of the emotional impact of reading grew out of the same *fin de siècle* ambience of concern for psychological interiority as did Freud's consideration of the psychopathology of everyday life. Despite the two having been contemporaries, despite their both being sophisticated and alert to new ideas arising around them, and despite their common interests, Proust and Freud did not appear to have read each other. Yet concern for many of the ideas that each developed independently was in the air at the turn of the century. When Freud and Proust were each crystallizing their discoveries, sensuality, interiority, femininity, mesmerism, dreams, and the unconscious were pervasive popular themes. Freud and Proust were immersed in the same atmosphere.

Giving shape to what was stirring, these two geniuses exploded with creativity. Freud's work, as we know, was so powerful as to become, in Auden's words, "a whole climate of opinion" (Auden 1939, p. 217). Even those who would come to oppose him had to use the language that Freud created. Proust had a like effect in literature. As Graham Greene put it, "For those who began to write at the end of the twenties or the beginning of the thirties, there were two great inescapable influences: Proust and Freud, who are mutually complementary" (quoted in White 1999, p. 2).

For Proust, reading offered an entrance to the inner life. "Reading," he wrote, "is for us the instigator whose magic keys open deep within us the door to those dwelling-places into which we would have been unable to penetrate" (Proust 1994, p. 36).

Of course, once engaged, both reader and analysand must struggle toward and against identifications, toward and against opening of hidden urges and fantasies. Speaking of his own reading, Proust was explicit that "the emotions aroused in me" while reading came from "the action in which I was taking part" (Proust 1981, Vol I, p. 91). As a result, he went on, such feelings evoked by reading have special power "since we have made them our own, since it is in ourselves that they are happening ... as we feverishly turn over the pages of the book, our quickened breath and staring eyes. And once the novelist has brought us to this state, in which, as in all purely mental states, every emotion is multiplied ten-fold, into which his book comes to disturb us as might a dream, but a dream more lucid and more abiding than those which come to us in sleep" (*ibid.*, p. 92).

In *À la recherche du temps perdu*, Proust provided a host of insights into human psychology, describing and examining desire, longing and loss, the quality of memory and the insufficiency of intentional memory for recapturing the past, jealousy and sexuality and perversion, falling into love and falling out of love. He offered incisive observations on emotions and on social interactions in almost infinite diversity. Yet it is with the narrow issue of reading that we are now concerned.

First, I shall report some of Proust's own thinking on the psychological power of reading. I will then turn to *À la recherche* in general before, in closing, relating aspects of the ending of this work to the termination phase of an analysis. It is true that just as any clinical analysis is singular, unique, and particular, so too is any personal reading. Yet despite the idiosyncrasies intrinsic to any given analysis or to any particular reading, both reading and analysis have commonalities inherent to their structure.

Proust on reading

To read or to analyze is in part to give oneself over to an other. That "in part" implies that there are limits of both depth and time – how deeply and for how long one loses oneself in identification before reintegrating. As one "*lends* an ear," a person listening or reading or analyzing partially defers self-definition and judgment in order to take in the other. However, at some point one's integrity of self-definition demands a drawing back, an implicit response of "Yes, but." One lets oneself go in order to take something in, but what is taken in is not swallowed whole; it is selectively chewed over and only then digested. That is so as you consider what I write; it is so when the lights come on between acts at the theater; it is so when an analyst emotionally steps back to think about what has been heard and felt; it is so when a patient contemplates an interpretation; and it is so when a reader pulls back after being lost in a book. The *becoming as-if-one-with* and the *separating from* are at the heart of both reading and analyzing. We know it well clinically when in a termination phase it is as if an analytic patient wakens from the dream of a transference neurosis.

Let us look into some of Proust's own thinking about reading, written before he embarked on *À la recherche*. In 1905, Proust wrote an essay on the nature of reading, an essay he later used as the introduction to his and Marie Nordlinger's translation into French of Ruskin's *Sesame and Lilies*. Ruskin, as a leader of the Arts and Crafts movement dedicated to restoring beauty to domestic life in the face of the effects of the machine age, had written on how reading could improve the lives of working people.

In his introduction, Proust turned from Ruskin's emphasis on the educational role of reading to the power of reading to develop and stir the imagination, to open the mind. While praising Ruskin, Proust's own thinking was in direct contrast to Ruskin's. Instead, his argument was similar to that offered by psychoanalysis when contrasted with conventional therapy: in lieu of shaping a mind by the transmission of content or by influence toward preferred points of view and behavior, what is offered is liberation by exciting new capacities for feeling and thinking. Proust, like Freud, emphasized inquiry and opening rather than education and indoctrination.

Proust's conceiving of this essay appears to be part of the process of his own personal growth and developing identity. In working on this piece he began with an idealized sense of Ruskin, a valuation that changed as Proust, in the process of writing, separated and distinguished his own ideas. The relation of loss to maturing of identity was a process that subsequently would itself become the organizing theme of Proust's later major opus. In *On Reading*, Proust already actualizes his personal individuating even as he describes the role of reading in that service (Proust 1994).

The essay begins with Proust describing how central reading was to his childhood: "On no days of our childhood did we live so fully perhaps as those we thought we had left behind without living them, those that we spent with a favourite book" (Proust 1994, p. 3). But Proust went further and brought forward dynamics of reading that underlie the idyllic image painted.

In contrast to Ruskin, who viewed reading as instruction, Proust saw reading as incitement. He considered the greatest power of reading came from a text's stimulation of the reader's mind, its opening of the mind to new possibilities far beyond the mere transmission of information. Incitement!

Is not inciting to new openness also the heart of the analytic situation? Proust emphasized that the author–reader conversation differs radically from ordinary conversation, just as does analytic conversation. That difference starts in the *asymmetry* (Proust's word) of give and take between author/analyst, on the one hand, and reader/analysand, on the other.

Just as psychological structural change requires more than transference cures, Proust similarly insisted on "incitement" as the power of reading to awaken and stir the mind. He wrote, "[Reading] becomes dangerous ... when, instead of awakening us to the personal life of the mind, reading tends to take its place" (White 1999, p. 36). He was saying what 14 years later Freud said when he warned, "The patient should be educated to liberate and fulfill his own nature, not to resemble ourselves" (Freud 1919, p. 165).

In his 1905 essay Proust (1994, p. 33) highlights another similarity between reading and analysis, addressing those difficult times when each seems insufficient in power. In this instance, he makes the comparison explicit:

> There are certain cases ... in which reading may become a sort of curative ... reintroducing a lazy mind in perpetuity into the life of the mind. Books then play a role for it analogous to that of psychotherapists with certain neurasthenics ... In certain conditions ... the patient is mired in a kind of impossibility of willing, as if in a deep rut, from which he cannot extract himself on his own ... He is incapable of willing those various actions, which he would be capable of performing.

Proust saw the special value reading can provide as beyond so limited a function, just as psychoanalysis holds to a depth of new openings beyond the symptom relief sought by general therapies. Also, just as Freud was concerned with what factors might render analysis interminable, so too Proust carefully thought about what might be called reading interminable, finding it the result of characterological passivity.

Proust even recognized the power of resistance, the defensive nature of falsely submissive rather than actively engaged reading. "What happiness, what respite for a mind weary of seeking for the truth within, to tell itself that the truth is located outside, in the sheets of an in-folio" (Proust 1994, p. 37). In reading and in analysis, idealization and disowning of personal agency serve as masks to substitute for actual growth.

Alert to this danger, Proust also spoke – as analysts do today – of the question of authority. While the author (or analyst) has significant partial authority, it is the reader who keeps the inner last word. In that sense, both reading and analysis differ from conventional conversational give and take. Proust again is explicit:

> Reading being *the exact opposite of conversation* in consisting for each one of us in having another's thought communicated to us while remaining on our own, that is while continuing to enjoy the intellectual authority we have in solitude and which conversation dispels instantly, while continuing to be open to inspiration, with our mind yet working hard and fruitfully on itself.
>
> (Proust 1994, p. 26; emphasis added)

Thus, the author/analyst does not provide the other's new world view but merely works to shape the possibility of its opening. Again, Proust:

> To make it [reading] into a discipline [i.e., instruction] is to give too large a role to what is only an incitement. Reading is on the threshold of the spiritual life; it can show us the way into it; it does not constitute it.
>
> (Proust 1994, p. 32)

Those words could serve as a motto for psychoanalytic discipline, for the analyst's facilitating insight rather than imposing an indoctrination, for the analyst's remembering that analysis exists for life, not life for analysis.

What matters ultimately is the reader's experience, transforming the words taken in to an emotional engagement; what matters ultimately is how the analysand digests the clinical emotional experience. Almost as if he were addressing an audience of psychoanalysts, Proust speaks of creative forward motion:

> But the most elevated conversation and the most insistent advice are of no use to it [the reader's mind] either, for they cannot produce this original activity directly. What is needed, then, is an intervention which, though coming from another, is produced deep inside ourselves, the impulsion of another mind certainly, but received in the midst of our solitude.
>
> (Proust 1994, p. 35)

Even in the reader's conversation with the author, one is always "in the midst of our solitude." It is the same in clinical practice where the engagement matters as it is digested and assimilated within the solitary privacy of a patient's mind. Psychoanalysis like "reading works only in the manner of an incitement" (Proust 1994, p. 35), one offered "in the midst of ... solitude."

Etymological development confirms our observations; the origin of the word "reading" itself reveals the process at hand. Long before the word referred, as now it most commonly does, to the supposedly passive taking in of what is written outside oneself, the word spoke of *actively* deliberating, considering, and attending to (*Oxford English Dictionary*). Reading originally implied a dominating activity. "The original senses of the Teut. verb are those of *taking or giving counsel, taking care or charge of a thing, having or exercising control over something,* etc." (*Oxford English Dictionary*; emphasis added). One must forego the activity of domination of the other in order to take in incitements that then can free one from defensive passivity and allow an active stance regarding impulses, urges, and fantasies.

The borderline between liberating and influencing by teaching is as hazy as that between psychoanalytic inquiry and therapy. Yet both work to stir a mind to activity, not to passive reception. Incitement of a mind from fixed knowledge and fantasy to ever more open possibilities was as central a goal for Proust in reading as for Freud in analyzing.

On reading Proust

We turn now to Proust's grand work, *À la recherche du temps perdu*, knowing how broad is the ocean from which we take so small a sample. (Dr. Johnson complained of this problem by saying that such examples reminded him of the pedant who, having a house for sale, carried a brick in his pocket as a sample.) Nonetheless, we can select cogent snippets for the sake of illustration.

At issue in *À la recherche du temps perdu* is the partial loss of self in an engagement with an other and the possibilities for change and growth that come from working through that loss. Shengold trenchantly observed, "Every step away from the primal everything toward the establishment of an identity must be paid for since it involves a loss" (1991, p. 9). The tale of Marcel is such a tale of desire, of profound longing for union, and ultimately of the disillusionment that liberates. An engaged reader can share the experience.

Proust uses authorial techniques that facilitate pulling the reader into the story. He blurs the lines between the protagonist Marcel, the narrator, and the author. The effect is akin to that of the analytic situation where the ties of conventional society are loosened to facilitate regression. Proust pulls the reader into a haze of boundaries with shifting identifications. Then, after prolonged observation, exploration, and investigation, he ends the journey in a manner like that of the termination phase of a successful analysis: waking succeeds dreaming, ghosts are recognized, new self images are sharpened, and the traveler has new strength to turn passivity into personal activity.

Behind the universe of observations about society and about human dynamics, this is a story of longing and loss. The ultimate desire driving the tale appears always to be that of establishing union, primarily and initially for Marcel with his mother and in derivative contexts with his grandmother, with aristocratic society, with his lovers, with Albertine. Desire is for union; horror is of separation and isolation; consolation is taken in imagining oneself as related.

In this novel as it was with his earlier essay, the struggles in the literary work reflect those in the author, with the written novel itself attesting to Proust's success. Reviewing biographies of Proust, Aciman (2002) saw conflict over intimacy as central to both Proust's life and his writing. Dealing in the novel with the death of his grandmother, Marcel lies sobbing in bed next to the wall on which boy and old woman had tapped their connections and thinks, "She was my grandmother and I am her grandson." Observing that Proust was able to start writing *À la recherche* three years after his mother died, only when no one was left to "knock back," Aciman saw the writing itself as an inner effort of reunion. The driving force of unconscious fantasy remains, but the power of disillusion and of accepting loss frees one for active creativity.

Now, back to *À la recherche* itself. To read Proust's great work is to take a journey through a magical hall of mirrors, a maze of reflections of life and on life, where one often feels lost in long hallways and then turns a corner into a moment of incisive clarity; where one often feels confused by endlessly shifting associations only to be charmed by a magically apt and frequently witty insight; where, through several wandering volumes, one wonders if there will ever be an end, arriving at last at an ending where there is a person changed, a character integrated, a life put into action. It is impossible to read Proust without at times feeling at sea, without sometimes feeling sad, but also without many times laughing aloud. In contrast to the reading of a case report, how very like it is to the actual experience of an analysis, the mostly confusing but generally moving travel through an individual psychoanalytic experience.

A labyrinth of mirrors is especially apt as a metaphor because the volumes are reflections and reflections on reflections. And as the reflections on reflections in a clinical analysis pull the emotions of the analyst into the experience of the stories the patient tells, so do these at times confusing multiple reflections pull the reader into Marcel's experience. Analyst and reader are ever oscillating, in and out, experiencing and becoming detached. Indeed, Proust both represents and demands that oscillation by creating *two* speakers, the narrator and Marcel, switching subtly back and forth between the two so that the reader loses some of the sense of himself and inevitably becomes both part of and apart from the emotional experiences. Inner and outer, self and other, illusion and reality – all become mixed in the transitional land of reading Proust and of an analytic hour.

In the book's famous opening line, Marcel tells us, "For a long time I used to go to bed early." The voice, to start, is the "I" of Marcel, the protagonist. Subtly, however, the voice shifts back and forth between Marcel and the narrator and also between Marcel, narrator, and reader. In the passage cited earlier on idyllic reading, Marcel reminisces about the pleasures of reading in childhood. He speaks of "the emotions aroused in me" and "the action in which I was taking part" (Proust 1981, Vol. I, p. 91). Then, turning to the reader, he slides over to "we." (How very like Sterba's [1934] use of the "we" to effect an ego split and analytic alliance.) Indeed, we cannot even be certain whether it is Marcel's or the narrator's voice we hear. What is clear is that the reader is now taking part. The words in the book are "It is in ourselves that they [the actions and emotions] are happening," that "the novelist has brought us to this state" (p. 92). Who are "ourselves" and who is speaking to whom? We have no choice but to be part of what unfolds.

Barthes (cited by White 1999, p. 164) speculated that Proust's capacity to tell the story in the first person so that "I" slides from author to narrator to hero was one of the conditions that permitted Proust to move from writing fragments to writing his great novel. The novel, like the psychoanalytic situation, calls forth ghosts by dimming the lights that shine on boundaries. The confusingly shifting voices come together with a singularity only in the integration that follows prolonged working out and working through, only in the "termination phase" of the final volume of the series, *Le temps retrouvé, Time Refound*.

Like a detective story, like an algebra problem, like a clinical analysis, much comes clear and comes to be seen differently only in the end. And what comes clear is now not only freshly understood, but changed, as Proust finally appreciates how present experience recreates the mind's sense of past relationships, "casting them in an original creation" (Proust 1981, Vol. III, p. 73). *Time Refound*, the final of the several volumes, provides a clarity that informs as Marcel moves from seemingly endless reflection to a capacity to act, indeed to the very writing of the novel as manifest proof of such activity.

Many have read the charming *Swann in Love* that opens the introductory volume *Swann's Way*, yet likely few have followed all the way to *Time Refound*. For those who do not have the necessary literary patience that matches the *sitzfleish* needed to stay with an analysis to its termination but who are genuinely interested to learn what Proust has to conclude, reading the last half of the last volume is invaluable. For there Marcel and narrator are no longer split, indeed Marcel and narrator and Proust are no longer split. United, character united, Marcel Proust can move from reflecting to acting, turning the inner reflections into the outer activity of writing. Marcel the character and Proust the man can act.

It is in *Time Refound* that the nature of memory is described, that its elusive evanescence is drawn out, and that its relationship to unfolding experience and sensation is critically defined. This is the area of most concern to us as we try to discover what as psychoanalytic practitioners we can learn from Proust.

Just as Proust demonstrates with his writing style the quality of free association, however, it seems appropriate to ramble just a bit more before ending, at last, with the matter of termination. In one more diversion concerned with both reading and analysis, I would like to add a few words about translation.

Memory and the sensation of experience, relationships, longing and disillusionment – these are identified as both the underlying subjects and the manifest content of the story. But with both Proust's work and clinical analysis, reflecting and translating are the processes by which we approach our subjects, take part in our subjects, and step back to add the insights that contribute to change in our subjects and change in ourselves. An author first translates a fantasy when he writes, and the reader translates it yet again when he carries what he reads into his own inner world. A patient translates emotional experience into words when he speaks; the analyst translates those words when he listens; he translates them further when he interprets; and the patient translates them yet again when trying to digest them. Translation is a problem always at work in a reading and always at work in an analysis, even when author/analyst and reader/analysand seem to share the same language. Study of translation may clarify processes present in all communications, even within what seems to be a single language. By way of example, let us briefly consider translation of just the title of the work at hand. *À la recherche du temps perdu*. In its first major English translation, those words were rendered through a line from Shakespeare, *Remembrance of Things Past*. Now, the title has been transformed into a schoolboy's more literal *In Search of Lost Time*. Each is a translation; each, being a translation, loses something.

In its poetic context, *Remembrance of Things Past* does approach the mood Proust likely intended, that of an emotional experience of loss and longing. Its great limitations are with the words "remembrance" and "things." As a noun, "remembrance" seems to speak more of content and subject than of effort and activity. The problem when those words stand on their own decreases when the Shakespearean sonnet from which the phrase comes is allowed to resonate: "When to the sessions of sweet silent thought/ I summon up remembrance of things past." Summoning those remembrances may well be the essence of Proust's title.

As we know from Proust as well as from clinical experience, successful summoning comes not from active seeking and logical interrogation but from a way of being open to sensations that allows and welcomes rather than chases after memory.

It is in that sense that Shakespeare's 30th sonnet fittingly expresses both Proust's ideas and classical analytic ideas about memory, about mental representation as standing for the lost object, the outcome of loss, longing, and summoning. Shakespeare's sonnet makes that explicit, saying "I sigh the lack of many a thing I sought" and ends with the couplet "But if the while I think on thee, dear friend,/ All losses are restored and sorrows end." The "things" that seems off the mark in the translated title of Proust's work refers not to objects in the colloquial sense of the word but in the psychoanalytic sense, that of emotional attachments. How at once both very Proustian and very Freudian, the irrelevance of objects as things-in-themselves rather than as carriers of meaning born in emotional relationships.

These days, Shakespeare's sonnets are not of such ready currency as to effect their power on modern readers. So we turn to the translation *du jour*, the translation in fashion but likely also due to suffer its own transience, that of *In Search of Lost Time*. Is that quite right? Perhaps, but a few words remind us of the need for modesty in the acceptance of any single understanding when dealing with a translation.

"*In* Search" and "*À* la Recherche." The English is "in," but the French "à" can mean not only "in," as in "à Paris" for "in Paris," but also "to" or "toward." The sense of effort, of reaching out toward, the very sense of stretching to try to find – all are diminished by the English word "in." And what of "recherche"? "To search" in French is "chercher," familiar in the common phrase "cherchez la femme" as well as "rechercher." "Rechercher" is properly translated as "to search," but to the Anglophone ear it strongly carries an implication of "research." "Research" in English has a scientific laboratory flavor that misses the usual effect of adding "re-" to a word. The word loses the flavor Proust likely was emphasizing, that of searching and then searching again and then searching still more. And what of "temps"? "Time" seems apt, but the word "temps" in French carries richer connotations of weather, of matters closer to emotional climate.

Rosenzweig (Scholem 2002, p. 118), himself a historically famous translator, wrote, "Only someone who is inwardly convinced of its impossibility can be a translator. ... There is no such thing as a simple linguistic fact." Beyond what is written or spoken on the lines, it is in the space between the lines that full meaningful engagement can come to life. It is there that there is room for new openings and growth through engagement in reading or in psychoanalysis. Writers and analysts can succeed in helping open others' minds only if they know and respect the limits of translation, the impossibility of precise communication.

A closing illustration: termination

Now, let us at last turn for an illustrative specimen to a particular moment in reading *À la recherche*. The process of change in Marcel in the book, the parallel process of change in an immersed reader, and the process of change in a psychoanalytic patient all resonate. For our own closing we narrow our attention to the closing of the story and to similarities with the closing of a psychoanalysis.

As it would be for a successful lengthy analysis, so is it also a bit silly to try to summarize *À la recherche* in a paragraph or two, but a quick statement may nonetheless be of benefit. The novel, as described, opens notably with the young Marcel's inability to fall asleep as he desperately longs for his mother's kiss. Then, over the course of almost 3000 pages, Marcel grows and spends his life seeking unavailable love, whether in the form of acceptance by the aristocratic world after whom he hungers or of possession of his desired Albertine, his detached longed-for lover, an equally unsatisfying other after whom he also hungers. En route, Marcel and the narrator make profound observations about people and society, but gradually and inexorably Marcel becomes bored, feels jaded, in the end feeling detached even from himself.

The final of the original 12 volumes is entitled *Le temps retrouvé: Time Refound* or *Time Regained*. In it, the weary older Marcel dispiritedly attends yet one more grand party, one destined to be the last in the book. Alighting from his carriage, Marcel feels himself trip on cobblestones; then, while waiting to join the gathering, he hears the ring of a teaspoon against a cup; and finally he feels the crispness of a napkin against his face. Each of these three sensations recalls a flood of previously lost memories, vital recollections similar to those recalled earlier after dipping a madeleine into tea. Now, however, Marcel is different, and that difference is crucial. Thinking back to his experience with the madeleine, Marcel now recognizes that the enjoyment of the earlier memory was pleasant but wasted. As Shattuck put it, "The ultimate moment of the book is not a *moment bienheureux* [a happy moment] but a recognition" (2000, p. 135). What counts is not transient reminiscence but the use to which one puts those memories, what analysts might call the working through of insight.

It is here character change crystallizes with an outcome that places all that went before in a new light. Here it is as it is in analysis. Interpretation has aptly been called "a commemorative event" (Hall, personal communication), but insight is more than a victory parade after long emotional battles. Full appreciation of the past permits new possibilities in the future. It is an opening into new prospects, new potentials, new beginnings.

When the musical performance that blocked Marcel from immediate entry into the party is completed, Marcel joins the crowd. Then, in a scene both brilliantly witty and piercingly sad, Marcel faces former friends, confused by how old they all look, troubled by realizing how old he must now appear to them. Seeing people more for themselves and recognizing himself more truly for who he now is come not as separate forces but as an integrated unitary process.

With appreciation of his own role in creating the world as a place in which he was bound ever to seek his missing mother, always chasing ghosts that always receded beyond his fingertips, Marcel now realizes more fully for the first time his own powers, what analysts speak of as his agency. "Ideas come to us as the successors to griefs, and griefs, at the moment when they change into ideas, lose some part of their power to injure our heart" (Proust 1981, Vol. III, p. 944). Marcel now realizes that all of his search – his working toward, his working out, and his working through – were preparation that made possible his own more freely self-determined life. At last he can act, and he knows that his way to do that is to write.

To read Proust's own behavior in his final years as reclusive is to misread it perversely. In the closing of the *magnum opus*, Marcel and Proust have come together. Proust's withdrawal from the social scene was for him not a withdrawal from life but, more truly, a turning *to* life. Now fervent for creative engagement and painfully aware of how little time he had, he threw himself into his newly possible work with unbound passion. Despite the conventional appearance of social withdrawal, Proust was choosing a life of action, the life of actively writing.

For brevity's sake, I outline only a bit of the parallel between the ending of *Le temps retrouvé* and the termination phase of an analysis. Dreams can become sources of replenishment rather than solely engulfing traps of quicksand; idealization as a way of obscuring longing and disappointment can give way to appreciation of loves lost; diminishing grandiosity and omnipotence can permit endless mourning to be replaced by grieving; and entanglement in the dream world of transference can diminish so that insistence on passive satisfaction can make way for activity in the world of finite actuality.

As already mentioned, boundaries have been hazy throughout the novel until its end, just as they are through so much of a clinical engagement when reality testing is set aside and the transference is felt to be fully true in its own right. Throughout the long text as throughout an analysis, the boundaries between the minds fade and sharpen, re-fade and re-sharpen, repeatedly.

A self becomes clearer as boundaries become clearer, both in *À la recherche* and in an analysis. Only once in the work does Proust (1981, Vol. III, p. 147) make the unity of Marcel and the author explicit. He does so when he is describing separateness rather than merger, speaking of one person's "possessing" another. Marcel thinks of Albertine's awakening as he watches her sleeping. Then Proust writes in the text,

Then she would find her tongue and say: "My—" or "My darling—" followed by my Christian name, which, if we give the narrator the same name as the author of this book, would be "My Marcel," or "My darling Marcel."

And only one other time in the work does Proust sharply break the frame and acknowledge himself as author of the world in the book being read. At that moment he turns directly to the reader of the book so as to name the family Larivière, the actual name of real people, not merely characters in the fiction of the book, heroes who he feels merit recognition in the world at large because of their contribution to the survival of France (Proust 1981, Vol. III, pp. 876–877). Putting into words and, importantly, giving both people and feelings their proper names are essential to sharpening hazy views, crucial to gaining inner freedom and crystallizing and integrating identity.

In *Le temps retrouvé*, Marcel and narrator and even Proust himself all come to face prior idealizations and to see others more for who they actually are rather than for whom one would have wanted and believed them to be. Such resolution opens passivity into possibilities of fresh activity without relentless regression into fixation. Letting go of an illusory nirvana brings with it a wider range of new possibilities in life, broadening ways of living, of feeling, of dreaming. Self and others, hopes and fears and regrets, permanence and transience – all can be faced with less determined distortion as *À la recherche* and as an analysis resolve. The mood at the end is one of appreciation but disengagement in order to go forth in the world.

The experience of an analytic journey or the engagement of reading a novel is similar to the passage through a dream, and the ending of each, with its return to the world of daily reality, entails both gain and loss. Waking ends the ephemeral atmosphere in which one had lived only a moment before.

Proust succeeded well in describing the joy and the sadness of that transition and in making clear the character change that ensued. As Marcel was able not only to experience moments like those with the madeleine – moments of sensation that ring so immediately true as to have become known throughout western civilization as "Proustian," so was he by virtue of his emotional inner journey also able to use those moments to become a new man, a man changed in a way that left him able to be more, not less, himself. Marcel and Proust both became newly able to act in self-determined ways. And the reader, a reader who gives himself over to experiencing the book and who lets in the book's incitements, comes to know anew both the experience of opening and awakening and that of the sadness of loss, the grief when a shared universe closes.

Success implies loss, but it is the very acceptance of that loss and renunciation of the demand for direct satisfaction that makes possible new life. That is so for waking from a dream, allowing one to face the break of day. That is so for foregoing the demands of transference longings, allowing an analysand to engage the possibilities of a current life. That is so for Marcel's letting go of his profound desire for his mother's kiss as if it would be actualized through acceptance in a society from which he felt excluded. It was a letting go that allowed him to become a creative adult, a man in his own right. Proust tells us all of that while Marcel awaits entry to what would be the final party in the book. The party is over. Marcel and Proust now each can write, and we move from being identifying participants to becoming witnesses apart.

A novel must come to its end, while a life after analysis, happily, can go on. Hans Sachs commented that in completing an analysis one has scratched the surface of a continent. Termination does not imply closure on essential human inner conflicts. Self-analysis replaces formal analysis, so that introspection can continue even as, and indeed because, core issues have been mastered. In contrast to transient commercial bestsellers, literary classics do not necessarily end with all conflicts finally resolved, all threads neatly tied together. Yet completion of reading a great work can leave a bittersweet satisfaction like that in ending an analysis, the sense of achievement of important insight and mastery even as more uncertainty lies ahead.

In closing

In writing on truth in fiction, Hanly noted that "psychoanalysis and great literature share a common object of observation. That common object is psychic reality. The greater the work of literature, the more it tallies with what is most fundamental to psychic reality" (2003). We analysts feel proudly protective of that which only psychoanalytic exploration can provide, yet credit must be paid to the valuable insight and growth that have been available through drama and fiction since time immemorial.

Like an analyst with an analysand, an author invites his reader into an inner world, facilitating engagement so as to incite the reader's mind. Freud and Proust were both geniuses of engagement and insight. And though both Freud and Proust have been accused of grandiosity, both indeed were modest in their full recognition of the dauntless challenge they faced.

Proust was explicit that

> the essential, the only true book, though in the ordinary sense of the word it does not have to be "invented" by a great writer – for it exists already in each of us – has to be translated by him. The function and the task of a writer [and, we can add, an analyst] are those of a translator.
>
> (Proust 1981, Vol. III, p. 926)

The task is incitement, the struggle to open a mind.

Like a successful analyst, Proust takes us with him and artistically captures much of our human universe as he struggles to summon lost remembrances. Finally, with time refound, like an analyst, Proust discovers that such refinding alone is not enough, that the uses of such refinding matter much. Proust began by having Marcel say that for a long time he used to go to bed early. Like a successful analyst, he ends by helping us awaken to life.

References

Aciman, A. (2002). Proust regained. *The New York Review of Books*, July 18, pp. 55–61.

Auden, W.H. (1939). In memory of Sigmund Freud. In *Collected Papers*. New York: Random House, 1979.

Bate, W.J. & Strauss, A.B., eds. (1969). *Samuel Johnson: The Rambler, Vol. 2*. New Haven, CT: Yale University Press.

Freud, S. (1919). Lines of advance in psycho-analytic therapy. *Standard Edition*, 17:157–168.

Hanly, C. (2003). On fictional truth. Unpublished.

Holland, N. (1968). *The Dynamics of Literary Response*. New York: Columbia University Press, 1989.

Holland, N. (1975). *5 Readers Reading*. New Haven, CT: Yale University Press.

Proust, M. (1981). *Remembrance of Things Past*. Three volumes. New York: Random House.

Proust, M. (1994). *On Reading*. London: Penguin Books.

Scholem, G. (2002). *A Life in Letters, 1914–1982*. Cambridge, MA: Harvard University Press.

Shattuck, R. (2000). *Proust's Way: A Field Guide to In Search of Lost Time*. New York: W.W. Norton.

Shengold, L. (1991). *"Father, Don't You See I'm Burning."* New Haven, CT: Yale University Press.

Sterba, R. (1934). The fate of the ego in analytic therapy. *International Journal of Psychoanalysis*, 15:117–126.

White, E. (1999). *Marcel Proust*. New York: Viking/Penguin Lives.

Chapter 14

Psychoanalysis and culture

The future strength of psychoanalysis will be determined less by what is newly discovered in the psychoanalytic consulting room than by how psychoanalysis engages with the culture at large.

For more than a century, individual psychoanalyses have led to the liberation of numberless individuals. The enrichment of the world through each personal analytic benefit, plus its spreading cumulative benefits through impact on others, is incalculable. Nonetheless, the full force of the Freudian revolution did not result primarily from the direct effects of individual analyses. While those were the source of analytic insights, it was the spread of the new ideas themselves and the new way of exploring the mind that changed the world.

Since Freud's time, the energies of the psychoanalytic movement have become constituted mainly around clinical analysis. Ironically, it is in those places where analysis has been tied most tightly to its clinical activities that the interest of new patients in analytic treatment seems to be drying up. Where psychoanalysis has unfolded most broadly throughout the culture, where analytic voices are most integrated into discussions of art, literature, politics, history and so forth – in those places individuals seem most readily open to accepting appropriate recommendations for analytic therapy.

The conclusion appears self-evident: psychoanalysis thrives best when it moves beyond guild-like preoccupations and focuses more of its energy on substantial engagement with the broader world in all its myriad aspects.

Realistic as is this argument, it remains essentially in the service of clinical concerns. Fortunately, behind considerations of the practical problems of the profession lie deeper motives within psychoanalysis, passions essential to the field itself. These are urges so central as to be in the very genetic makeup of psychoanalysis: profound curiosity about how humanity works plus the powerful desire to advance with understanding and thus enrich (not just heal) the world. These drives now demand return of psychoanalytic resources to the world of culture in its countless incarnations.

Schneider (2010) argued (1) that analysis of culture generated new psychoanalytic knowledge, (2) that such learning from analysis of culture could inform new understandings for clinical analytic technique, and (3) that analysis of culture is essential to the survival of established psychoanalysis in a changing world.

Blinders to any aspect of human life are antithetical to a psychoanalytic attitude of inquiry. For the sake of illustration of both relevance and potentialities, I select but one illustration, choosing from an endless number of possibilities. It is the impact of virtual reality on the psyche.

We are in these times confronted by a disquieting natural experiment in development. Today a growing child is offered the possibility of engagement with a world that can *seem* to be human but that *is not*, the world of virtual reality. What happens to the developing "I" when the seeming "Thou" of others is actually a nonhuman program? What then happens to the capacity for sensitivity to others?

A child comes into the world equipped with curiosity and with instincts to mastery, as well as with nascent executive functions. How those inner forces, along with other innate drives, meet the outer world, and how they are dealt with by that outer world are the tales of character development and interpersonal history. Principles of morality may be more shaken by the creation of virtual others than they were by the death of God.

Virtual reality simulates both actual and imaginary worlds; being engaged with virtual reality feels very much like actually "being there." The reason sexual drives are significant in the genesis of neurosis has been speculated to be that they are the only drives that can be self-satisfied, relieved through fantasy and masturbation. Does the new opportunity for engagement with an artificial virtual other now present a newly developed parallel for aggression? Might the new ability to seem to satisfy immediate object hunger or to destroy the other in a virtual reality interfere with hitherto normal development of self and capacity for relatedness?

We have learned much from both clinical analytic investigation and from disciplined infant observation. Yet such investigations remain in a relatively early stage, perhaps necessarily early since the world in which a child now grows is itself changing qualitatively. We cannot wait for another generation to mature before studying the effects of early involvement with virtual reality three decades later in adults.

Analytically sophisticated serious workers in other disciplines are already making major advances, a prime example to be found in *Alone Together: Why We Expect More from Technology and Less from Each Other* by Turkle (2011), director of the MIT Initiative on Technology and Self. How does character alter when people expect less from each other, indeed even less know otherness?

There is much to do and much to learn. Applied psychoanalysis of literature, film, history, art, biography, etc., already exists. Islands of psychoanalysts do such work, many actively engaged in conversations with workers in other fields, learning and teaching, working together with others to advance knowledge in common. Their contributions are valuable, although the institutional support they have been given has been slight.

Psychoanalysis will always require its tap root to be fed from the depths of individual clinical analytic inquiries. With that source secure, to bear most fruit the analytic plant must also grow above ground where it can be best nourished by the light of actively engaged exchanges with other cultural disciplines.

It is time for such psychoanalytic engagement with the entire world of educated inquiry and creativity to resume its proper place alongside clinical work at the forefront of psychoanalytic activities. As Schneider (2010, p. 23) aptly observed, "Freud the *clinical psychoanalyst* would not have existed at all without the Freud who was deeply connected with culture, and, conversely, Freud the *psychoanalytic cultural theorist* is indissociably connected with Freud the *clinician*."

References

Schneider, G. (2010). Culture and psychoanalysis. *International Psychoanalysis*, 18:22–23.
Turkle, S. (2011). *Alone Together: Why We Expect More from Technology and Less from Each Other*. New York: Basic Books.

Chapter 15

The mind beyond conflict

Whimsy

As I was walking up the stair
I met a man who wasn't there
He wasn't there again today
Oh, how I wish he'd go away.
(Mearns 1922)

Without the safety to let one's mind play, without the freedom to think any thought just for the fun of imagining, we might find that childhood rhyme terrifying. Yet most of us hearing it are amused, not frightened. Although the poem threatens both the dependability of what one sees with one's own eyes and the logic of what one thinks with one's own mind, the little doggerel delights by being whimsical. Indeed, it is a pleasure not because it denies logic and senses, but because it toys with them as if they were mere playthings.

Many years ago, I tried to think through some of the development of a sense of humor, both the nature of humor itself and the gift of laughter (Poland 1996). Yet each time I tried to grasp whimsy, I was stopped, unable to hold it in my hands.

In the many years since then, I have continued to think about the subject. When I saw something whimsical, I was amused; but whenever I tried to reason out the nature of whimsy, I felt bemused. How could it be that something could give me so very much pleasure yet I could never grasp it? I tried. I failed. I tried again and I failed again. Over and over and over.

As a psychoanalyst, I am familiar with missing the point, with having to listen repeatedly before I begin at last to realize what is being said. (Whenever my vanity has me feel I have overcome that weakness, analysands with whom I work quickly remind me of it. As one remarked with exasperation, "You can be brilliant at being stupid.")

Sometimes, the problem has been my listening too hard, my trying to hear too much. Just as there are images that can be seen only from the corner of one's eyes and there are messages that can be read only between the lines, so are there experiences that can be appreciated only by valuing what is not directly noticed and recognized. At times, the most important messages come to one in ricochet fashion.

That, of course, was my problem in thinking about whimsy. I was so determined to take hold of its nature that I long resisted the realization that its ungraspability may be the very essential point.

Whimsy is a wit soufflé – light, sweet, and quickly disappearing. Made too rich, it falls flat; made too sweet, it is saccharine and precious. To succeed, even to survive, it must be delicate, light, and evanescent. Humor helps, but humor is not essential. On the other hand, fear, danger, loss, and unhappiness can have no place. As in playing with balloons, it is the pleasure of lightness that counts the most. Ideally, one could play with a balloon from which the containing rubber skin had been removed. Soap bubbles, where nothing of the soap remains but its shining iridescence. The smile without the Cheshire cat.

There is an old popular song advising one to "catch a falling star and put it in your pocket." That line has whimsy without being droll. It is not whimsical because it is a metaphor, nor even because it is an effective metaphor; it is whimsical to the extent that it floats.

The poem of the man on the stair who isn't there and yet who won't go away is whimsical not because it is paradoxical or ironic, but because in a way that seems lighter than air it suggests that even reality, one's senses, and logic can be playthings.

What does the dictionary tell us? Webster (1973) calls whimsy a whim or caprice, "a fanciful or fantastic device, object, or creation." More modern Encarta (2009) gives two definitions: the first is an "endearing quaintness or oddity," and the second an "impulsive notion, an idea that has no immediately obvious reason to exist."

A whim or caprice is born from a person's inner impulses, a desire or wish unburdened by the constraints either of the laws of reality or the restrictions of convention and morality. A caprice is where one "just feels like it," apart from inner imperatives or the demands of outer reality: "I felt like doing a somersault." The oddity lies in the absence of convention and familiarity; the endearing quality speaks to the setting aside of danger from inside or outside, from self or other.

However, even though the lightness is a product of creative style, the energy must have arisen from an inner impulse – yet with whim it must be an impulse not driven by urgency. A caprice can never be an urge driven by compulsion. "No immediately obvious reason to exist": the game is afoot for the fun of the game. Like a person's dancing simply for the pleasure of feeling the music of movement rather than the need to perform, and like a wit's expressing a pun for the play of the words rather than the import of the message, whimsy arises from desire embodied in the pleasure of expression and expressive mastery rather than conflictual, vital need. Or, if there is a need, it is like the need for unencumbered luxury we all feel at times. Perhaps it is akin to a satisfied infant's playing with its mother's nipple. Contentedness and the fun of playing rather than insistent resolution of conflicts are necessary conditions for whimsy.

No, it is not reasonable to assume there can be any human activity entirely removed from underlying urges. Even sublimation has its sources. Yet must the pressure of drive and the demands of execution always imply inexorable conflict? Many forces combine to result in any seemingly singular instant of behavior or feeling. Often those forces would clash before yielding to each other in a final outcome of compromise, but there are moments when forces do not clash head-on. Rather, they aim mostly in the same direction, as if some would tilt a bit more to the right and others a bit more to the left, while chiefly reinforcing each other.

Aggression and sexuality, narcissism, the internalized voice of criticism and restriction, the constraints of reality – all of these are readily apparent when we think of conflict and compromise. How easy it is for us to leave for last in line – if not to forget entirely – the instinct to mastery, with its attendant pleasures of expression and even creativity, at times the fruit of internalized voices of admiration and encouragement.

Whimsy, thus, may result not only from the liberation following peaceful resolution of conflict; it may also thrive in less conflicted areas where security, encouragement, love, and constitutional talent have flourished. When sublimation is permitted free sway, the instinct to mastery (Hendrick 1943) yields the pleasure of function fulfilled. Such is the land where whimsy dwells. Whimsy may derive from substantial conflict mastered or it may mainly express more autonomous skills. Some whimsies are born free, some achieve freedom, and some have freedom thrust upon them.

Whatever the underlying urges, conflicts, and fantasies, the very nature of whimsy is the playfulness of contentedness, the freedom when the instinct for mastery has succeeded and the individual can take pleasure in its functional pleasure. The shadow of more urgent drives may at moments still be evident. However, when those conflictual elements are so untamed as still to be recognizable, we recognize antics and pranks more than whimsy.

I realize now that the incident that triggered my earlier study of the development of the sense of humor was itself a moment of whimsy nascent, a manifestation of delight in growth and the instinct for mastery. "The 16-month-old child walked into the living room, bent over, put a piece of bread on her foot, looked up at the adults present, announced 'Shoe,' and burst out laughing" (Poland 1996, p. 178). The broad delight the child's "joke" elicited was the shared pleasure in a new skill, one that evidenced both mastery and the capacity for enjoyment in creative play.

Clinical analysis not only can relieve symptoms, but also can unleash striking growth when one is liberated from long-standing inhibitions. A young reporter came for analysis paralyzed by indecisiveness. His need for absolutes and his inability to integrate mixed feelings left him frozen in the face of needed life decisions. It was with marked embarrassment that gradually his humor came to be exposed. He felt it to be "silly," the inane humor of a little boy, a humor that showed him to be cute but not an adult among adults. He first offered his "silly" humor as a symptom to be removed.

As oedipal conflicts were analyzed, as the young man was able to venture beyond his clinging to juniority and able to risk feeling and acting like a man among men, he began to value his native wit and whimsy, enjoying rather than squelching them. With his father away at war, he had been raised by a mother who did not seem responsive to his budding masculinity, who did not react warmly to his incipient charm. His humor, like his sexuality, were treated as signs of smallness and weakness, qualities to be overcome.

Now, feeling more respectful of himself and more secure in the world of adults, he became able to expose his humor in both social and professional circles. He was no longer ashamed of the childlike aspects of his imagination, and his increased freedom for fantasy allowed him a humor both creative and light. His capacity for whimsy was no longer inhibited.

I wonder whether one could ever satisfy the queries of an insurance company that new freedom for whimsy was evidence justifying the expense of a clinical analysis. Perhaps the problem is not merely with minds devoted to bookkeeping, but with the nature of whimsy itself. Whimsy is too light ever to allow strings to be attached. Whimsy must float free.

Even when whimsy may first be born in the stark emotional wars of early conflict, the resultant whimsy itself can only come into the light when no longer bound to those anxious roots. Greenacre (1955) incisively analyzes as equivalents of central screen memories core schema she elucidates and illustrates across the work of Lewis Carroll. Her conjectures about the underlying issues in Carroll's psychology are convincing. Nonetheless, much of the poetry that was the end product of Carroll's mastery and creativity can be read with unfettered pleasure as successful whimsy.

Sterne (1759–1769) has Tristram Shandy wonder whether the limitations of his life resulted from what was lost during his conception by his father's preoccupation with whether the clock had been wound. Sterne's humor achieves whimsy by virtue of its being delightful as playful thinking, an idea colored by but not bound by reality. Whatever origins are inferred or speculated, whether such origins are discovered psychoanalytically or themselves imaginatively conceived, the presence of whimsy is determined by emotional liberation from such thorny beginnings.

Yet even as whimsy would soar free from its origins, it may secondarily be put to other uses. Something can itself be conflict free and yet be put into the service of other conflicts, although the essence of whimsy is then lessened or lost. When something light is put to such secondary purpose, the person with so tendentious a goal will disavow what previously had been whimsical. "This is no mere whimsy of mine" proclaims the heaviness of one's argument as something not to be blown away as froth, as something that commands consideration and must have force. Caprice melts in the fire of battle.

With so much of life shaped by self justification, by positioning oneself in the world of others, by scoring points in debate, it is no wonder that successful whimsy seems out of place in the world of adults, that it so often is left aside to child's play, where supposedly innocent children are thought to know no better.

References

Encarta (2009). Whimsy. Retrieved from http://encarta.msn.com/encnet/refpages/search. aspx?q=whimsy.

Greenacre, P. (1955). "It's my own invention": a special screen memory of Mr. Lewis Carroll, its form and its history. *Psychoanalytic Quarterly*, 24:200–244.

Hendrick, I. (1943). Work and the pleasure principle. *Psychoanalytic Quarterly*, 12:311–329.

Mearns, W.H. (1922). Antigonish (or the little man who wasn't there). Retrieved from: http://en.wikipedia.org/wiki/William_Hughes_Mearns.

Poland, W. (1996). The gift of laughter: on the development of a sense of humor in clinical analysis. In *Melting the Darkness: The Dyad and Principles of Clinical Practice*. Northvale, NJ: Aronson.

Sterne, L. (1759–1769). *The Life and Opinions of Tristram Shandy, Gentleman*. Mineola, NY: Dover Publications, 2007.

Webster (1973). *Webster's New Collegiate Dictionary*. Springfield, MA: G. & C. Merriam Co.

Chapter 16

Pathologizing mental processes
Whimsy

> As I was walking up the stair
> I met a man who wasn't there
> He wasn't there again today
> Oh, how I wish he'd go away.
> (Mearns 1922)

As is my custom, I shared my discussion of that charming piece of doggerel with colleague friends, ever eager to hear helpful thinking. This time, however, along with valuable ideas, one reaction I heard unsettled me. Indeed, it startled me so strongly that for a while I withdrew from what I had written so as to have more time to reflect on my possibly seriously mistaken reasoning.

The disquieting response came from someone whose thinking I deeply value, whose thinking I never take lightly and certainly would never easily dismiss. What was so troublesome was not merely that she disagreed with my line of thought but that she felt it to be so deeply wrong as strongly to urge me *not* to publish my ideas, trying as a friend to protect me from the humiliation she was convinced was bound to ensue.

I valued my friend's critique, read it over and over, slept on its implications, and struggled to consider possible personal blind spots that might have led me astray. Nonetheless, my observations that a mind could be freed from its inevitable roots in psychological conflict and could then have areas of unencumbered play, even creative and enjoyable play, persisted.

Considerable time passed before I recalled something else about that specific friend, and that memory cast our apparent disagreement in a new light, one sad but cogent. What finally returned to my mind was that many years earlier my dear friend, a survivor of the horrors of the Holocaust, had lost a beloved brother in that evil. A loved brother lost in such a way, stolen and destroyed, left a wound that could never heal.

Emerson (2001, p. 199) wrote, "The only thing grief has taught me, is to know how shallow it is." Grief can truly be so devastating as to leave territory uninhabitable by the mind for a lifetime, areas of thinking and feeling that can never, never ever, be free or fit for play. "I met a man who wasn't there/ He wasn't there again today." For one who has suffered unfathomable loss, those words telling of a man who isn't there yet never goes away speak uncontainable heartbreak and mourning without end.

What to me was playful doggerel was to my friend a graveside *cri de couer*. That severe trauma can be so devastating as to make a territory forever a source of pain nonetheless does not rule out the possibility that some conflicts can be resolved, that their resolution can itself become a nutrient for full playfulness and fresh creativity.

Before settling on such an explanation, uncertainty commands one caveat. I very well may be wrong in what I now say are the implications for our different views of what is doggerel for me and perhaps unremitting grief for my friend. Attention must be paid to the risk of being self serving when finding congenial hypotheses.

Respecting the caveat, still the distinction between my personal delight in my understanding of conflict free whimsy and my friend's horror of such a view as necessarily a misreading stands and even highlights the considerations about freedom from conflict I propose. The repudiation of mental processes unencumbered by origins in conflict is, I believe, a view more pervasive in our field than often is appreciated. There seems to be a bias structured within analytic thinking, a bias that any turning of attention to non-conflictual thinking and play must be essentially defensive.

In his discussion of dreams, Freud (1900, p. 621) said that it is instructive to observe the much trampled soil from which our virtues proudly spring. We have generations of clinical experience laboring persistently and profitably to dig beyond the resistances under the topsoil of the mind, knowing that some work requires such labor that, like Freud, we speak at times of hitting bedrock.

A mind is supple, ever working to protect its secrets, and there is good reason for caution in our concern that seeming resolution may itself be subtle defense. One consequence, at times as faulty as it is understandable, is that as analysts we work so hard to explore the much trampled soil that we may often forget to consider, value, and examine the flowers that bloom from the roots in the soil.

A historically distant incident is illustrative, capturing in print the too common quality of repudiating anything that might threaten the imperishability of conflict. It appears in the intense reactions and debate that followed the appearance of Ives Hendrick's (1942) seminal paper on the instinct to mastery, the ego's function to resolve and move beyond instinctual urgencies. It is a publication ultimately deemed so valuable as to be republished 65 years later by *The Psychoanalytic Quarterly* (Hendrick 2007).

Hendrick's suggestion was that the workings of the adult mind, the adult ego, were not simply reproductions of infantile processes, nor that infantile processes necessarily had the censorious conflicts present in adults. He suggested that the mind had a pressure to master instincts and conflicts.

The idea of a mind's instinct to mastery seemed to trouble accepted analytic canon. A league of opposition arose, including some of the most significant thinkers of the day, such as Edward Bibring, Thomas French, Karl Menninger, and Robert Waelder. Much of the dispute now seems theoretical and perhaps dated, having to do with the relationship of the ego to the id, specifically with whether satisfactions from an ego based function didn't provide "forms of pleasure which are not themselves instinctual gratifications" (Hendrick 1943, p. 561). It was as if any consideration of the mind at work that did not end with crucial instinctual roots was distracting, somehow threatening to diminish the centrality of those sources.

Two particular problems that color and constrict our minds are so built into the nature of the psychoanalytic field that they may well be termed intrinsic flaws. One is general, having to do with the theoretical nature of thinking. The other, a problem perhaps unique to analysis, has to do with the very nature of psychoanalytic data.

First, let us consider the misuse of theory. In speaking of the distress stirred by Hendrick's contribution, I described an aspect of the hostile reaction as theoretical. Theory can be, of course, implicit, structured into any thought even when not noticed. Only an empty mind is devoid of all bias.

There is a price paid for such already present understanding. It is the narrowing of curiosity that can result from the comfort of previous understanding. As has been said, an understanding is a place where the mind comes to rest.

Theory organizes the accumulated knowledge of experience. Phenomenology, the actuality of experience, is altered as it is abstracted in the process of being described, then further altered with each increased level of abstraction. At times, actuality often seems to be lost at very high levels of inferential abstraction.

Theory certainly is essential, our way of accumulating knowledge, finding commonalities and distinctions, making categories, allowing our minds to work – yes, even to play – with ideas. Theory reminds us to look to areas we might otherwise ignore; it lets us open new questions for exploration.

We absolutely need theory, but we do not need absolute theory. Theory is always intrinsically wrong, always betraying the singular and particular nature of every unique experience. One could not analyze without an educated and informed readiness to look for what might otherwise seem absent, yet analytic inquiry turns too quickly to the analyst's confirmation of favored theories if the analyst allows theory to dominate open exploration.

Too often, the conclusions of analytic investigation can be predicted if one knows the theoretical school of the presenting analyst. Too often, theory protects an analyst from the anxiety of ignorance and uncertainty. Insufficient knowledge of psychoanalytic theory may be more minor a problem than is the analyst's misuse of theory to avoid the lost and helpless feeling of not understanding. The reassurance that comes from old understandings can relax the search for new.

Second, let us consider the nature of analytic data. Much has been learned from the study of culture in its broadest manifestations, spread horizontally across all aspects of human life and vertically across all time periods of history. There is a reason, however, that such study is termed "applied analysis."

Psychoanalytic Terms and Concepts, sponsored by the American Psychoanalytic Association and prepared and deeply researched by a broad swath of psychoanalytic scholars, defines applied analysis as "Use of insights and concepts gained from clinical psychoanalysis to enlarge and deepen the understanding of various aspects of human nature, culture, and society" (Moore & Fine 1990, p. 27).

The idea, broadly implicit in our literature, is explicit there: the primary data of psychoanalysis are those bits of knowledge gained in the specific context of clinical psychoanalytic experience.

The primary data of psychoanalysis are clinical. They derive from close examination of observations of associations with reflections on the interacting subjectivities of both partners in a highly disciplined psychoanalytic situation. Data that are most essential and determining develop in a clinical situation.

Unfortunately, the consequence of having our primary data derive from clinical work is the tendency of psychoanalysis to pathologize life. Freud called his masterpiece *The Psychopathology of Everyday Life* rather than *The Psychodynamics of Everyday Life*. He spoke of infantile polymorphously *perverse* sexuality rather than infantile polymorphously *normal* sexuality.

The tendency to see things always in terms of pathology is shaped and reinforced by having clinical work as our basic laboratory. This distortion of pathologizing what we see is present across our field. That certainly is evident when we consider the mind at play, when we turn to creativity.

When we consider creative artists, whatever their genre, we find our studies powerfully driven to the conflictual roots that are resolved within the creative acts. That, of course, emphatically matters, but it does not inform us about, and indeed it distracts us from, the nature of creative imagination and how creativity, sublimation, and free mental play work.

Too often these post-ego-psychological days, sublimation seems passé, like an old style now thought naively unfashionable. We must find a way so that when we search the index of our knowledge, the listing for "How the mind works" does not say "See Pathology."

"As I was walking up the stair / I met a man who wasn't there / He wasn't there again today / Oh, how I wish he'd go away." Without the safety to let one's mind play, without the freedom to think any thought just for the fun of imagining, we might find that childhood rhyme terrifying. Neither theoretical biases nor clinical preoccupations with pathology should blind us to the working of a mind amusing itself toying with impulses and ideas.

References

Emerson, R.W. (2001). Experience. In *Emerson's Prose and Poetry*, eds. Joel Porte & Saundra Morris. New York: W.W. Norton & Company, p. 199.

Freud, S. (1900). *The Interpretation of Dreams. S.E.* 4, ix–627.

Hendrick, I. (1942). Instinct and ego during infancy. *Psychoanalytic Quarterly*, 11:33–58.

Hendrick, I. (1943). The discussion of the "instinct to master" – a letter to the editors. *Psychoanalytic Quarterly*, 12:561–565.

Hendrick, I. (2007). Instinct and ego during infancy. *Psychoanalytic Quarterly*, 76:387–414.

Mearns, W.H. (1922). Antigonish (or the man who wasn't there). Retrieved from: http.//en.wikipedia.org/wiki/William_Hughes_Mearns.

Moore, B. & Fine, B., eds. (1990). *Psychoanalytic Terms and Concepts*. New Haven, CT: Yale University Press.

Chapter 17

Polymorphously normal sexuality

At times, the clinician leaves his office and is fortunate enough to wend his way to the theater. One exceptional venture led to rare enchantment. I came across so riveting a performance that it not only moved me but sharpened my hazing perspective once I returned to seeing patients in the office. Ideas about gender and adolescence, gender and early infancy, gender and the delights of life were all clarified by the evening at the theater.

Adolescence is a time of glorious but painful agonies when, in the face of great uncertainties about oneself, a gender identity gels. The pressure to settle that sexual identity, however, is not the only force exploding tumultuously within the young person. For while adolescence is subject to the compelling command of both lusty and romantic desires, it is also a time when everything is thrown off balance by a tidal pull toward individuating self-definition, often manifested by a rash readiness to discard established constraints.

As gripping as are the feminine and masculine urges of adolescents and the pressure for independence, behind these remains the desire for fusion, for an oceanic unity of being, for a self fully at one with the whole human fabric and, concomitantly, for a sexuality not differentiated by gender. It is often forgotten that there is a unity that precedes individuation and a sexuality that is non-gendered but comes before both bisexuality and male/female identity and indeed extends more broadly than that simplistic dualism would suggest. Growth does not dissolve these prior states, which continue to lie behind and alongside the later aspects more familiar to our view.

This early sexuality, one that might be called polymorphously normal (as opposed to polymorphously perverse), can nowadays be seen most easily from a distance. Shakespeare, whose breadth of view is ever astonishing, not only brings us a mimesis of the life we know but also, awakening us from the cultural fashions of the present, reminds us of early states we have learned to obscure. It is manifest in his protean nature and his ability to bring to life female characters that can successfully be portrayed by males.

The place of undifferentiated sexuality in Shakespeare's plays informs us of its origins in individual development. This parallel demands fresh notice, because the "progress" of civilization since Shakespeare's day has brought with it repression as well as liberation. Open recognition and appreciation of an underlying *ungendered* sexuality has become culturally hidden. Perhaps "ungendered sexuality" more properly should be thought of as an infinitely variable range of gender identities. Reclaiming comfortable access to such unfettered equal-opportunity sexuality enriches our understanding of our patients and ourselves, as well as of Shakespeare.

Much of the above became clear when the clinician attended (perhaps too detached a word for the engagement he and others in the audience actually experienced) a specific performance of an already well-known and well-loved play, *Twelfth Night* (1971). It is a play he had read innumerable times through life's proverbial ages from school days on, one he had already seen many times produced by companies from the severely amateur to the most professionally accomplished, and one that had never ceased to delight him. This particular performance, directed by Mark Rylance for the Globe Theatre in London, was different because all efforts were aimed at bringing the play to life in a way that conformed as closely as possible to how it would have been staged in Shakespeare's time.

Seeing *Twelfth Night* in the theater that evening amazed, raised unexpected questions, and stimulated fresh thoughts. The effect was to induce the clinician to revisit not only his sense of Shakespeare but also his understandings of sexuality. *It suddenly seemed clear that Freud's thinking was closer to Shakespeare's than to conventional twentieth- and early twenty-first-century psychoanalytic thinking.* As modern fashions and postmodern theories have turned away from drives and libido, much of great value has been left behind.

It is improbable that any single evening in the theater could change the views of someone who had attended innumerable performances of Shakespeare for more than six decades. How could a single production lead to the reevaluation of all that had gone before? But such was the effect of a play staged as Shakespeare and his contemporaries had likely staged it, likely seen it when first it was on the boards.

Having traveled cross-country specifically to see this production of *Twelfth Night* as reincarnated by the Globe Theatre, I quickly recognized I was not alone in my reaction. Reviews and personal reports from others had attested not only to the play's success but to its stunning impact on the audience. My evening at the theater, both my own reaction there and the apparent response of the audience as a whole, amply confirmed those reports. The Globe combines performances on a high artistic level with maximum historical accuracy. Costumes are replicas of those used by Shakespeare's players; the format of the performances, including the actors' dancing before and between acts, is as it was done in the original; and, of course, male actors played all the parts.

Twelfth Night, as all know, deals with lovers' struggles to come together, with sexual identity as a central theme. It is a romance, a comedy with tragedy reduced to a subplot. In the play, a union is sundered when twins are shipwrecked and separated. The sister, Viola, disguises herself as a young man to serve in the Duke's court. As the Duke's emissary, now called Cesario – an apparent man who is actually a woman (played by a boy) – Viola is sent as a surrogate to woo Olivia, who herself then falls in love with the messenger. Gender misidentifications compound. The woman Olivia tries to seduce the messenger, the presumed man Cesario. Frustrated, Olivia asks Cesario to teach her how to woo. In response, Cesario ventures a love letter of seductive beauty, but that has been described as a letter a woman might send another woman ("Make me a willow cabin at your gate / and call upon my soul within the house ..."). All of this unfolds with a man playing Olivia and a man playing Viola playing Cesario, the role of a woman playing the role of a man.

Masculine identities and feminine identities interact, compete, reverse, and shift. Indeed, that had been the extent of the clinician's sense of the flow until he saw Shakespeare played in Shakespeare's style. This time the emotional impact was different, and not just for the clinician; the entire audience exploded with laughter, overwhelmed with enthusiastic excitement, and at the end seemed not to want to leave the theater. Such had been the consistent response to other performances of this staging in cities across the international tour, both in England and in America. The effect led the clinician to think anew about individual gender identity.

Psychoanalysts know that a large part of the appeal of young adolescents to more mature adults is their seeming bisexuality. What had engulfed the audience was not merely a flow of male and female identities but also an easy unboundaried open sensuality. When Freud first saw this quality clinically, he called it polymorphous perversity. Shakespeare's play brought to life as it was in Shakespeare's own time awakened appreciation of the developmentally normal nature of such gender diffusion. This mutable sensuality that was more safely open in a truly Shakespearean production and more readily accepted and enjoyed in Shakespeare's time suggests the simultaneous presence of multiple levels of sexual functioning, including a protean ungendered sexuality, one that structures into a unique and particular constellation with the formation of each and singular character formation.

Analysts have come to appreciate ever better the infinite varieties of individual gender identity, whatever the endless variety of combinations. What unfolded clearly in the play and in the audience reactions was recognition of a diffuse fluidity that was cannot be separated simplistically into male and female aspects. Rather, what was clear was a *not-yet-gendered* rush for sensual excitement, for stimulation and satisfaction, an exhilarated urge for both thrill and union that is fluid and indifferent to gender. Sensuality blossoming but not yet shaped or even outlined. (In *A Midsummer Night's Dream*, indeed, this diffuse early sensuality is indifferent to species as well as to gender barriers.)

An audience led to set aside the restraints of modernity quickly realized another reason Shakespeare's plays were so popular in his day. They played to an audience unencumbered by the burden of modern shame. Shakespeare's bawdiness caught the temper of the times, a human temper now more constrained by modern mind-sets of narrow masculine and feminine delineation. Yes, such forces clearly are also present in Shakespeare, but beyond them much in the plays is made of erotic attraction indifferent to gender, lust for its own expansive delight.

A male playing a female character on the stage could be appreciated as being male, as being female, as being mixed male and female, and as personifying the lightness of sexual excitement unweighted by gender. Undifferentiated primordial sexual excitement, early libido, is an innate emotional drive constituent of the oceanic oneness that is part of human psychic reality. Beyond heterosexuality and homosexuality and their various permutations lies a core of earliest polymorphous sensual and sexual enthusiasm.

Reference

Shakespeare, W. (1971). *Twelfth Night or What You Will*. New York: Penguin Books.

Part V

Endings in poetry, psychoanalysis, and life

Chapter 18

What play did Shakespeare write when he wrote *Twelfth Night?*

Ever since I emerged from childhood during high school years, *Twelfth Night* (1971) has been for me a standard alongside which I could measure my growth, like the door post where my parents had earlier marked my changing height. I first found the play, a classroom assignment, pleasing, never suspecting I would go on through the years to see it performed many times, to read it repeatedly, and always find in it new levels that would mark and measure for me the alterations of my own unfolding life. It seemed as if the play extended its reach along with me as my life progressed.

In the exploding heat of adolescence, it was the excitement of seeking and finding love, especially love in its physical fulfillment, of which the play spoke loudest. More softly spoken and more comforting in effect was what then seemed its main subtext, uncertainty of gender identity both faced and resolved.

In later adolescence, during college years, the power of physical excitement was tamed sufficiently so that I next saw *Twelfth Night* as suffused by pleasures of playfulness manifested in its astonishing richness of word play. That was evident in the very names of the major characters, Viola and Olivia and Malvolio, but it extended broadly and deliciously throughout the text. Shakespeare played with words in the delighted way an infant, having discovered its fingers, watchfully plays as it exercises its power to move them.

During each decade of personal growth, new wonders appeared in *Twelfth Night*. As the years passed, as I thought I had myself developed a more settled character, I expected fewer changes of dramatic significance. I assumed I had mined the play and perhaps life for most of their variety. I imagined I knew both the play and myself well enough that no great surprises were left to be uncovered.

Fortunately, even if painfully, such was not the case. It was not until middle age, perhaps when I was in my fifties, that I let myself see, or more probably was able to see, how dark a strain ran through the play. Likely that arrived around the same time I came to realize mortality was not an abstract concept that merely concerned other people. For the first time I recognized the cruelty that appeared and grew within the second half of the play.

Malvolio was indeed a pretentious ass, and playing off his pomposity had seemed a fine delight, no more than his fair comeuppance. What started as mockery, however, I newly realized lapsed into nakedly mean, ruthless malice. Just as I was forced to accept in my own world the persistent presence of disappointment, a view of the universe far different from the wonders of delight I had imagined in my adolescent idealism, so too the play now exposed evil, not only its brutality but also its eternal presence.

Perhaps I should not have been surprised. I wondered, had that heartlessness always been present in the play? Had that really been there all along, obscured only by my being unable to see it? Logically, the answer must be Yes, but that certainly is not how it felt.

Matters turned darker yet. In my sixties I found that on rereading the play or seeing it again, I could not blind myself to something I never before had noticed. The fact is that *Twelfth Night* is not simply a comedy, one that satisfies by having everything happily resolved at its end. No, cruelty, it declares, demands its satisfaction as much as does love. In the midst of the happy unions with which the play closes, Malvolio stalks off proclaiming, and with just cause, "I'll be revenged on the whole pack of you."

Twelfth Night had been an endless delight for me through each period of my life. It took a long while before I recognized that it has also consistently served as a precious interpretive companion, one profoundly valuable to mark the self analysis by which I struggle to mature, trying to make maturity keep up with age. Along with the kindness of strangers, I also have always depended on the interpretations of *Twelfth Night*.

Logic insists that the play cannot actually have changed and grown as have I myself. If the contrary must be true, if such a thought is unrealistically solipsistic on my part, if the play has always been the constant text Shakespeare wrote centuries ago, then yet again, what a wonder Shakespeare is.

In addition to his unique genius for capturing the breadth of human experience and sublimating that with language-changing poetical beauty, his capacity to cover the range of an individual's progress while aging and doing so in a single unvarying text is an added cause for admiration.

How conscious could Shakespeare possibly have been of the full sweep of a human life that he subtly mirrored in a play penned for the pleasure of the queen and her court as they celebrated the closing of the Christmas holiday?

Having known writers of fiction, I have been privileged to watch the ways their creative imaginations and authorial gifts combined to yield works of more richness than they themselves consciously could have known. I assumed it likely was the same for the Bard, more than merely ordinary mortal though he seem.

What is the truth? More than commonplace mortal in other qualities, may not the reach even of Shakespeare's consciousness also have been greater than is possible for the rest of us? Other aspects of this play, less subjectively personal to me, suggest that is so.

Twelfth Night, the name we seem always to use for the play, is actually an abbreviation of the full title Shakespeare gave his work: *Twelfth Night or What You Will*. The first half merely identifies the occasion for which the play was penned. The customarily overlooked name by which its author identified what he was offering his audience was the title's second half, *What You Will*. Playing with us, he seems to say, "Make of this what you can." *What You Will.*

Knowing his awesome genius for word play and knowing a bit of his own sense of himself, Shakespeare seemed to be stating that final message as one of his, Will's, personal own as well as one addressed to the audience.

The play has an epilogue, one in which Shakespeare makes manifest a person's progress through the journey of life. After the tale is done, after the story has been told, the clown comes forward to state the theme of the differing stages of an individual life. Although less often cited than is Jacques' statement about the seven ages of man, *Twelfth Night*'s epilogue is just as explicit. The clown sings a review of his life, starting "When that I was and a little tiny boy" and ending "When I came unto my beds." Each stage has its issues, its pleasures, and its pains. The refrain for each stage is one of mixed acceptance and defiance, "Hey, Ho, the wind and the rain."

The clown then speaks the play's last words. For an instant, Shakespeare, the author, steps out from behind the persona of a dramatic character and speaks openly for himself:

> A great while ago the world began,
> Hey, ho, the wind and the rain,
> But that's all one, our Play is done,
> And we'll strive to please you every day.

"Our play" and our lives – ever changing, eventually but inevitably ending. Shakespeare knew so very much. He captured and expressed so very much that only slowly and partially, little by little, each of us comes to learn and appreciate for ourselves, truths intrinsic to life, discoveries made and grasped differently across our changing ages. Finding him personally so very helpful, we are left to wonder how much he himself might have known consciously of what clearly he knew deeply.

What play did Shakespeare write when he wrote *Twelfth Night*?

Reference

Shakespeare, W. (1971). *Twelfth Night or What You Will*. New York: Penguin Books.

Chapter 19

Ephemera

Unfinished thoughts on endings and death

We are such stuff as dreams are made on, but of what are dreams made? Deep and desperate longings, haunting memories, and the light of creative imagination. These all are at once both transient wisps of inner experience and yet the very stuff of life, as real as experience can ever be, as central as our identities, as permanent as our lives.

What is permanence in our lives, our selves? As Arlow said in the letter cited at the very start of this volume, "The *self* [is] a unique, unprecedented event in the history of the universe, an awareness of the continuity of experience in a unique entity, one that never existed before and will never exist again." Individuality, not grandiose presence but singular particularity, gives meaning to life, that meaning manifest as it has its place in both relationships and creativity.

Any conclusion prior to death is unfinished. Although for one person after death the rest is silence, the conversation of life goes on ... for the world, but not for that person.

Psychoanalysis and poiesis,[1] the journey of self inquiry that is psychoanalysis and the poetic activity that is creativity, both work to enrich the meaning of life, giving life significance in the face of inexorable endings.

Such stuff as we are becomes our dreams and our poetry, and such mortal stuff as we are, each of those must at some point end, as noted by Caston (2007), who turned attention to those endings and to where Eros and Thanatos openly wrestle as death is foreshadowed. Starting implies stopping, just as living implies dying. Our personal inconceivable endings become approachable by looking at the endings of those of our creations we have learned to love, psychoanalysis and poetry.

Before turning directly to those endings, it is fitting first to consider what the endings conclude, the qualities that constitute psychoanalysis and poetry. Such is apt because, despite their different universes, the two share a common aim, that of reaching through words for the essence of personal being beyond words. Psychoanalysis strives in the name of therapy and science; poetry, in the name of art. The direction of each is the same, and, similarly, their having to come to their ends reminds us of death no matter the distractions we struggle to conjure.

Psychoanalysis

First, psychoanalysis. Whatever broad psychotherapeutic techniques may be used clinically, it is concern for the unconscious and determined efforts to expose and explore the power of the mind outside awareness that define psychoanalysis and give it its uniqueness. The unconscious is the name we give those inner forces that at once shape who we are and simultaneously keep us forever ultimately unknowable to ourselves. It is that ultimate unknowability that matters here as we struggle to be at peace with the stranger who drives us from within, as we labor to tame enduring inner forces while knowing such a task can never be complete. Although self knowledge is always partial, even partial candid emotional openness extends a person's freedom. One can come to know oneself better even as one never can know oneself fully.

By attending to verbal associations and to the special relationship of the clinical engagement, a successful analysis succeeds in facilitating an analysand's greatest and most candid self knowledge, helping that person *approach* inner essences with decreasing defensiveness and with increasing courage, at times even with calm.

An intrinsic irony appears. As analysts we use words, both the associations we hear and our own spoken interventions, to try to approach, open, and grasp as best we can what matters that ultimately lies beyond words. Whatever emotional engagements we also address, the analytic situation remains a universe in which we reach through words to experiences, forces, and feelings that lie immeasurably deep in our essential cores, that words can never fully grasp or contain.

Poetry

What of poetry? Just as all psychotherapy is not psychoanalysis, so too not all language is poetry. Poetry is language with profound power to move one emotionally, language affectively effective. To define poetry we must distinguish it from prose, for just as psychotherapy can at times be psychoanalytic in its nature, so too can prose at times be poetic. Yet psychoanalysis and poetry have characteristics that distinguish them, no matter how those qualities may at times be present in other forms. Each reaches beyond, psychoanalysis beyond superficial meanings and change, poetry beyond mere passing of messages. In their reach, psychoanalysis and poetry are both transcendent.

In light of historical struggles over distinctions between poetry and prose, my abbreviated statement here may seem as arbitrary as may the shortened version of psychoanalysis just preceding. For our limited immediate needs, I draw on a compelling and cogent discussion by Yves Bonnefoy (2005). A poet and a translator of poetry writing in both French and English, Bonnefoy had the benefit of cross-cultural experience when considering what is poetic whatever its manifest form. Laboring to see how different mind-sets developed in the worlds of contrasting languages, he compared English and French ways of thinking and using language. His conclusion, one that seems valid, is that verse (measured meter and rhyme) cannot alone define poetry.

Verse is the English tradition. As Bonnefoy makes clear, the tonic stresses and iambic meter so important in English in speech as well as verse are absent in French. Such formality of form has diminished to the extent that in French regular verse has almost disappeared. (One valuable side effect in French literature has been a heightened search for what is poetic expressed in prose.)

His and our concern is not that of an Anglo-French competition but of a wish to tease out what is defining and unique of poetic expression. To that point, Bonnefoy emphasizes what is poetic to lie in the relationships of experience and language in a way that is intuitive and intimate, a way in which words are used to escape from the alienation of conceptual thinking. "Poetry is an act by which the relation of words to reality is renewed; it is not the simple production of meanings or of a verbal object" (Bonnefoy 2005, p. 4).

I take Bonnefoy's use of the word "reality" to come close to what analysts mean by psychic reality, "unconscious desire and its associated phantasies" (Laplanche & Pontalis 1973, p. 363). As psychoanalysis reaches for the authenticity of experiential emotional insights, valuable even as they are inevitably partial and insufficient, poetry too rises toward insights beyond those of logical formulations. Indeed, as Arlow (1979) pointed out, the roots of transference and metaphor are the same, that of carrying something across, from one level to another.

It is not that there is more or less poetry in one language than the other, rather that each language has come to use different forms for what best approaches emotional essences. Parenthetically, such cross-cultural literary comparisons may help inform us even of psychoanalytic questions, especially as we wonder about the comparable successes of sensitive clinicians from vastly discrepant schools. Our understanding may grow most fully if we try to match clinical openness to analysands with similar regard for the concepts of those from other analytic schools, not limiting ourselves to the narrow native languages our minds inhabit. Bonnefoy serves us well as a model for regarding contrasting psychoanalytic forms without the constraint of allegiance to the theories of our conceptual homelands.

Whether the poetic form is relatively free from structural format such as verse, as appears to be the case in modern French literature, or whether as Bonnefoy implies "prose and poetry separate more naturally and constantly in English than in French" – each style offers a vantage point for comparison from which each can reflect on itself.

Common aims, different forms

My effort has been to place psychoanalysis and poiesis on equal footing as human endeavors that share central goals and inevitable insufficiencies. As Caston (2007) also noted, a person is not a text. Words can stir feelings and can reflect feelings, they can express feelings and can contain feelings, they can be awesomely complex and can be piercingly simple. Words can never tell all.

Whatever has unfolded and whatever has been told, there comes a time for even the best of analyses and the best of poems to conclude. Being different even if parallel processes, each must end faithful to the laws of its own form.

Psychoanalysis does not have the range of choices open to poetry. The poet can tailor the closing of a poem, seeking the effect desired. The vitality of life, in contrast, demands that psychoanalysts, despite their own inevitable human wish for tidy completion, recognize the openness of unresolved issues. As has been said, when we complete an analysis, we have scratched the surface of a continent.

Another distinction between clinical analysis and poetry, also noted by Caston, is that only the former opens a sense of dread as part of the realization that the ending is being approached. To be an individual is to be sensitive to relationships, to be ever caught in the conflicting pressures for intimacy and separateness. Getting "into analysis" and getting "out of analysis" sharpen the presence of those conflicts.

While I generally do not think in terms of categories, there is an advantage in considering a termination phase. That is the name I use for the period after the moment it is emotionally clear to a patient that the analysis one day will come to an actual end. For me, the termination phase starts at that instant, no matter how early in the work it arrives.

Indeed, some of the most painfully powerful termination experiences I have encountered were ones that began with the initial consultation, analyses in which separation and the inevitability of death were primary terrors center stage from the moment of the first "Hello." In the shadow of that realization, everything carries a different and highly freighted significance, one that comes from knowing that unconscious wishes and external actualities all exist within the same world with neither undoing the other.

Whatever their differences, endings in both psychoanalysis and poetry ring most true when integral to what has gone before. Smooth endings may feel more congenial but whether smooth or rough-hewn, authentic endings are preferable to artificial ones. As has been observed, nothing straight can ever be made from the crooked timber that is humanity. At their best, poetry and psychoanalysis are most true to themselves when tuned to authenticity rather than reassurance.

Facing the end

To love is to be vulnerable to loss. To long is to seek a love already lost. To embark on an analysis is to open oneself to the hurts of loss and longing. What courage it takes.

Beginning ineluctably implies ending. The gifts of our species – the power for symbolic representation, language and the ability to delay action long enough to play with ideas – these gifts bring with them the curse of the knowledge of our individual deaths. It has been said that every man knows he will die, yet no man believes it. The knowledge, distance it though we try, will not disappear.

We can, indeed, learn from the structure of poetry about the implicit structure of clinical analysis. It could not be otherwise, because poetry is not a universe external to us but is, like the psychoanalytic venture, a human creation. Our minds shape endings not solely for the sake of reality testing but to make experience digestible. We learn from examining poetry and analysis because in them we see the working of our own minds mirrored.

How we yearn for happy endings. Like the heroic prostitute of *Never on Sunday*, we want even Greek tragedies to end happily, with the words "And they all went to the seashore." The fundamental adaptive principle learned from long psychoanalytic experience is that each person functions the way that one does because it is the best way of getting along in the world as that person sees it. So every aim, manifestly cruel or self-destructive though it may seem, takes adaptive gratification, a happy ending, as its goal. Furthermore, on one level any ending is a happy ending because uncertainty evidences our smallness and our helplessness. We take the anguish of the world as random and disordered or we face the dreadfulness of Death itself. Putting an ending on things comforts us about safe conclusions, whatever other meanings may also be implied.

Despite his long-windedness, we love Proust not only for his wisdom but also for his showing us passivity turned to activity, with Marcel maturing and able to write. Despite his esoteric obscurity, we love Joyce not only for what he says of the human condition but also for his holding randomness to a place within human connectedness and continuing sexuality. Kafka also tells us about our human world, but how many love him? He forces us to face intolerable helplessness without safe ending.

Does our therapeutic zeal lead us to put an unduly happy face on endings in order to salve our own anxieties of uncertainty and helplessness? Might we do better with a bit less encouraging inspiration and a bit more respect for the verities of loss and death? Those are questions not only for psychoanalytic technique but for living life itself.

The narcissism of our being, no mere vanity, is at stake. Wondrously and wonderfully, prisoners did play music in death camps, yet such amazing behavior was not miraculous. The prisoners were killed, they died, even if their music lingered on. Our own narcissism has us insistently optimistic, perhaps even perversely optimistic. We try to forget that it is Death who says, "*Et in Arcadia, ego sum.*" It is Death who says "and in Paradise, there too am I." Narcissism can tolerate only so much in the battle of Eros against Thanatos. As humans we need to know love to be able to survive and even flourish in the presence of death.

How can one face the end, not simply the possible pain of death but more crucially the very thought of nonbeing? How can one keep one's mind in the face of dreaded dissolution? We survive little endings as if to show ourselves we will somehow go on endlessly. With wit and with sobriety, with cruelty and with love, with symptoms and with faith, with anything we humans can devise we try to distract death from us or, at the least, distract ourselves from death. Therein lies creativity.

Denial and disavowal are paradoxical defenses, because their very negation proclaims the existence of what they would deny. Yeats's (1919) "rough beast" slouching to be born in Bethlehem reminds us of the imperishable imminence of death in its very act of offering the hope of continuing life. The existence of Eros implies the existence of Thanatos just as the existence of Thanatos implies the existence of Eros. Beginnings imply endings, and the "rough beast" slouching to be born carries both.

Yes, we indeed are such stuff as dreams are made on, and like dreams we are by nature transient. We would have it otherwise, but unable to make it so – despite science or art – we come to cherish what matters most. Transience bears with it poignancy, sharpening of emotional sensitivity. What grows more vulnerable grows more dear.

An analytic termination is a death in the family: the relationship mattered deeply and the loss is real. A wise analysand once touchingly commented, "I'll look at reality – but only as a tourist!" That is as good as it gets, as good as we have reason to hope for, even for ourselves.

We analysts must be cautious that we do not, for our own needs, exaggerate the hopefulness in successful analytic terminations. After the sorrow over ending, the happiness of new beginnings does not imbue immunity against future terrors. Strengths and creative potentials are to be honored but not converted into magical amulets for mutual reassurance.

I do not believe my terminating analysands misunderstand the words that accompany my final handshakes when I say, "I wish you well." By then they know well that I regard them, that is, that I try to see them for themselves. And they know that I genuinely regard them, that is, that I hold them in regard, valuing them for themselves. And they also know that I do not believe my wishes have power to alter either their situations or their futures, that is, that my regard includes the caring not of a ministering parent or powerful physician but of a separate equal other person, one who shares the human condition. So they even know that no matter how they might also wish that my wish had magical power, it is not such magical power that I imply.

An analyst's honest regard is what I believe ultimately matters most in an analysis. It is the personal and professional derivative of the love that is at the center of Eros, that which allows one to go on despite the imperishability of Thanatos and the inevitability of individual death. It is a regard founded as much as a person's can ever be on appreciating the benefit of the reality principle as a mature version of the pleasure principle. Such regard, rooted in one's recognition for an other, is weakened when altered into inspiration.

Our minds create shapes to make experience bite size and digestible, so we ever have beginnings and we ever have endings, ever having each present in the other. Generations must pass to make room for new generations. Analytic terminations have endings in them, endings akin to death, or else the analysand is deprived of what he or she can go on to do alone in introspective growth, those things that could not be done while the analyst was still a living presence. The possibilities of new beginnings deserve to be honored; the actualities of endings also merit their full respect.

In another poem confronting and expressing both loss and continuity, Yeats captured that balance. He knew love and life were transient, that they came to their ends, and that as long as life lasted, love would continue to live and die. Knowing the transience of love, he entitled one of his most tender poems "Ephemera" (Yeats 1884). His closing speaks a truth for psychoanalysts as well as poets, for all of us:

> Before us lies eternity; our souls
> Are love, and a continual farewell.

Note

1 Defined in the *Oxford English Dictionary* as "Creative production, esp. of a work of art ... [as in] 1971 G. Steiner *In Bluebeard's Castle* ... The equivocations between poiesis ... the artist's, the thinker's creation – and death."

References

Arlow, J.A. (1979). Metaphor and the psychoanalytic situation. *Psychoanalytic Quarterly*, 48:363–385.

Bonnefoy, Y. (2005). Beyond words. *Times Literary Supplement*, August 12.

Caston, J. (2007). Poetic closure, psychoanalytic termination, and death. *Journal of the American Psychoanalytic Association*, 55:7–30.

Laplanche, J. & Pontalis, J.B. (1973). *The Language of Psycho-Analysis*. New York: W.W. Norton.

Steiner, G. (1971). *In Bluebeard's Castle: Some Notes Toward the Redefinition of Culture*. New Haven, CT: Yale University Press.

Yeats, W.B. (1884). Ephemera. In *The Collected Poems of W.B. Yeats*. New York: Macmillan., 1959

Yeats, W.B. (1919). The second coming. In *The Collected Poems of W.B. Yeats*. New York: Macmillan, 1959.

Chapter 20

Slouching towards mortality
Thoughts on time and death

For me, it felt in my life like the break of day. I was in my late twenties, married and with two young children, at long last moving out from life fully bound by outer structures: college, medical school, internship, residency, and the then required two years' uniformed service time. Eager to take full ownership of life, I was shocked when the doctor at my service discharge physical announced I should not resign from the service. "Why?" I demanded. Her words still echo: "Because your wife will need widow's benefits."

That was one of three different times doctors in separate circumstances told me I likely had a fatal disease. Each of those times had a happy outcome, yet I know a time will come with a different ending. The ease with which now I reflect on transience is far from the cold terror that attends the imminent presence of death.

Death is a fact; its subjective impact varies with distance. I move a touch closer, from times that worked out well to one that did not. Standing at the bedside of a hospitalized friend on a day we both knew would be one of his last, I mentioned Prospero's line, "Every third thought will be my grave." My friend fell momentarily silent, then smiled and said, "I like that – every third thought, not every second."

Death's proximity concentrates one's mind. Desire to distance attention to the imminence of my own demise is apparent in the path I followed essaying this concept. Customarily, when writing, I start with a disorganized draft of rambling thoughts, modify them repeatedly, and finish with a polished statement very different from its uncertain start.

This time was different. Instead of tacking, repeatedly altering course, while sailing continuously forward, this time I started, stopped, started anew and differently, doing so repeatedly and creating a series of distinctly different statements. Only retrospectively did I recognize how hesitantly I had ventured, working my way cautiously as I approached the subject. My first accounts were objective, academic. Only with struggling could I work my way to the subjective, the more personal.

Now I retrace that journey with three dissimilar short statements: the first, on time and the evolutionary uniqueness of our species; the second, on the place of impermanence in an individual's developmental line; and, finally, on confronting the awareness of one's own passing out of time, passing from life. First, the species; next, the individual; and last, one's self.

Time and the human species

Change is the quality that defines time. Regardless of scale, the nature of time is progressive alteration, existence always carrying a before, during, and after movement.

Whether other animals, other species, have awareness of personal death is something we cannot directly know. We do, nonetheless, have reason to recognize that impermanence is an essential organizing principle that defines our species. A biological verity lies behind the famous statement often attributed to Kafka that the meaning of life is that it ends.

The evolutionary advance that marks us a species apart, *Homo sapiens*, lies in our minds, precisely in our capacity to form symbols. Less imprisoned by rigid instincts than our evolutionary predecessors, we have power to break the link between stimulus and response – or at least to interrupt it. As a result, we can delay reflexive reactions, create meanings, play with possibilities, and choose our reactions.

Not so bound by rigid reflexes, we capture perceptions and take them into our minds as mental representations. Capturing perceptions and experiences in symbols and words, we make meanings, meanings that then define us. A person is a meaning-making mammal. This is the quality that, I believe, led general semanticists accurately to define our species as "time binding."

We recognize time and its passage. We have memories; we reflect on events; we discuss them; we pass what we have learned on to others. The human is a time binding animal.

The evolutionary miracle of symbolically internalized time binding, like all evolutionary advances, carries its own intrinsic flaw. The essence of time is that it passes. If all were static, there would be no time. Time passes, and therein lies the ironic flaw of our species.

Even as we lay down memories, reflect on events, and pass what we have learned on to others, time passes. Time's being out of joint is built into the human condition. The moment we register an experience in mind or form a word, that representation or word is in some part wrong. The word fixes something as stable in our minds while the world continues to change.

That pace of change can be so slow that often we need not notice the slippage between our representational world and the universe of outer reality. Still, slippage is always there, ever present and normal, not a disconnection existing solely in the neurotic distortions of "then" and "now" on which we focus our clinical attention.

When psychoanalysts speak of character, they refer to the relative permanence of a person's psychic structure over time – a seeming permanence that, in fact, is relative. It is easy to forget that psychic structure means no more than a relatively stable set of functions.

The inexorable permanence of impermanence is built into the nature of our species, into everything we think. We are time binding, with the result that our mental representations, our symbols and words, are always temporally a bit askew. Life implies movement. Transience is in the very structure of our minds.

An individual's developmental line

Let us move from the species to the individual and the life pattern of any individual. From the day of birth through the ever changing years of growth and into what we favor by calling the prime of life, even before time starts clearly to advance too rapidly to ignore, there are early hints of the ultimate chill that awaits the end of day. Mostly, painful awareness of our impermanence lies outside our notice when we are young.

"Mostly" is not "always." When fears of disappearance intrude severely, we think of mental disorders. We adopt a detached clinical stance and speak of childhood phobias, or we parse the provenance of depression. We do so validly, but also at times a bit defensively. We are too quick to pathologize. Just as beginning always implies ending, so living implies dying. Implications of ending are intrinsic to normal life, affecting us whether or not they impinge on consciousness.

Although Eros prevails as life begins, fears inevitably accompany growth. Whatever the security, still loss intrudes – loss of the breast, loss of body parts, loss of the other, losses of every variety, even loss of one's very self.

Fears of disappearing appear in child's play, from an infant's peek-a-boo, to early childhood's hide-and-seek, later to the older child's game of musical chairs. Reality requires a maturing child to master an ever mounting awareness that not only do things change but that at times they disappear and do not always reappear. From the start Eros must battle Thanatos, its endless rival.

Without surveying the threat of loss of self across a lifetime, I call attention to that particular developmental phase when awareness of personal transience loudly commands attention. Unlike earlier stages, this period has not been studied closely enough to have its own recognized name. "Midlife crisis" is not what I have in mind, although that crisis of recognizing mortality often serves as the opening into this phase. For shorthand and without any chronological precision I will simply call it "the sixties."

Repeated observations reveal that for many the sixtieth is the most frightening birthday of their lives. I have seen it in friends, colleagues, patients, and myself. Turning sixty heralds one's being old in a way never before accepted.

Mortality is insistently proclaimed; it commands notice. Death seems to hover in the air. The experience may not be linked directly to the birthday, but somewhere around this period a person's awareness of vulnerability of being comes more to the fore. Appreciation of the fleeting nature of one's own life then tenaciously colors one's being. One's sense of self changes.

Some fracture in the face of this new challenge, shriveling with meanness or anger, becoming bitter with jealousy of the young. Others find new energy and blossom, starting new ventures as if life now offers possibilities never before dared. Those who achieve acceptance rather than mere resignation find the fear of death start to fade.

For these people, their sixties are like a second adolescence, an unexpected opportunity to loosen and reshape earlier character styles, an occasion opening innovative possibilities in life. Unlike "second childhood," a phrase often used disparagingly to deny one's own vulnerabilities by mocking the loss of powers in others, "second adolescence" connotes no demeaning repudiation, as it names a developmental possibility for a late-life fresh growth spurt, even a new capacity to transcend the character constrictions of one's earlier life.

Having moved from the time patients told me I was "too young to understand" to that of being thought "too old to understand," I am now often consulted by many in their sixties, seventies, and even eighties – successful people who are keenly introspective as they confront aging, each alert to the evanescence of life. One, a therapist in his mid-sixties, when asked why he was consulting me at that particular moment, offered an answer both simple and profound: "Because now I'm old enough."

The threat of ending can spark new beginnings. Recognizing transience can open the risk-taking needed for new creativity. In addition to several friends who published their first novels after turning sixty, I think of many others who found their own singular fresh outlets for imaginative originality.

Respecting the fact of death as a fact of life can dissolve fears and inhibitions. Just as the burst of pubertal sexuality opens an adolescence of new possibilities for one's childhood way of being, so can the sixties' burst of awareness of the ephemeral nature of life open fresh possibilities and even courage for new adult freedoms.

Mastering the realization of mortality is not easy. Taming personal narcissism is difficult work. Nonetheless, aging does not dictate inevitable depression. Loss, yes; grief, yes; mourning, yes; but depression, no.

Thanatos can add wisdom as well as fear. In Freud's words, "Transience value is scarcity value in time" (1916, p. 305). New appreciation of poignancy can also add subtle richness to aesthetic sensibility. Perhaps even more valuably, one's basic acknowledgment of the otherness of others can enlarge into more fully cherishing the very distinctiveness of those others from oneself.

Facing Thanatos stirs the defiant vitality of Eros. Whatever physical limitations age brings, there also can be a bold resurgence of vitality, a resilience, an emotionally mature vigor that is put into the service both of one's self and, significantly, of loved ones who will live on beyond one.

I do not want to distort or obscure the agonies of what can be the wreckage of old age by painting it in the pastels of youth. On the other hand, it would be equally wrong to fall into the common fallacy of pathologizing all of life. Despair is not the preordained outcome of recognizing the ephemerality of life. Not only does the heart have its reasons; it also has its creative strengths. Acceptance opens doors that are closed by resignation. Indeed, with acceptance of the evanescence of life, the question of whether there is life after death comes to matter less than does determination for life before death. Awareness of mortality can rouse one's active claim on the life one has.

One's own dying

At last, perhaps inevitably left until last, attention to the evolution of our species and consideration of an individual's developmental lines must yield. What
is personal and immediate will not disappear, despite our avoidance. Reality is
what will not go away. We return to the actuality of death, death for me and death
for you. Each of us will die, each and all, a fact unforgettable even if at times
unrememberable.

We whistle past the graveyard, making light of death – as in a friend's comment that the average age in his condominium is deceased. Death's appearance in
humor is more often implicit than explicit, as in that jest. Nonetheless, whatever
its form, humor deriding death acknowledges death's very undeniability. There is
no pardon from "time's thievish progress to eternity" (Shakespeare 1609, Sonnet
77, line 8).

Death will not be deterred. Our own narcissism has us try to forget that it is
Death who states, "Et in Arcadia ego sum." One's own death is not a reality easily
absorbed; narcissism can tolerate only so much. Nonetheless, there is no exception to the rule of Thanatos: I die; you die; he, she, it dies.

Words commonly offered to soften the sad sense of approaching loss are the
poet's "If Winter comes, can Spring be far behind?" (Shelley 1819). That hopeful
encouragement, however, lends itself to contrary meanings.

Whose spring arrives after winter's passing? If it is implied that we ourselves
enjoy returning spring, we then deny personal death even as we pretend otherwise.

Yet, the saying that values springtimes still unborn holds true if comfort comes
from knowledge of the continued lives of others we love, if we are led not simply
to deny our personal passing but to recognize the satisfaction that comes with our
passing on the baton of continuing life.

From the growing number of patients who die while I still live, I mention
just one, one who carried into action in our encounter this caring forward for the
next generation.

D. and I were both young when first we worked together analytically almost
a quarter-century ago. At that time he stayed engaged for only about three years
before deciding to interrupt his analysis, to go off, in Goldsmith's felicitous
phrase, "in search of superfluity."

D. found success in that search, great financial success as well as success in
establishing a new family, a new wife and son and daughter, all before returning
in his mid-forties to resume his unfinished analytic introspection.

The death of his father while D. was quite young, indeed his deeming himself
to have grown up as if never having had a father, contributed to his intense concern for how he would father his own children. He was particularly anxious over
his determination to be for his son the good father he himself had never known.

Our analytic work together proceeded well until at 49 D. developed a fatal illness. He worked assiduously to protect his children as the effects of his disease and
repeated hospitalizations washed over the family for the three years until his death.

Some months before he died, D. asked me for a promise, one that was deeply important to him. He asked that after he died, at whatever time his son chose, whether sooner or later, I would meet once with him to talk about D., about D. as a man, about D. as a father, about D.'s profound regard for his son. It was as if I were to give a testimony of authenticity to his love for the son. Indeed, more than that, in contrast to the unresolved resentment he felt for what he had taken to be his own father's disinterest manifest in abandoning him by dying, D. wanted his son to know the genuineness of his respect for the lad, for the son as a separate person with great value of his own.

The death of my patient and my mourning for him came, and time went on. Many months later I was called by D.'s 15-year-old son. I spent a single two-and-a-half-hour session with him in which we discussed his grief and his ambivalence, his guilt and his imaginings about his father. I think I was of help to him, but I am certain that for me those were among the most emotional hours I have experienced in more than 50 years of practice. I was the stand-in carrying the message of caring respect from a dead father to his adolescent son.

What had this meant to D., my patient? One element of our shared enactment, his and mine, had to have been his fantasied power to act after death, a derivative of early omnipotence. Much more important, I believe, was the greater ease to face death that he found in this token satisfaction of his wish to reinforce his son's flourishing after he was gone.

Generosity of spirit, creative generativity, is the way Eros defies Thanatos, the way one generation can deeply regret its own death yet be comforted by the continuation of loved others. This is no mere trick, no disguised belief that we ourselves will see through their eyes, nor is it the foolish false fantasy of continuing as if we ourselves are still actually alive through the memory of others.

Rather, it is what genuine love of the other brings, the knowledge that while we will be no more, we can find contentment, even pleasure, in the joys yet to come to our children and grandchildren, professional as well as personal, and beyond them to those yet to come newly into life who follow us.

In final closing

"Every third thought will be my grave." Then, every second. Who knows for any of us how many final thoughts will be the grave, how many final thoughts will be of our caring for an other, that love of others in whose continuation we take joy even as we ourselves disappear?

What I have in mind and intend is descriptive, not at all inspirational. I report observations that appear to be consistent: not only does generosity of spirit bring its own great richness to life, but also, beyond the soothing fantasy of being remembered by others, generous genuine love of those others in their own right offers the chief ease in death.

Life is a flow of generations. As our parents' generation died, leaving the world to us, so will we pass on, leaving the world to those who follow. What is a generation but a community of contemporaries? And what is the essence of that word "generation" but a group defined by engendering those who follow? A generation engenders. It generates.

Eros is the god of love; Thanatos, the god of death – the two endlessly engaged in the passage of time. For us, it is generosity of spirit for those yet to come that allows Eros to allay the agony of Thanatos.

References

Freud, S. (1916). On transience. *S.E.*, 14:305–307.

Shakespeare, W. (1609). Sonnet 77. In *Shakespeare's Sonnets*. London: Folio Society, 1977.

Shelley, P. (1819). Ode to the west wind. In *Shelley: Selected Poetry*. London: Penguin Books, 1985, pp. 160–162.

Index

For Product Safety Concerns and Information please contact our EU
representative GPSR@taylorandfrancis.com
Taylor & Francis Verlag GmbH, Kaufingerstraße 24, 80331 München, Germany

www.ingramcontent.com/pod-product-compliance
Lightning Source LLC
Chambersburg PA
CBHW070711280326

41926CB00089B/3827

9 781138 097766